PARLIAMENTARISM

For eighteenth- and nineteenth-century authors such as Burke, Constant, and Mill, a powerful representative assembly that freely deliberated and controlled the executive was the defining institution of a liberal state. Yet these figures also feared that representative assemblies were susceptible to usurpation, gridlock, and corruption. Parliamentarism was their answer to this dilemma: a constitutional model that enabled a nation to be truly governed by a representative assembly. Offering novel interpretations of canonical liberal authors, this history of liberal political ideas suggests a new paradigm for interpreting the development of modern political thought, inspiring fresh perspectives on historical issues from the eighteenth to early twentieth centuries. In doing so, Selinger suggests the wider significance of parliament and the theory of parliamentarism in the development of European political thought, revealing how contemporary democratic theory, and indeed the challenges facing representative government today, are historically indebted to classical parliamentarism.

WILLIAM SELINGER is Lecturer in European History, 1700–1850 at University College London. He is a historian of political thought whose work has focused on the development of modern theories of democracy, representative government, and the state. His articles have appeared in a variety of political theory and intellectual history journals. Prior to publication, this book was awarded the Annual Montreal Political Theory Manuscript Award, 2017.

IDEAS IN CONTEXT

Edited by

David Armitage, Richard Bourke, Jennifer Pitts, and John Robertson

The books in this series will discuss the emergence of intellectual traditions and of related new disciplines. The procedures, aims, and vocabularies that were generated will be set in the context of the alternatives available within the contemporary frameworks of ideas and institutions. Through detailed studies of the evolution of such traditions and their modification by different audiences, it is hoped that a new picture will form of the development of ideas in their concrete contexts. By this means, artificial distinctions between the history of philosophy, of the various sciences, of society and politics, and of literature may be seen to dissolve.

The series is published with the support of the Exxon Foundation.

A list of books in the series can be found at the end of the volume.

PARLIAMENTARISM

From Burke to Weber

WILLIAM SELINGER

University College London

CAMBRIDGE
UNIVERSITY PRESS

University Printing House, Cambridge CB2 8BS, United Kingdom

One Liberty Plaza, 20th Floor, New York, NY 10006, USA

477 Williamstown Road, Port Melbourne, VIC 3207, Australia

314-321, 3rd Floor, Plot 3, Splendor Forum, Jasola District Centre, New Delhi - 110025, India

79 Anson Road, #06-04/06, Singapore 079906

Cambridge University Press is part of the University of Cambridge.

It furthers the University's mission by disseminating knowledge in the pursuit of education, learning and research at the highest international levels of excellence.

www.cambridge.org
Information on this title: www.cambridge.org/9781108468855
DOI: 10.1017/9781108585330

First published 2019
First paperback edition 2020

A catalogue record for this publication is available from the British Library

Library of Congress Cataloging in Publication data
NAMES: Selinger, William, 2019– author.
TITLE: Parliamentarism : from Burke to Weber / William Selinger.
DESCRIPTION: Cambridge, United Kingdom ; New York, NY : Cambridge University Press, 2019. | Series: Ideas in context | Includes bibliographical references and index.
IDENTIFIERS: LCCN 2018061716 | ISBN 9781108475747 (hardback : alk. paper) | ISBN 781108468855 (paperback : alk. paper)
SUBJECTS: LCSH: Representative government and representation–History. | Cabinet system–History.
CLASSIFICATION: LCC JF1051 .S4 2019 | DDC 321.8–dc23
LC record available at https://lccn.loc.gov/2018061716

ISBN 978-1-108-47574-7 Hardback
ISBN 978-1-108-46885-5 Paperback

Contents

Acknowledgments

When I entered graduate school, I never imagined that I would write a book like this one. For inspiring me to begin this journey, and for assisting me on it, I am thankful to a great many individuals.

My first debt is to my dissertation committee, especially Richard Tuck, who taught me an entirely new way of thinking about history and politics, and Eric Nelson, who strongly encouraged me to focus on Parliament, when I could not yet see where that might lead. Cheryl Welch and Harvey Mansfield shared their knowledge about Tocqueville and so much else – I learned an enormous amount from their comments and erudition. Michael Frazer was a source of insight and encouragement, and he constantly urged me to reflect on how themes in this book persisted into the twentieth and twenty-first centuries.

I met Richard Bourke and Sam Moyn after the dissertation was already completed. However, I feel toward both a similar debt as toward my graduate school mentors. Each read a complete draft of the manuscript out of no other motivation than intellectual generosity and offered invaluable suggestions as I worked to transform the dissertation into a book.

In both the Department of Government and Committee on Degrees in Social Studies at Harvard, I was blessed with wonderful colleagues and interlocutors. I had stimulating conversations about this project with Jacob Abolafia, Eric Beerbohm, Kenzie Bok, James Brandt, Jonathan Bruno, Katrina Forrester, Ana Keilson, Jim Kloppenberg, David Lebow, Jennifer Page, Rebecca Ploof, Arjun Ranamurti, Justin Reynolds, Jacob Roundtree, Michael Rosen, Nancy Rosenblum, Mira Siegelberg, and Don Tontiplaphol. I am especially thankful to Hannah Callaway, John Harpham, Madhav Khosla, Rita Koganzon, Sungho Kimlee, and Adam Lebovitz for reading large portions of the manuscript and offering indispensable feedback. Greg Conti has been an extraordinary interlocutor. I cannot even begin to count how many drafts he has read of various chapters or how many of the ideas in the book emerged through our conversations.

I am also grateful to UCL and the broader scholarly community of London for welcoming me as a colleague. This book has benefited from conversations I have had over the last year with Richard Bellamy, Angus Gowland, Maurizio Isabella, Gareth Stedman Jones, Paul Sagar, Peter Schröder, and Georgios Varouxakis. I am excited for many further conversations in the years to come.

I was fortunate to be able to present an earlier draft of the book at the Annual Montreal Political Theory Manuscript Workshop. I would like to thank Jacob Levy, Arash Abizadeh, Ryoa Chung, Daniel Weinstock, Robert Sparling, Victor Muñiz-Fraticelli, Catherine Lu, Briana McGinnis, Travis Smith, Dominique Leydet, Yves Winter, and the other scholars who read the manuscript and offered truly invaluable comments and suggestions.

Liz Friend-Smith at Cambridge University Press has been a pleasure to work with, as have the series editors at *Ideas in Context*. I am especially grateful to David Armitage and Jennifer Pitts for their interest in publishing the book when it was still a work in progress as well as for their suggestions on how to improve it. The manuscript was also greatly improved by the comments I received from two anonymous readers. I would also like to thank Henry Brooks for his excellent work on the bibliography and Heather Jones for producing a fantastic index.

A part of Chapter 2 was previously published in "Patronage and Revolution: Edmund Burke's Theory of Parliamentary Corruption and His *Reflections on the Revolution in France*," *Review of Politics* 76 (2014); while parts of Chapters 5 and 6 appear respectively in "*Le grand mal de l'époque*: Tocqueville on French Political Corruption," *History of European Ideas* 42 (2016); and "Fighting electoral corruption in the Victorian era: An overlooked dimension of John Stuart Mill's political thought," *European Journal of Political Theory* (forthcoming). I thank the journals for giving me permission to reproduce this material here.

For fruitful conversations about the book (or for sharing work with me that was not yet publicly available), I would like to thank Teresa Bejan, Aurelian Craiutu, Anelien de Dijn, Hugo Drochon, Bryan Garsten, Jeffrey Green, Alex Gourevitch, Nick Juravich, Patchen Markell, Iain McDaniel, John McCormick, Isaac Nakhimovsky, John Pocock, Noah Rosenblum, Geneviève Rousselière, Lucia Rubinelli, Rahul Sagar, Stephen Sawyer, Melissa Schwartzberg, Nadia Urbinati, Nathan Tarcov, Adam Tooze, Julianne Werlin, and Frederick Whelan. No doubt there are other individuals I am forgetting.

It is time to record debts of a more personal order. Had *fortuna* not sent Emily Warner into my life, I never could have written this book. Partly that is because she taught me how to think about the past, but far more, it is because of the magic she has brought to life in the present and the excitement I have for our future together.

My parents and brother have always been my greatest source of love and support. The last several years have been no exception. For that reason, this book is dedicated to them.

Introduction

In the introduction to his now classic book, *After Virtue*, Aladair MacIntyre proposed a striking thought experiment. Suppose that the study of the natural sciences is prohibited. Then, generations later, a movement emerges with the aim of reviving them – but by this point nobody has any scientific training, and "fragments" of books and articles are all that remain. What would happen next? According to MacIntyre, many people would begin using scientific terms and ideas in conversation. They would argue over "the respective merits of relativity theory, evolutionary theory, and phlogiston theory." But what it actually meant to do scientific research would remain ungraspable. "Almost nobody" would realize "that what they are doing is not natural science ... at all."[1]

This book is motivated by the following conviction: we have failed to understand much of European political thought during the eighteenth and nineteenth centuries in the same way that MacIntyre's imaginary individuals failed to understand natural science. We read authors such as Edmund Burke, Benjamin Constant, Germaine de Staël, François Guizot, Alexis de Tocqueville, and John Stuart Mill. We argue about how to properly interpret their texts and over the meaning of "liberalism." But we have forgotten the concrete, overarching project in which these figures all were involved, the one that made their thought intelligible. That project was parliamentarism.

For each of the authors just named above, the defining feature of a free state was that it contained a space for parliamentary politics – an assembly in which political actions were discussed and deliberated and in which executive officials were held responsible. To create a secure space and a lasting culture of parliamentary politics, they defended a specific political framework, one based on the English constitution.

---

[1] Alasdair MacIntyre, *After Virtue: A Study in Moral Theory* (Notre Dame: 2007), 1.

Its characteristic practice was that ministers holding the highest-ranking executive offices served in the legislature and were responsible to the legislature for their positions. This has remained the *sine qua non* of parliamentarism down to the present day.[2] It is to parliamentarism (also known as *parliamentary government*) what universal suffrage is to democracy. However, before the twentieth century, parliamentarism was understood radically differently than it is now. In the first place, the presence of a constitutional monarch was viewed as not merely incidental to a parliamentary government but nearly indispensable. Prominent authors championed parliamentary republics, but they were careful to include a functional substitute for constitutional monarchy. Most importantly, whereas parliamentarism since the early twentieth century has accommodated a powerful executive who sets the agenda in parliament and engages in many forms of independent governance, prior to then, it was widely believed that parliamentarism's *raison d'être* was to make executive officials decisively subordinate to the legislature.[3]

The classical structure of parliamentarism about which Burke, De Staël, Tocqueville, and others wrote extensively (and, indeed, through which they articulated their core political beliefs and arguments) was defined by the following four elements:

---

[2] Kari Palonen writes that "the responsibility of the government to the parliament is the key political issue in the history of parliamentarism in that it distinguishes parliamentary from non-parliamentary regimes." As we will see, this responsibility arose in tandem with the involvement of the highest-ranking government officials in parliament. See Kari Palonen, "Parliament as Conceptual Nexus," in *Parliament and Parliamentarism*, ed. Pasi Ihaleinen, Cornelia Ilie, and Kari Palonen (New York: 2016), 8. For a classic statement on parliamentarism emphasizing both sides of this practice, see Karl Loewenstein, "The Balance between Legislative and Executive Power: A Study in Comparative Constitutional Law," *University of Chicago Law Review*, vol. 5, no. 4 (1938), 590.

[3] This shift, which I will return to in the Conclusion, has been widely discussed by historians and political scientists. For the growing power of the prime minister in twentieth-century Britain, see Richard Heffernan and Paul Webb, "The British Prime Minister: Much More than 'First Among Equals,'" in *The Presidentialization of Politics: A Comparative Study of Modern Democracies*, ed. Thomas Poguntke and Paul Webb (Oxford: 2005), 26–52; and for the government's increasing role in setting the agenda of Parliament since the late nineteenth century, see Kari Palonen, *The Politics of Parliamentary Procedure: The Formation of the Westminster Procedure as a Parliamentary Ideal Type* (Opladen: 2014), 199–244. In France, a parallel shift (which occurred somewhat later in time) is analyzed in Nicolas Roussellier, *Le Parlement de l'éloquence: La souveraineté de la délibération au lendemain de la Grande Guerre* (Paris: 1997). For the turn to the executive more generally during the twentieth century and the decline of older presumptions about the primacy of parliament, see Marcel Gauchet, *L'avènement de la démocratie*, vol. 3: *À l'épreuve des totalitarismes, 1914–1974* (Paris: 2010), 627–634; Pierre Rosanvallon, *Le bon gouvernement* (Paris: 2015); Bernard Manin, *Principles of Representative Government* (Cambridge: 1997), 193–235.

An *elected legislative assembly* that was the most powerful actor in the state.

Ministers who held the highest-ranking executive offices while serving in the legislature and who could not remain in office without parliamentary support (i.e., the practice of parliamentarism or parliamentary government *in the narrow sense*).

A *constitutional monarch* who rarely exercised his official prerogatives but instead shaped the political process through moral (and in some cases financial) influence.

A system of competing political parties that struggled for power in parliament.

This structure originated in eighteenth-century England. By the turn of the twentieth century, it had spread across Europe – indeed, across the globe. It was championed by an astonishing array of political thinkers, especially ones associated with the movement of *liberalism*.

For the proponents of this structure, its decisive advantage was that it enabled a nation to truly be governed by a representative assembly. Parliamentarism gave the assembly greater powers and more public legitimacy than any other constitutional actor. It made legislative deliberation *the* crucial factor in political decisions, while the highest-ranking executive officials had to prove themselves before parliament if they wished to remain in office. But parliamentarism did more than just provide representative assemblies with the capacity to rule. It made such assemblies fit for ruling. The practice of constitutional monarchy and the presence of ministers in parliament were believed to ameliorate the worst pathologies that had historically been associated with legislative bodies. These practices (i.e., ministers in parliament and constitutional monarchy) prevented the legislature from acting tyrannically or being seized by a violent faction. Once a system of political parties was properly integrated into this framework, it was thought that the worst effects of legislative corruption and gridlock could likewise be overcome.

Between the 1760s and the turn of the twentieth century, the prospect of a nation being genuinely governed by a representative assembly – through parliamentarism – was viewed as entirely realistic. I will argue that this prospect underlay the political thought of that entire age. The true project of figures such as Edmund Burke, Germaine de Staël, Alexis de Tocqueville, and John Stuart Mill was parliamentary rule. For in their eyes, to live in a state ruled by a parliament was to be *free*. Under parliamentary rule, each political decision was preceded by substantial debate and deliberation, so the pros and cons of every action were discussed. Moreover, the executive officials who carried out those decisions were strictly responsible to the assembly. The exercise of coercive power was thus debated in advance and held accountable in retrospect. Political decisions were made *responsibly* and *deliberatively* rather than arbitrarily: the defining condition of a free state.

The aim of this book is to recover the great theories of parliamentarism that were produced in Britain and France during the eighteenth and nineteenth centuries. Many of those theories were composed by authors with whom we are still familiar – such as Constant, Tocqueville, and Mill. But by putting parliament at the center, I hope to make these canonical authors strange and unfamiliar all over again. I will situate them not only within the wider discourse about parliamentarism that flourished during that period but also within the world of parliamentary politics itself. It is often overlooked that nearly all the major French and British liberal theorists who wrote in the eighteenth and nineteenth centuries were actively involved in parliamentary affairs. Burke, Constant, Tocqueville, and Mill all ran for parliamentary office – as did Henry Brougham, Thomas Macaulay, Duvergier de Hauranne, François Guizot, Charles de Rémusat, Walter Bagehot, and James Bryce. With the notable exception of Bagehot, they all ended up as elected representatives. These figures were profoundly shaped by the rhetorical culture of parliament. But they also struggled with the real pathologies of parliamentarism including corruption and cabinet instability.

During the century and a half prior to the First World War, the theories of parliamentarism explored in this book constituted Europe's most important constitutional tradition. In addition to Britain where parliamentarism emerged over the eighteenth century, and France, where it was introduced in 1814, parliamentarism was adopted in Belgium, Spain, Holland, Italy, Sweden, Denmark, Greece, Serbia, Canada, and Australia.[4]

---

[4] These nations' constitutions are documented in *Summary of the Constitutions and Procedures of Foreign Parliaments*, ed. Reginald Dickinson (London: 1890); however, for Serbia (not included in the compilation), see Alex Dragnich, *The Development of Parliamentary Government in Serbia* (New York: 1978). The parliamentary traditions of thought that developed in many of these nations are explored in the essays in *Parliament and Parliamentarism*. For the constitutional practices of Canada and Australia in the nineteenth century, a classic work is Alpheus Todd, *Parliamentary Government in the British Colonies* (Boston: 1880).

In Germany,[5] Japan,[6] Russia,[7] and Austria-Hungary,[8] the champions of a more liberal polity argued for parliamentarism. It was the spread and durability of parliamentary regimes that undermined the widespread belief (strengthened by the experience of the French Revolution) that liberal values and a vibrant political sphere were too dangerous to contemplate in most of Europe.[9] By the end of the nineteenth century, insofar as it seemed increasingly obvious that European nations were capable of free government, this was the achievement of parliamentarism.[10]

Today this extraordinary legacy has been largely forgotten by historians of political thought.[11] For over a generation, the dominant narratives about eighteenth- and nineteenth-century constitutionalism have not been about *the spread of parliamentarism* but rather the *rise of democracy*.[12]

---

[5] A particularly rich debate over parliamentarism unfolded in Germany where a constitution close to the model examined in this book was adopted in the Frankfurt National Assembly of 1848 but never instituted. A classic history is Friedrich Meinecke, *Cosmopolitanism and the National State*, tr. Robert Kimber (Princeton: 1970), 250–374. See as well Andreas Biefang and Andreas Schulze, "From Monarchical Constitutionalism to a Parliamentary Republic: Concepts of Parliamentarism in Germany since 1818," in *Parliament and Parliamentarism*, 62–80. For discussions of parliamentarism following German unification, see Mark Hewitson, "The *Kaiserreich* in Question: Constitutional Crisis in Germany before the First World War," *Journal of Modern History*, vol. 73, no. 4 (2001), 725–780.

[6] For the extraordinary movement in favor of parliamentarism in nineteenth-century Japan, see Kyu Hyun Kim, *The Age of Visions and Arguments: Parliamentarianism and the National Public Sphere in Early Meiji Japan* (Cambridge: 2007).

[7] Paul Miliukov was the most eloquent liberal proponent of parliamentarism in Russia; however, the coalition in favor of this regime also came to include socialist radicals such as Peter Struve. See Melissa Stockdale, *Paul Miliukov and the Quest for a Liberal Russia, 1880–1918* (Ithaca: 1996); Klaus Fröhlich, *The Emergence of Russian Constitutionalism, 1900–1904* (The Hague: 1981).

[8] See, for instance, Jonathan Kwan, *Liberalism and the Habsburg Monarchy, 1861–1895* (Basingstroke: 2013).

[9] The skepticism about free government following the French Revolution is a central theme in James Kloppenberg, *Toward Democracy: The Struggle for Self-Rule in European and American Thought* (Oxford: 2016), 554–658.

[10] Of course, uncertainty remained, which would be confirmed by the "crisis of parliamentary democracy" in the early twentieth century. However, for a broad survey this achievement, see Jürgen Osterhammel, *The Transformation of the World: A Global History of the Nineteenth Century*, tr. Patrick Camiller (Princeton: 2014), 584–605, 915–917.

[11] One scholar who has insisted upon the importance of parliamentarism in the history of political thought is Kari Palonen. See in particular Kari Palonen, *From Oratory to Debate: Parliamentarisation of Deliberative Rhetoric in Westminster* (Baden-Baden: 2016), 155–197. Palonen has also been integral to the research program that culminated in the collection of essays *Parliament and Parliamentarism*. Palonen's reading of Weber as a theorist of parliamentarism is particularly astute; see *A Political Style of Thinking: Essays on Max Weber* (Colchester: 2017).

[12] It is striking, for instance, that in the impressive *Cambridge History of Nineteenth-Century Political Thought*, there is no entry on parliament or parliamentary government. See *The Cambridge History of Nineteenth-Century Political Thought*, ed. Gareth Stedman-Jones and Gregory Claeys (Cambridge: 2013). In recent decades, there has been interest among scholars of French liberalism in the rival accounts of constitutional monarchy and parliamentary government offered in nineteenth-century France. See Pierre Rosanvallon, *La monarchie impossible: Les Chartes de*

When scholars take up the major constitutional theorists of that era, say Constant, or Tocqueville, or Mill, it is to elucidate their views on democracy – not parliamentarism.[13] The same is true of the more general intellectual movement of *liberalism*. Scholars either emphasize how liberal theorists opposed universal suffrage and popular sovereignty – the two crucial elements of a democratic regime[14] – or they seek out resources in classic liberal theory for harmonizing popular sovereignty and universal suffrage with constitutionalism and the rule of law.[15] But in either case, the question of democracy is at the center.

What is so striking about parliamentarism is that it simply cannot be understood within this framework. Parliamentarism was manifestly not equivalent to constitutional democracy. Britain, the exemplar of a successful parliamentary regime, did not have anything near universal suffrage during the period examined in this book: on the eve of the First World War, 40 percent of adult British men still did not possess the franchise.[16]

1814 et de 1830 (Paris: 1994); J. A. W. Gunn, *When the French Tried to Be British* (Montreal: 2009); and Pasquale Pasquino, "Sur la théorie constitutionelle de la monarchie de Juillet," in *Francois Guizot et la culture politique de son temps*, ed. Marina Valensise (Paris: 1991), 111–122.

[13] The dominant emphasis in American scholarship has been on the ways in which these figures sought to harmonize liberal constitutionalism with democratic sovereignty. See, for instance, Stephen Holmes, *Benjamin Constant and the Making of Modern Liberalism* (New Haven: 1984); Bryan Garsten, "Representative Government and Popular Sovereignty," in *Political Representation*, ed. Ian Shapiro (Cambridge: 2009), 90–110; and Nadia Urbinati, *Mill on Democracy: From the Athenian Polis to Representative Government* (Chicago: 2002). The literature making some version of this argument about Tocqueville is too vast to even begin to survey. For a discussion of the "Tocqueville revival" in both the United States and France emphasizing this point, see Cheryl Welch, *De Tocqueville* (Oxford: 2001), 217–253.

[14] The scholarship making this point has tended to focus on how liberal theorists concretely responded to demands for greater popular participation – which was frequently with staunch opposition. See Pierre Rosanvallon, *Le sacre du citoyen: Histoire du suffrage universel en France* (Paris: 1992); Pierre Rosanvallon, *Le peuple introuvable: Histoire de la représentation démocratique en France* (Paris: 1998); Alan Kahan, *Liberalism in Nineteenth-Century Europe: The Political Culture of Limited Suffrage* (New York: 2003); Aurelian Craiutu, "Guizot's Elitist Theory of Representative Government," *Critical Review*, vol. 15, no. 3–4 (2003), 261–284; and Gregory Conti, *Parliament the Mirror of the Nation: Representation, Deliberation, and Democracy in Victorian Britain* (Cambridge: 2019).

[15] This more optimistic approach to the relationship between liberalism and democracy tends to focus on the conceptual relationship between democracy and representation – and how representation can enhance or invigorate popular participation. See Pierre Rosanvallon, *La démocratie inachevée: Histoire de la souveraineté du peuple en France* (Paris: 2000); Nadia Urbinati, *Representative Democracy: Principles and Genealogy* (Chicago: 2006); as well as Urbinati, *Mill on Democracy*; Marcel Gauchet, *La condition politique* (Paris: 2005), 277–384; Kloppenberg, *Toward Democracy*; Bryan Garsten, "From Popular Sovereignty to Civil Society in Post-Revolutionary France," in *Popular Sovereignty in Historical Perspective*, ed. Richard Bourke and Quentin Skinner (Cambridge: 2016), 236–269.

[16] This percentage is taken from T. A. Jenkins, *Parliament, Party, and Politics in Victorian Britain* (Manchester: 1996), 19. For the legislation leading to universal male suffrage (and the introduction of voting rights for women), see Robert Blackburn, "Laying the Foundations of the Modern Voting

Many of the greatest theorists of parliamentarism explicitly preferred a regime of restricted suffrage. But it would be equally misleading to think of the theory of parliamentarism as simply a vehicle for opposing democracy. There were seminal authors who accepted or even favored democracy while also championing parliamentarism. Mill, Tocqueville, Dicey, and Weber all believed that the classical structure of parliamentarism could be modified to accommodate universal suffrage.

What makes it easy to mistake the classical theories of parliamentarism for theories of democracy is that they promoted a powerful representative assembly. It was widely argued that a parliament could not effectively deliberate on behalf of the common good or hold executive officials accountable unless all the major interests and standpoints in society were represented. At its best, *parliament* was the "express image" or "mirror" of the nation it represented. But like parliamentarism itself, this conception of a representative assembly was never equivalent to democracy. It was articulated by certain proponents of universal suffrage and popular sovereignty. However, especially prior to the late nineteenth-century movement for proportional representation, this conception was expressed even more frequently by authors who had no desire for democracy and who were convinced that democracy would lead to assemblies less representative of society.[17]

To understand the classical theories of parliamentarism, we cannot begin with the debate over democracy. We must start from a different but no less pressing question that preoccupied eighteenth- and nineteenth-century thinkers. This was how to establish liberty in a modern European state that contained a professional military and centralized political authority. One powerful answer was to make the centralized authority clearly subordinate to a representative assembly. This meant that all laws were to be debated in parliament, and all government actions were to be evaluated in parliament. When necessary, a majority of representatives would have the power to remove executive officials from office and deprive the government of funding. It was through an assembly of this kind that,

---

System: The Representation of the People Act 1918," *Parliamentary History*, vol. 30, no. 1 (2011), 33–52.

[17] For the mirror theory of representation, its frequent antagonism with democracy, and the importance of proportional representation as an attempt to "square the circle" of democracy and representation, see Conti, *Parliament the Mirror of the Nation*; Robert Saunders, *Democracy and the Vote in British Politics, 1848–1867: The Making of the Second Reform Act* (Burlington: 2011). The French side of this story is explored in Rosanvallon, *Le peuple introuvable*.

in the words of Adam Smith, "a system of liberty" was established in eighteenth-century England.[18]

But this raised an additional question: how to prevent such an assembly from itself becoming a threat to liberty? One of the best-known eighteenth-century answers to this question was provided by Montesquieu, who, in his *Spirit of the Laws*, argued that the defining feature of a free state was that each constitutional power was equally checked by the others. Thus, in England, according to Montesquieu, the House of Commons was checked by the monarch's veto and the House of Lords.

In recent years, scholars have argued that Montesquieu's account of the English constitution was the foundation of liberal constitutionalism across Europe.[19] This book contends that the opposite is true. The theory of parliamentarism, which would become the dominant liberal constitutional theory in the century following the French Revolution, emerged out of dissatisfaction with Montesquieu's account. Already in the eighteenth century, a wide array of thinkers had rejected Montesquieu's understanding of the English constitution. They contended that the system of checks and balances depicted in *The Spirit of the Laws* was wholly ineffective at containing the House of Commons. The powers that enabled the Commons to hold government officials responsible – above all, its control over revenue – could not be matched by the other branches of the constitution. This was why the Crown never once made use of its veto after 1708. Nor was this a negative development: any constitutional change that made the Crown equal to the House of Commons risked undermining the supreme achievement of parliamentary control over the executive, which was what preserved English liberty.

The authors who developed this line of reasoning included Edmund Burke and Jean Louis de Lolme. They argued that the House of Commons was moderated not by the Crown's veto but rather by two other mechanisms, which Montesquieu failed entirely to note. The first was the regular presence of the Crown's ministers in Parliament, where they intervened in debates, shaped Parliament's agenda, and defended the interests of the government. The second was the institution of monarchy itself. The great

---

[18] Adam Smith, *Lectures on Jurisprudence*, ed. R. L. Meek et al. (Indianapolis: 1982), 269.

[19] Among recent texts tracing liberal constitutional theory back to Montesquieu, see Annelien de Dijn, *French Political Thought from Montesquieu to Tocqueville: Liberty in a Levelled Society?* (Cambridge: 2008); Urbinati, *Representative Democracy*; Aurelian Craiutu, *A Virtue for Courageous Minds: Moderation in French Political Thought, 1748–1830* (Princeton: 2012); Jacob Levy, *Rationalism, Pluralism, and Freedom* (Oxford: 2014); and Garsten, "From Popular Sovereignty to Civil Society in Post-Revolutionary France," 260–262.

danger of a legislative assembly was not that it would engage collectively in tyranny but rather that it might be seized by an individual or faction seeking to usurp the state. The presence of a constitutional monarch, even one who did nothing, served as an imposing symbolic barrier to usurpation. By moderating the ambition of its leading individuals and factions, a constitutional monarch moderated the assembly as a whole.

What was so remarkable about parliamentary government and constitutional monarchy was that the restraint these practices imposed on the legislature emerged as part of the very process of legislative deliberation. These practices did not rely on an outside power's direct veto, and they did not require the Crown to exercise prerogatives equal to those of the House of Commons. But even as these practices maintained the essential condition of a modern free state, the subordination of the executive to the legislature, they created several ways through which the Crown might influence the decisions at which the legislature arrived. For nineteenth-century champions of parliamentarism, its great advantage would continue to be the manner in which it simultaneously empowered and moderated the legislature. Parliamentarism secured the most expansive possible space for parliamentary politics. It enabled a nation to truly be governed by a deliberative and representative assembly. But crucial conditions were in place that made this powerful assembly unlikely to threaten the political order.

The event that made parliamentarism the dominant paradigm of a free state across Europe was the French Revolution. At its outset, the French National Assembly rejected the parliamentary model that was emerging on the other side of the Channel and instead instituted a modified system of checks and balances. But this project, the Constitution of 1791, failed dramatically, leading a range of authors including Jacques Necker, Germaine de Staël, Simonde de Sismondi, Benjamin Constant, and François Guizot to turn to parliamentarism. They would develop the definitive accounts of this constitutional paradigm, which influenced liberal thought across Europe and the globe.

The first half of this book explores the emergence of parliamentarism in British and French constitutional theory. *Chapter 1* shows how the basic elements of parliamentarism first began to cohere in eighteenth-century Britain. *Chapter 2* homes in on Edmund Burke. While Burke defended each of the crucial components of parliamentarism – a powerful representative assembly, the presence of responsible ministers in Parliament, a constitutionally limited monarch, and a system of political parties – from his earliest years in British politics, he would also argue for them in response to the French Revolution. Burke is thus the crucial figure connecting the theories of a parliamentary regime that emerged in eighteenth-century Britain with those that would come to predominate in France after the Revolution. *Chapter 3* examines the French Revolution more comprehensively. The most important ideological legacy of that event, I contend, was that it made parliamentarism the dominant constitutional paradigm in European liberal thought.

The second half of the book considers several of the great nineteenth-century theorists of parliamentarism. *Chapter 4* takes up Benjamin Constant, whose account of this constitutional model was the most influential of any European thinker. *Chapter 5* considers Alexis de Tocqueville. In *Chapter 6,* I turn to John Stuart Mill, situating him among a range of other Victorian intellectuals. I contend that each of these three figures viewed parliamentarism as the crucial political framework for securing liberal values. Another important theme running through *Chapters 5* and *6* is the contrast between parliamentarism and the American constitutional model. I show that not only Walter Bagehot but also John Stuart Mill and even Tocqueville preferred parliamentarism. In the *Conclusion* to the book, I examine the famous "crisis of parliamentarism" that erupted at the close of the nineteenth century when widespread doubt about this political form began to emerge. I then discuss the legacy of classical parliamentarism in the twentieth century and beyond.

As the foregoing summary should make clear, this book is not a comprehensive intellectual history of parliamentarism. While Max Weber plays an important role in the conclusion, my focus will generally be limited to Britain, where parliamentarism first emerged, and France, where (during the French Revolution and its aftermath) the greatest debate over the merits of parliamentarism unfolded. It was in these two nations that the formative theories of parliamentarism were produced: many of the parliamentary traditions that arose elsewhere in the nineteenth century were indebted to ideas first worked out in France and Britain.[20] But this book obviously cannot stand in for much-needed scholarship on other traditions of parliamentary thought.

---

[20] Heinz Eulau notes that in Germany, "the works of Constant and Guizot were constantly consulted in liberal circles" when it came to parliamentarism. See Heinz Eula, "Early Theories of Parliamentarism," *Canadian Journal of Economics and Political Science*, vol. 8, no. 1 (1942), 44. The importance of their influence in Italy is emphasized in Nadia Urbinati and David Ragazzoni, "Theories of Representative Government and Parliamentarism in Italy from the 1840s to the 1920s," in *Parliament and Parliamentarism*, 243–261.

Even when it comes to France and Britain, my goal is not to provide a comprehensive intellectual history of parliamentarism but rather to capture what one might call its *logic* – the chain of interconnected reasons that led so many individuals to believe parliamentarism was the best or even the only framework for securing political liberty in modern European states. As I have intimated, the logic of parliamentarism went broadly as follows. Political liberty requires a powerful legislative assembly. And a powerful legislative assembly requires parliamentarism: it requires constitutional monarchy, responsible ministers who serve in the assembly, and (as we will see shortly) a system of political parties.

To explore this approach to modern constitutionalism in all its richness and complexity, I have sought to strike a careful balance between historical breadth and the detailed examination of particular texts. The backbone of the book is formed by a relatively limited number of authors. Burke, de Lolme, Necker, de Staël, Constant, Tocqueville, Mill, Bagehot, and Weber are the central figures, and their ideas are explored in depth. However, these nine authors did not write in isolation. They were in dialogue with a wide array of other writers and political actors. Parliamentarism was not merely an intellectual construct; it was a structure that was implicated in every aspect of everyday politics. It is impossible to understand how any single theorist reflected upon it unless we reconstruct the larger political and intellectual world in which he or she was writing. That means taking a contextualist approach. My goal is for the history in this book and the textual interpretations in this book to be mutually enhancing so that my readings of the central authors are not only made intelligible by the contexts in which they are situated but also reveal and illustrate those very contexts.

While the nine authors at the heart of this study provided powerful arguments for a parliamentary regime, they also recognized its genuine puzzles and pathologies. If this book's central line of argument reconstructs their case for parliamentarism, an important auxiliary thread follows the *dilemmas of parliamentarism.* The first such dilemma concerned the role of the monarch. Could a king be constitutionally limited and subordinate to the legislature if he were actively involved in making political decisions? Or must the monarch delegate all his active powers to ministers – keeping only the social and symbolic trappings of royalty? Most eighteenth-century authors envisioned an *active* monarch, although one whose actions were comprehensively supervised by parliament, but beginning with Benjamin Constant, the idea of a *neutral* constitutional monarch would become increasingly attractive in European thought. Constant defended a monarch who played no active role in political decisions. "The king reigns but does not govern" became the mantra associated with his theory.

Constant titled the monarch the "neutral power." By this, he meant that the king's proper role was to serve not as a participant *in* the political process but rather as the referee *of* the political process. Ministers were not the agents of the monarch, as they had been viewed during the eighteenth century. They were simply the members of parliament who happened to win the support of a parliamentary majority and thus laid claim to the top executive positions. In making political decisions, they were to have complete autonomy from the king. Constant's conception of constitutional monarchy was picked up by numerous authors, including John Stuart Mill and Max Weber. Yet it would be rejected by others – most notably Alexis de Tocqueville and François Guizot – who thought it unnecessarily sacrificed the strength and stability of the executive.

If the first great dilemma of parliamentarism was the role of the monarch, the second was corruption. As parliamentarism developed in eighteenth-century England, the Crown made use of all its financial resources to ensure ministers had sufficient support in the House of Commons. Pensions, jobs, and favors were offered to members of Parliament as well as to the electorate. When France adopted a parliamentary government in 1814, patronage emerged as an equally widespread practice there. In both nations, it was widely argued that parliamentarism required patronage. Without it, no ministry would be able to command sufficient parliamentary support to stay in office, and the monarch would lose his most important tool for influencing representatives. Eliminating patronage would lead, at best, to endemic cabinet instability, and, at worst, to the Crown being overpowered by the legislature.

The authors who defended patronage also claimed a particular practice had emerged to mitigate its worst effects: *political parties*. They argued that as parliament came to be divided among competing parties, representatives were naturally grouped together by their opinions and principles. Patronage was an instrument for strengthening those already existing bonds – rather than a means of corrupting representatives who otherwise would have disagreed with the government. The function of political parties was to prevent cabinet instability while ameliorating corruption, thus overcoming the two great pathologies of parliamentarism. However, critics of patronage believed that even with a system of political parties, the threat of corruption remained quite real. By allowing ministers to gain political support through appealing to the personal financial interest of representatives, patronage undermined speech and persuasion in parliament. It put at risk the very values of responsibility and deliberation that parliament existed to secure.

With this issue as well, Benjamin Constant's writings marked a profound turning point. The neutral monarch envisioned by Constant had no need of "influence" to secure his minimal position in the state. The only remaining justification for patronage was the threat of cabinet instability. However, Constant was confident that this obstacle could also be overcome. Like the defenders of patronage, he believed the struggle over ministerial office in parliament would lead to a system of political parties. But Constant took an additional step: he argued this struggle would ultimately come to involve the public as well as the legislature. The party or coalition that won the confidence of *the nation* would be sure to have a strong basis of legislative support. In the modern parliament, *public opinion* rather than patronage would be the foundation of strong ministries and durable majorities.

For Constant, the monarch's role was simply to ensure that this process worked smoothly. He dismissed ministers when they were at odds with parliament, dissolved parliament when a majority could not be found or public opinion seemed undetermined, and served as a *ne plus ultra* who prevented any individual or faction from contemplating usurpation. In large part because Britain under Victoria would seem to powerfully instantiate Constant's theory, his would become the foremost nineteenth-century vision of parliamentarism – and therefore the most important ideal of constitutional government across Europe. While corruption and monarchical involvement never disappeared, they would come to seem less essential to a stable parliamentary regime.

By tracing the theory of parliamentarism from the French Revolution to the early twentieth century, this book offers a new perspective on the history of liberalism. To be clear, my contention is not that liberalism was (let alone is) coterminous with parliamentarism. While many self-described liberal authors advocated parliamentarism, others showed little interest in doing so. One thinks of Herbert Spencer.[21] Still others preferred

---

[21] See Herbert Spencer, "The Man versus the State," in *The Man versus the State: With Six Essays on Government, Society, and Freedom* (Indianapolis: 1982), 24–30. Spencer had previously offered an argument in favor of parliamentary bodies; however, one far narrower than is examined in this book. See Herbert Spencer, "Representative Government: What Is It Good For?" in *The Man versus the State*, 331–382.

the American constitutional model.[22] But if *parliamentary liberalism* was only one strand of liberal thought in this period, I hope to demonstrate that it was an exceptionally compelling and influential one. As the term *liberalism* came during the nineteenth century to signify a broad commitment to individual freedom, human progress, and political pluralism, a range of authors believed that parliamentarism was the most realistic institutional method for securing those values.

Moreover, the very activity of parliamentary politics seemed to provide one of the most powerful demonstrations of liberal values in action. Parliament was a space defined by discussion and pluralism. Its procedures forced individuals with vastly different priorities and interests to come to a common decision through argument and speech. In a genuinely liberal society, it seemed apparent that such a body would naturally stand at the center of political life. A powerful representative assembly was viewed as the crucial element that had been missing in traditional European monarchies. It was equally absent in the more novel "Caesarist" regimes that emerged in nineteenth-century France and Germany.[23]

The profound historical affinity between nineteenth-century liberalism and parliamentarism was well known among scholars writing prior to the Second World War. Guido de Ruggiero and Harold Laski, the two most important historians of liberalism during the first half of the twentieth century, both thought that the rule of parliament had been central to the liberal ideal.[24] Not only parliamentary government but also constitutional

---

[22] See, for instance, Frédéric Bastiat, "Parliamentary Conflicts of Interest," in *Collected Works of Frédéric Bastiat*, vol. 2, ed. Jacques de Guenin, tr. Jane Willems and Michael Willems (Indianapolis: 2012), 376. In Chapter 5, I will also consider Édouard Laboulaye, a figure who likewise advocated the American constitutional model in nineteenth-century France. For British authors attracted to American constitutionalism, one can begin with M. J. C. Vile, *Constitutionalism and The Separation of Powers* (Indianapolis: 1998), 110–118.

[23] The "Caesarist" regimes of France and Germany both had elected assemblies. But they could not influence and control the government as under parliamentarism. By the end of Napoleon III's regime, a form of parliamentary responsibility was being introduced in France. The classic study of this process is Theodore Zeldin, *The Political System of Napoleon III* (London: 1958). For debates over the constitutional character of the German Empire and its differentiation from parliamentarism, see Hewitson, "The *Kaiserreich* in Question." For broad overviews of the nineteenth-century concept of Caesarism, see Melvin Richter, "A Family of Political Concepts: Tyranny, Despotism, Bonapartism, Caesarism, Dictatorship, 1750–1917," *European Journal of Political Theory*, vol. 4, no. 3 (2005), 221–248; Peter Baehr and Melvin Richter, "Introduction," in *Dictatorship in History and Theory: Bonapartism, Caesarism and Totalitarianism*, ed. Peter Baehr and Melvin Richter (Cambridge: 2004), 1–26.

[24] See Harold Laski, *The Rise of European Liberalism: An Essay in Interpretation* (London: 1936), 157–158; Harold Laski, *Parliamentary Government in England* (New York: 1938), 1–52; Guido de Ruggiero, *The History of European Liberalism*, tr. R. G. Collingwood (London: 1927), 254–274, 303–304, 364–365, 380–391.

monarchy was recognized for its significance; Ruggiero even noted how formative the turn away from Montesquieu had been in the development of liberal thought.[25] According to Ludwig von Mises, "parliamentarism, as it has slowly developed in England ... since the seventeenth century, and on the European continent since the overthrow of Napoleon and the July and February Revolutions, presupposes the general acceptance of the ideology of liberalism."[26] This point was also expressed by Carl Schmitt, who claimed that "the belief in parliamentarism, in government by discussion, belongs to the intellectual world of liberalism,"[27] and by Friedrich Meinecke, who emphasized the long-standing liberal belief "that constitutionalism and parliamentarism are or ought to be identical."[28]

Since the Second World War, the relationship between liberalism and parliamentarism has gradually disappeared from the historiography of modern political thought. One especially striking demonstration of this has been the response to Quentin Skinner's well-known "neo-Roman" or "republican" theory of liberty. Skinner discerned in the parliamentarian cause of the English Civil War a distinctive account of political freedom, consisting of the following propositions. First, to be a free individual requires living in a free state. And, second, what is characteristic of a free state is that power is concentrated in a representative assembly. In particular, the "discretionary or prerogative powers" of government must be subordinate to the assembly.[29] Skinner's argument initiated an extensive debate. Some critics have expressed skepticism that he truly unearthed an alternative to liberalism.[30] Others have sought to show how liberal thought was itself shaped by "republican" concepts.[31] What has rarely been noted, however, is

---

[25] Ruggiero, *The History of European Liberalism*, 56–60, 158–165, 215–216, 254–274. These practices were also strongly emphasized by Carl Schmitt, writing at the same moment as Ruggiero. See Carl Schmitt, "The Guardian of the Constitution," in *The Guardian of the Constitution: Hans Kelsen and Carl Schmitt on the Limits of Constitutional Law*, tr. Lars Vinx (Cambridge: 2015), 150–160; Carl Schmitt, *Constitutional Theory*, tr. Jeffrey Seitzer (Durham: 2008), 308–378.

[26] Ludwig von Mises, *Liberalism*, tr. Ralph Raico (San Francisco: 1985), 170.

[27] Carl Schmitt, "On the Contradiction between Parliamentarism and Democracy," in *The Crisis of Parliamentary Democracy*, tr. Ellen Kennedy (Cambridge, MA: 1985), 8.

[28] Friedrich Meinecke, *Weltbürgertum und Nationalstaat* (Munich: 1908), 460. Quoted in Eulau, "Early Theories of Parliamentarism," 48.

[29] Quentin Skinner, *Liberty before Liberalism* (Cambridge: 1998), 51; Quentin Skinner, "A Third Concept of Liberty," in *Proceedings of the British Academy*, vol. 115 (2002), 250–255. Skinner's famous argument is that this conception of liberty was derived from Roman law and mediated by Renaissance authors such as Machiavelli.

[30] See, for instance, Charles Larmore, "Liberal and Republican Conceptions of Freedom," *Critical Review of International Social and Political Philosophy*, vol. 6, no. 1 (2001), 96–119.

[31] See, for instance, Andreas Kalyvas and Ira Katznelson, *Liberal Beginnings: Making a Republic for the Moderns* (Cambridge: 2008).

that for much of the nineteenth century, the parliamentarian ideas Skinner so brilliantly reconstructed simply were the ideas of liberalism.[32]

The very term *liberal* was first used (in its modern sense) in conjunction with demands for parliamentary rule that were not dissimilar from those of Henry Parker. The *liberales* were the defenders of the Spanish constitution of 1812, a constitution that was written with the aim of ending absolute monarchy and that had, as its most important institutional innovation, a powerful representative assembly. Titled the *Cortes*, this assembly was to pass all laws, control all taxation, hold executive officials responsible, and come to its decisions through open public deliberation.[33] For over a generation, the *liberales* battled the supporters of absolutism in Spain.[34] It was during this struggle that the term *liberal* would spread through Europe and be self-consciously adopted by figures such as Constant, De Staël, Tocqueville, and Mill.[35] They viewed parliamentarism as the crucial institutional framework that would enable assemblies like the *Cortes* to take up their rightful position in European states. Rather than discovering an alternative to liberalism, Skinner's true achievement, as a historian of neo-Roman liberty, was to unearth several of the crucial foundations of liberalism.[36]

---

[32] It is possible to follow out the seventeenth-century ideas that Skinner examines to a more radical conclusion that none of the authors I examine would accept: the total rejection of monarchy and the insistence on a republic. However, Skinner was disinclined to center his recovery of neo-Roman liberty on this line of thought. His focus is explicitly on the parliamentary theory of a free state in which monarchy is compatible with liberty so long as the monarch is fully constrained by law and parliament; see Skinner, *Liberty before Liberalism*, 22–23.

[33] This constitution also introduced a more equitable criminal justice system and ended the inquisition. See "The Political Constitution of the Spanish Monarchy. Promulgated in Cadiz, the Nineteenth Day of March, 1812," in *Cobbett's Political Register*, vol. 26 (London: 1814), 25–32. The parliamentarian arguments for this constitution and their legacy are analyzed in José María Rosales, "Parliamentarism in Spanish Politics in the Nineteenth and Twentieth Centuries: From Constitutional Liberalism to Democratic Parliamentarism," in *Parliament and Parliamentarism*, 277–291.

[34] This struggle is examined in Isabel Burdiel, "Myths of Failure; Myths of Success: New Perspectives on Nineteenth-Century Spanish Liberalism," *Journal of Modern History*, vol. 70, no. 4 (1998), 892–912.

[35] Jennifer Pitt documents the self-conscious use of this term by Mill, Constant and Tocqueville during the early nineteenth century. See Jennifer Pitts, *A Turn to Empire: The Rise of Imperial Liberalism in Britain and France* (Princeton: 2006), 260. For her explicit invocation of what she calls *principaux libéraux*, see Germaine de Staël, *Considérations sur les principaux événemens de la révolution Françoise*, t. 2 (Paris: 1818), 103. J. C. D. Clark has effectively traced the English history of the term *liberalism* and how it arrived in England as a result of the struggle in Spain. See J. C. D. Clark, *English Society, 1660–1832: Religion, Ideology and Politics During the Ancien Regime* (Cambridge: 2000), 6–8. Helena Rosenblatt provides a more general European history of the term, which emphasizes its early association with the struggle for legislative assemblies in Sweden as well as Spain; see Helena Rosenblatt, *The Lost History of Liberalism: From Ancient Rome to the Twenty-First Century* (Princeton: 2018), 41–87.

[36] This was, after all, the distinctive thesis of "Whig History" when it flourished in the nineteenth century: that the liberal state Britain became under Victoria could be traced back to the parliamentarian cause of the seventeenth century. For a discussion of this dimension of Whig historiography, see P. B. M. Blaas, *Continuity and Anachronism: Parliamentary and Constitutional Development in Whig Historiography and in the Anti-Whig Reaction between 1890 and 1930* (The Hague: 1978), 111–214.

I noted earlier how the rise of democracy has come to overshadow the spread of parliamentarism in the historiography of modern political thought. Until recently, one might have been tempted to think that this is entirely for the best – that the democratic structures which emerged during the twentieth century have created a stable new foundation for liberal values, rendering classical theories of parliamentarism obsolete. It is only now becoming apparent how far from true this is. The challenges that led to the classical theory of parliamentarism are still very much with us. How to achieve proper legislative supervision and control over the executive, how to create a space for legislative debate and discussion that does not threaten the constitutional order, and how to evaluate the challenge legislative corruption poses to public political life – these are among the central political problems of the twenty-first century.

Nor have we found a solution to these challenges that is really superior to that of Constant and Mill. For all practical purposes, we continue to think that a modern state is not genuinely free or liberal unless it has a representative assembly that can control the budget, oversee the executive, deliberate autonomously, and regularly engage with public opinion. Yet instead of moderating representative assemblies through the influence of constitutional monarchy and parliamentary government, we have instead let them be increasingly *displaced* by constitutional courts and administrative agencies. The result is a veritable "crisis of representation," which recent populist movements have proven adept at exploiting. The only true safeguard against populism in power seems to be a capable parliamentary opposition, just as the most plausible way to prevent its emergence is a vibrant process of parliamentary politics in which the nation sees itself represented. Put simply, we have not escaped the logic of classical parliamentarism. While this may be surprising to us, it would not have shocked many of the formative theorists of twentieth-century democracy – Max Weber, James Bryce, the American Progressives, Hans Kelsen, Joseph Schumpeter – who were profoundly influenced by the theory explored in this book. As I will show in the Conclusion, that theory is no longer a living constitutional option. It has been rendered impractical by the growing power of the executive, which coincided with the triumph of mass democracy. But it is by no means dead either. Through reckoning with the logic of classical parliamentarism, we might gain a better vantage point on the challenges of contemporary politics – which may prove to be nothing more than the old challenges of parliamentarism in a new form.

CHAPTER I

The Eighteenth-Century House of Commons

In his 1748 treatise *The Spirit of the Laws*, Montesquieu penned the most influential eighteenth-century account of the English constitution. Indeed, his account is so well known, it requires only the briefest summary. He argued that the English constitution was composed of three separate powers that checked each other through their respective prerogatives.[1] The House of Commons checked the Crown through its control over revenue and its impeachment power. In turn, it was checked by the House of Lords, which had to approve all legislation, as well as by the king's absolute veto.[2] Because these different prerogatives were relatively balanced, equilibrium resulted. However, Montesquieu warned that if any prerogative held by the Crown were seized by Parliament, or vice versa, the English constitution would be endangered.[3] It would also be endangered if any of the three powers lost its basis of support in English society.[4]

Montesquieu's account of the English constitution has been widely heralded as the intellectual origin of liberalism. Confronted by the excesses of the French Revolution, or so the story goes, Edmund Burke, Germaine de Staël, Benjamin Constant, and Alexis de Tocqueville all turned to Montesquieu. Along with the American Founders, they restored a sense of appreciation for the balanced constitution, which has subsisted in liberal thought down to the present.

In this chapter, I will begin the process of telling a very different history. I will demonstrate that in the decades leading up to the French Revolution,

---

[1] For the history of this theory before Montesquieu, see Vile, *Constitutionalism and The Separation of Powers*, 58–82.

[2] Montesquieu, *The Spirit of the Laws*, ed. Anne Cohler et al. (Cambridge: 1989), 164. For an astute analysis of how this makes Montesquieu less than fully committed to the "separation of powers," see Craiutu, *A Virtue for Courageous Minds*, 50–53.

[3] Montesquieu, *Spirit of the Laws*, 161–165.

[4] As I will discuss later in the chapter, he thought that the decline of the aristocracy had seriously endangered England by depriving the House of Lords of its traditional role and setting up a dramatic conflict between the Crown and Commons.

the insufficiency of Montesquieu's account of England was keenly felt. Put simply, a great many observers believed the English constitution was *not* actually balanced and that the prerogatives of the House of Commons were decisively superior to those of the Lords and Crown. This was both celebrated and lamented. On the one hand, an influential tradition of argument held that it was the House of Commons in particular that preserved liberty. This implied that its constitutional position *should* be the most heavily fortified. On the other hand, it was widely recognized that the House of Commons could itself become a threat to liberty. As it became apparent that the English constitution tilted toward the House of Commons, there was thus widespread uncertainty about its future.

I will argue that what ameliorated this uncertainty was the growing recognition that England possessed several practices Montesquieu had overlooked, which restrained the House of Commons, but did not require the Crown and Lords to exercise prerogatives equal to it. The first such practice was the involvement of ministers in Parliament. The second was the sheer presence of a constitutional monarch. A range of authors would become convinced that through these two practices, England could enjoy the benefits of a powerful legislative assembly without any risk of legislative usurpation. There was no need for a monarch with powers equal to those of Parliament, such as Montesquieu had envisioned. For much of the eighteenth century, this line of argument remained still inchoate. However, over the subsequent chapters of this book, we will see it develop into the classical theory of a parliamentary constitution.

This chapter will proceed as follows. I will begin by analyzing the powerful position of the House of Commons in the eighteenth century. I will examine the widespread argument that this institution made possible English liberty as well as the challenge that the House of Commons posed to the theory of the English constitution as a system of equally balanced powers. I will contend that it was in the context of this challenge that eighteenth-century authors began seriously reflecting on the developing practices of parliamentarism – the strict responsibility of ministers to Parliament, the emergence of a parliamentary opposition, the presence of a limited constitutional monarch, and the regular involvement of ministers in Parliament. I will consider each of these practices in turn. I will also discuss the profound dilemma of parliamentary corruption, which developed in tandem with the practice of ministers serving in the House of Commons. Because the aim of this chapter is to lay the general groundwork for what follows, it will range more widely than future chapters. However, I will devote concerted attention to the political struggles that occurred during the ministry of Robert Walpole and to Jean Louis de Lolme – the great eighteenth-century theorist of constitutional monarchy.

The Rise of the House of Commons and the Ideal of a Deliberative Assembly

The story this book tells is unthinkable without Parliament's unprecedented position in English politics after 1688. Throughout the eighteenth century, Parliament met regularly and determined taxation and the budget. Armies could not be maintained without its permission, and the king would eventually become dependent upon Parliament even for his personal discretionary funds. Most remarkably of all, the exercise of these powers went relatively unchallenged. In the seventeenth century, Parliament and the Crown had been in a perpetual contest of strength. Charles I ruled for 11 years (1629–1640) without calling a parliament, while Charles II kept the same one in being for 18 years (1661–1679) without an election. These actions sparked violent opposition, but in 1688, the conflict was largely settled.[5] The Bill of Rights enshrined into law that kings could not legislate, govern, raise money, or maintain an army without Parliament and that Parliament must meet regularly.

The new significance of Parliament after 1688 is indicated by the unprecedented surge in legislative activity that occurred. In the two centuries between 1485 and 1688, Parliament passed a total of 2,700 measures, while between 1688 and 1801, a period little over half as long, 13,600 measures were passed.[6] Whether one considers the number of bills passed or the number debated, the striking conclusion is that Parliament was 10 times more active as a legislative body during the eighteenth century than in previous centuries.[7] It was only during the eighteenth century that Parliament truly became a *legislative assembly*, not merely an extended council the Crown was forced to consult.

---

[5] For general historical studies of seventeenth-century British politics and the settlement of 1688, see Mark Kishlansky, *A Monarchy Transformed: Britain, 1603–1714* (London: 1996); Steven Pincus, *1688: The First Modern Revolution* (New Haven: 2009); J. C. D. Clark, *Revolution and Rebellion: State and Society in England in the Seventeenth and Eighteenth Centuries* (Cambridge: 1986), 68–163; Harvey Mansfield, "Party Government and the Settlement of 1688," *American Political Science Review*, vol. 58, no. 4 (1964), 933–946.

[6] Julian Hoppit, "Patterns of Parliamentary Legislation," *Historical Journal*, vol. 39, no. 1 (1996), 109.

[7] Ibid.

The stunning increase in parliamentary activity during the eighteenth century was due to the increasing length and frequency of parliamentary sessions and to the improvement of parliamentary procedures.[8] It also testifies to the growth of the English state itself.[9] Parliament was involved in building a transcontinental empire, and it was increasingly enmeshed in local and regional concerns across England.[10] While the eighteenth century saw a 10-fold increase in legislative activity, there was nearly a 20-fold increase when it came to bills dealing with local communities or individual persons.[11]

Julian Hoppit summarizes the growth in parliamentary activity as follows: "before the Glorious Revolution, the legislative output of Parliament was infrequent, unpredictable, and numerically inconsiderable. There was a transformation, a revolution, as a consequence of the events of 1688–1689. In legislative terms, by the early eighteenth century Parliament had a new place in the social, economic and political life of the country."[12] According to Geoffrey Holmes, "to an extent unparalleled before 1688," government in eighteenth-century England was *government through Parliament.*"[13] "Parliament after the Revolution became an indispensable part of the machinery of the state."[14]

This transformation was recognized by contemporary observers. According to the influential humanist George Savile, the Marquess of Halifax, "parliaments are now grown to be quite other things than they were formerly. In ancient times they were little more than great assizes; a roll of grievances; magna carta confirmed; privileges of holy church preserved; so many sacks of wool given; and away."[15] That was nothing like

---

[8] Ibid., 112–116. It was during this same period that there emerged regular election procedures. See Mark Kishlansky, *Parliamentary Selection: Social and Political Choice in Early Modern England* (Cambridge: 1986), 12–22, 105–122.

[9] The expansion of the English state during this period is examined in John Brewer, *The Sinews of Power: War, Money and the English State, 1688–1783* (London: 1989); J. H. Plumb, *The Growth of Political Stability in England* (London: 1967), 105–132.

[10] For the way that Parliament dealt with these new responsibilities, see Hoppit, "Patterns of Parliamentary Legislation," 116–125; Joanna Innes, "Legislating for Three Kingdoms," in *Parliaments, Nations and Identities in Britain and Ireland: 1660–1860*, ed. Julian Hoppit (Manchester: 2003), 15–48; David Armitage, *Foundations of Modern International Thought* (Cambridge: 2013), 135–153.

[11] Hoppitt, "Patterns of Parliamentary Legislation," 117. This trend was noted by Blackstone and other influential jurists. See David Lieberman, "Codification, Consolidation, and Statute," in *Rethinking Leviathan: The Eighteenth-Century State in Britain and Germany*, ed. John Brewer and Eckhart Hellmuth (Oxford: 1999), 359–390.

[12] Hoppit, "Patterns of Parliamentary Legislation," 125.

[13] Geoffrey Holmes, *British Politics in the Age of Anne* (London: 1987), 217.   [14] Ibid.

[15] George Savile, "Some Cautions Offered to the Consideration of Those Who Are to Choose Members to Serve in the Next Parliament," in *Works*, vol. 1, ed. Mark Brown (Oxford: 1989), 323.

the modern parliamentary assembly in which there were innumerable "traps and gins laid for the well-meaning country-gentleman."[16] Halifax was seconded by an anonymous pamphleteer who also wrote that "parliaments are grown quite other things than they were in those days." For there were now "the conveniences and inconveniences of every bill to be argued … grievances to be redressed, the government to be secured, mismanagements to be punished, property to be asserted, and money to be appropriated as well as raised."[17]

The House of Lords retained considerable importance across the eighteenth century.[18] But many observers believed that the House of Commons held a crucial advantage: the power of the purse. Only the House of Commons could initiate or amend bills that had to do with taxation and the budget. This power had been acquired through a complicated historical process. Grants of money had required parliamentary consent since the Middle Ages, but it was also expected that the Crown would primarily live off the revenue of its vast properties and would turn to Parliament only in "extraordinary" cases. By the seventeenth century, these properties were no longer capable of supplying the Crown with sufficient revenue to live on, while the costs of war and empire were causing the expense of government to grow rapidly.[19] Just as the Crown was becoming regularly dependent upon Parliament for revenue, the House of Commons successfully asserted against the House of Lords that it alone could initiate and amend bills funding the government.[20] Any demand for money by the Crown had to be expressed before the Commons.[21] Because the turn of the eighteenth

---

[16] Ibid.

[17] Anon., *The Subjects Case: Or Advice to All Englishmen, Who Have the Right of Electing Members to Serve Their Country in the Next Parliament, to Be Held at Westminster, on Thursday the 6th Day of Febr. 1701* (London: 1701), 10.

[18] For the role of the House of Lords in this period, see John Cannon, *Aristocratic Century: The Peerage of Eighteenth-Century England* (Cambridge: 1984), 93–125; Corrine Weston, *English Constitutional Theory and the House of Lords, 1556–1832* (London: 2010), 56–120; J. C. D. Clark, *English Society, 1688–1832: Ideology, Social Structure and Political Practice during the Ancien Regime* (Cambridge: 1985), 200–231.

[19] See Kishlansky, *A Monarchy Transformed*, 61, 83–88, 231–232. For a comprehensive account of how parliamentary grants came very gradually to supersede the Crown's traditional revenue, see C. D. Chandaman, *The English Public Revenue, 1660–1688* (Oxford: 1975).

[20] See Paul Einzig, *The Control of the Purse: Progress and Decline of Parliament's Financial Control* (London: 1959), 112–114; P. D. G. Thomas, *The House of Commons in the Eighteenth Century* (Oxford: 1971), 65–71.

[21] The process through which this occurred is described in the major text on parliamentary procedure from the eighteenth century; see *The Liverpool Tractate: An Eighteenth-Century Manual on the Procedure of the House of Commons*, ed. Catherine Strateman (New York: 1937). For a scholarly discussion, see Romney Sedgwick, *The House of Commons 1715–1754* (Oxford: 1970), 4–5. Note that although the House of Commons had to approve any money bill, it was conventional by the

century saw the "financial revolution" – the emergence of a modern system of debt finance to fund the growing English state – fiscal policy became essential to the government's existence like never before. The House of Commons was therefore placed in a position of extraordinary power.[22]

Historians emphasize that the House of Commons would not really make use of this position or effectively oversee government expenditures until the nineteenth century.[23] But sophisticated eighteenth-century observers recognized the seismic shift that had occurred and the new potentialities that had been created. De Lolme argued that in an age "when everything is rated by pecuniary estimation, when gold is become the great moving spring of affairs," no other actor could match the House of Commons.[24] According to Edmund Burke, "since the Revolution at least – the power of the Nation has all flowed with a full tide into the House of Commons. The power of the state nearly melted down into this house."[25] David Hume went one step further. He argued that because of its financial prerogatives, "the share of power, allotted by our constitution to the House of Commons, is so great, that it absolutely commands all the other parts of the government."[26]

As we will see, the powerful position of the House of Commons would inspire deep concern – it would profoundly challenge Montesquieu's account of the English constitution as a system of balanced powers. However, it was also widely celebrated. A range of authors believed that a free state was simply impossible in modern Europe without a powerful representative assembly like the House of Commons. For these analysts, the value of the House of Commons was most on display at two moments. The first was in the lead-up to laws being passed; the second was after the passage of a law, as it was being executed. Prior to the act of legislation, the House of Commons served as a *deliberative assembly*. It was a space in which the merits of a bill could be debated and discussed from the widest

---

eighteenth century that such bills were initiated by ministers (i.e., at the request of the government) rather than by ordinary members.

[22] Classic discussions of the "financial revolution" and the central position it created for the House of Commons include Brewer, *Sinews of Power*, 89–161, 221–269; P. G. M. Dickson, *The Financial Revolution in England: A Study in the Development of Public Credit, 1688–1756* (London: 1967).

[23] See Henry Roseveare, *The Treasury: Evolution of a British Institution* (London: 1969), 86–97; Basil Chubb, *The Control of Public Expenditure: Financial Committees of the House of Commons* (Oxford: 1952), 8–29.

[24] Jean Louis de Lolme, *The Constitution of England*, ed. David Lieberman (Indianapolis: 2007), 64.

[25] Edmund Burke, "Speech on Parliamentary Incapacitation," in *Writings and Speeches*, vol. 2, ed. Paul Langford and William Todd (Oxford: 1981), 234.

[26] David Hume, *Essays Moral and Political*, ed. Eugene Miller (Indianapolis: 1985), 44.

variety of perspectives. Following the act of legislation, the role of the House of Commons was to supervise and control the executive officials who enforced the laws. In every state, the executive posed the most immediate threat to liberty, because it exercised direct coercion over individuals. The House of Commons served as the "control" on the executive. It supervised the highest-ranking ministers and prevented them from acting arbitrarily.

Bernard Manin has questioned whether the value of deliberation was associated with representative assemblies during the eighteenth century, as it manifestly would be during the age of liberalism.[27] In fact, this value had been associated with Parliament even in the seventeenth century. During the English Civil War, opponents of the Crown argued that because the monarch was a single person, he was a less capable ruler than Parliament, which came to its decisions through a discussion in which many individuals contributed their opinions. As Henry Parker characteristically put the point, "I think every man's heart tells him, that in public consultations, the eyes of many choice gentleman out of all parts, see more than fewer."[28] This argument was reiterated by Algernon Sidney, who wrote that "a house of commons composed of those who are best esteemed by their neighbors in all the towns and counties of England" would govern better "than such a man, woman or child, as happens to be next in blood to the last king. Many men do usually see more than one; and if we may believe the wisest king, *In the multitude of counsellors, there is safety.*"[29] Milton would similarly write that "Parliament is the supreme council of the nation, set up by a completely free people and furnished with full power for this very purpose; to consult together over the most important matters."[30]

Such arguments continued to be expressed during the eighteenth century. However, they would be articulated in a very different context. It was no longer the specter of a powerful monarch that inspired the defense of parliamentary deliberation but rather the specter of greater popular control

[27] Manin, *Principles of Representative Government*, 183–192.
[28] Henry Parker, *Observations upon Some of His Majesties Late Answers and Expressions*, in *Tracts on Liberty in the Puritan Revolution, 1638–1647*, ed. William Haller (New York: 1979), 177. See as well, Henry Parker, "The Case of Shipmony Briefly Discoursed," in *The Struggle for Sovereignty: Seventeenth-Century English Political Tracts*, vol. 1, ed. Joyce Malcolm (Indianapolis: 1999), 117.
[29] Algernon Sidney, *Discourses Concerning Government* (New York: 1979), 424.
[30] John Milton, *A Defence of the People of England*, in *Political Writings*, ed. Martin Dzelzainis, tr. Claire Gruzelier (Cambridge: 1991), 218.

over Parliament.[31] Throughout the eighteenth century, a variety of English radicals argued that electors should be able to determine exactly how their representatives in Parliament voted.[32] Opponents of this practice warned that it would harm parliamentary deliberation – undermining what one author called "the mutual debates and consultations of ... representatives."[33]

One impetus behind the movement in favor of electoral mandates was precisely a sense of wariness about the growing power of the House of Commons. "Our ancestors," James Burgh wrote in his influential book *Political Disquisitions*, "were provident, but not provident enough. They set up parliaments, as a curb on kings and ministers; but they neglected to reserve to themselves a regular and constitutional method of exerting their power in curbing parliaments."[34] From the beginning of the eighteenth century, direct popular control was seen by many authors as the best way to "curb" the House of Commons.[35] However, in the 1770s, a more radical argument would also become widespread: without mandates, it was impossible to ensure that laws truly expressed the popular will.[36] "The consent of the whole people, as far as it can be obtained, is indispensably necessary to every law, by which the whole people are to be bound," Burgh wrote.[37] In a large nation like England, this could only occur if the people directly determined how their representatives voted. Mandates would

---

[31] Opposition to mandation and claims for the superiority of parliamentary over popular judgment were not absent in seventeenth-century parliamentarian pamphlets, however. See, for instance, Sidney, *Discourses Concerning Government*, 451; Charles Herle, "A Fuller Answer to a Treatise Written by Doctor Ferne," in *The Struggle for Sovereignty: Seventeenth-Century English Political Tracts*, vol. 2, ed. Joyce Malcolm (Indianapolis: 1999), 247.

[32] For discussions of the campaign for mandates, see Mark Goldie, "Situating Swift's Politics in 1701," in *Politics and Literature in the Age of Swift* (Cambridge: 2010), 31–51; Richard Tuck, *The Sleeping Sovereign: The Invention of Modern Democracy* (Cambridge: 2015), 198–203; Paul Kelly, "Constituents' Instructions to Members of Parliament in the Eighteenth Century," in *Party and Management in Parliament, 1660–1784*, ed. Clyde Jones (New York and Leicester: 1984), 169–189.

[33] Humphrey Mackworth, *A Vindication of Rights of the Commons of England* (London: 1701), 38.

[34] James Burgh, *Political Disquisitions*, vol. 1 (Philadelphia: 1775), 6.

[35] A crucial moment in the development of this argument occurred in 1701, when five residents from Kent who presented a petition to the House of Commons were condemned by the House for being "scandalous and seditious" and arrested. This event led to a mass outcry against the abuse of the legislature's power, and in response, a number of pamphlet writers – including Daniel Defoe and John Somers – argued that a popular check was needed over the House of Commons. For a discussion of this event, see Goldie, "Situating Swift's Politics in 1701."

[36] See Richard Price, *Two Tracts on Liberty*, in *Political Writings*, ed. D. O. Thomas (Cambridge: 1992), 24–25; Burgh, *Political Disquisitions*, 185; Catherine Macaulay, *Observations on a Pamphlet Entitled "Thoughts on the Cause of the Present Discontents"* (London: 1770), 14–19.

[37] Burgh, *Political Disquisitions*, 3.

recreate the kind of popular lawmaking that had been characteristic of classical republicanism.[38]

One of the most influential eighteenth-century opponents of mandates was the Reverend Anthony Ellys, who based his case to a considerable extent on the value of the House of Commons as a deliberative body.[39] Ellys argued that parliamentary representatives "use all of the freedom of speech in enquiry, consultation, and debate upon any matter, that is necessary, in order to form laws, for the welfare of the public."[40] His attack on mandates was a defense of this deliberative process, which enabled a representative to have "very great advantages for forming his judgment" that were not possessed by his constituents.[41]

One crucial "advantage" of parliamentary deliberation that Ellys identified was *information*. He argued that "by the representatives being at liberty to follow their own judgment, in Parliament," they attained "the great light to be had by the mutual information which such numbers of gentlemen, coming together from all parts of the nation, may give to each other."[42] Representatives also could request information from the government through "the right of the House of Commons to demand any public papers ... relating to the state of the nation, and to apply to the king for others."[43]

A second "advantage" was more rhetorical in character. Ellys claimed that through deliberation, representatives were exposed not only to a wider range of facts than their constituents, but also to a wider range of viewpoints. They were forced to grapple with "the various views of things that may arise from their debates and reasonings" and from "examinations of evidence in the house."[44] Through the very process of deliberation, in

---

[38] Rousseau was fully in agreement with English radicals about the importance of mandates. He pointed to "the negligence, the carelessness, and I dare say the stupidity of the English Nation which, after arming its deputies with the supreme power, adds not a single restraint to regulate the use they might make of it." He recommended that Poland, in contrast with England, institute legally binding instructions to determine how representatives voted. On any matter not completely unforeseen, Rousseau argued, a representative must vote "according to the express will of his constituents." Such a practice would close the gap between representative government and direct popular rule by giving regular citizens power over the laws by which they were to be governed. It would ensure "the immense advantage of never having the law be anything but the real expression of the nation's wills." See Jean Jacques Rousseau, "The Government of Poland," in *The Social Contract and Other Later Political Writings*, tr. Victor Gourevitch (Cambridge: 1997), 201, 202.

[39] Richard Bourke notes Ellys' significant influence on Burke's well-known speech at Bristol, which was also famously centered on Parliament being a "deliberative assembly." See Richard Bourke, *Empire and Revolution: The Political Life of Edmund Burke* (Princeton: 2015), 380.

[40] Anthony Ellys, *The Spiritual and Temporal Liberty of Subjects in England*, vol. 2 (London: 1765), 108.

[41] Ibid., 123.   [42] Ibid.   [43] Ibid.   [44] Ibid.

other words, an issue came to be seen from multiple perspectives. Even if no new facts were revealed, the meaning of an existing fact could shift in the course of debate, revealing consequences that had not been previously apparent. An author contemporary to Ellys, who was also writing in opposition to mandates, expressed this advantage of parliamentary deliberation in particularly evocative terms: "we know that things which considered in one light appear just and reasonable, may when they are considered in another light be unfit, and impracticable. The manner of the House of Commons is to view and examine the matters which come before them in all lights."[45]

As Kari Palonen has demonstrated, "to view and examine matters in all lights" was an aim cultivated by the House of Commons' procedures. Since the sixteenth century, speakers in the House of Commons have had to alternate *pro et contra*, ensuring a continuing contest between opposing viewpoints.[46] This was the cornerstone of parliamentary procedure during the eighteenth century. To ensure further variation in perspective, a representative could not speak more than once.[47] Finally, debates were stretched out over multiple days, so that there was time for new arguments to be generated. For a bill to be passed, it had to be read on three different occasions, and each reading could potentially be followed by a full discussion.[48]

The House of Commons' claim to be a deliberative assembly was also grounded in its social and geographic makeup. There were procedures in the House of Lords to ensure that debates occurred *pro et contra* and were stretched out over time. But for most of the eighteenth century, the Commons had nearly three times as many members as the Lords, and they represented a far greater variety of interests and localities.[49] The argument that the House of Commons was distinctive within the English constitution because it served as an "express image" or "mirror" of the

---

[45] Anon., *A Second Letter to a Member of Parliament Concerning the Present State of Affairs* (London: 1741), 28.

[46] See Palonen, *The Politics of Parliamentary Procedure*.

[47] In committee debate, members were allowed to speak more than once. Ibid., 126–131.

[48] Ibid., 178–195. The connection between parliamentary procedure and the practice of rhetorical persuasion is emphasized in Thomas, *The House of Commons in the Eighteenth Century*, 5–13, 45–64. An eighteenth-century source that gave prominent attention to this theme in its discussion of Parliament was the *Encyclopedia*. See Chevalier de Jaucourt, "English Parliament," in *Encyclopedic Liberty: Political Articles in the Dictionary of Diderot and D'Alembert*, tr. Henry Clark and Christine Dunn Henderson (Indianapolis: 2016), 451–462.

[49] Palonen, *The Politics of Parliamentary Procedure*, 36.

people was forged in the Civil War period.[50] It would continue to be widely expressed in the eighteenth century and justified the notion that the House of Commons was a uniquely deliberative body. Members of the House of Commons "come from all parts and corners of the kingdom," one author wrote, making known "the interest and grievances of every place and country."[51] Ellys similarly emphasized that that representatives "com[e] together from all parts of the nation."[52] This fostered both the diversity of viewpoints and the exchange of information that he associated with parliamentary deliberation.

To institute the direct popular control over the House of Commons that radicals like Burgh favored would mean the end of meaningful parliamentary deliberation. "To what purpose would this be," one author asked about debates between parliamentary representatives, "if, before their coming to Parliament, the point was settled for them in their instructions."[53] Nobody doubted that the House of Commons could arrive at a mistaken decision. However, it was feared that the voters who elected that body were even more prone to mistakes. Ellys argued that because electors did not directly participate in the exchange of facts and opinions characteristic of parliamentary debate, they were likely to have "but narrow and partial, or probably, in many cases, false, views and accounts of things."[54] They were not positioned "to judge ... what is most advantageous and conducive to the common good" or to "understand what is the true state and condition of the nation."[55]

The foregoing statements about deliberation and representation in the eighteenth-century House of Commons may sound surprising, as parliamentary politics during that period has long been associated with corruption and exclusion. In addition to the Crown's patronage, which I will be discussing later in the chapter, the House of Commons was elected through a highly limited franchise. Only 15–120 percent of adult males could vote.[56] Scholars have also emphasized that many eighteenth-century

---

[50] For a discussion of the classical English "mirror" theory of parliamentary representation, see Quentin Skinner, "Hobbes on Representation," *European Journal of Philosophy*, vol. 13, no. 2 (2005), 155–184; Eric Nelson, *The Royalist Revolution: Monarchy and the American Founding* (Cambridge: 2014), 60–107.

[51] Mackworth, *A Vindication of the Rights of the Commons of England*, 38.

[52] Ellys, *The Spiritual and Temporal Liberty of Subjects in England*, 123.

[53] Anon., *A Second Letter to a Member of Parliament Concerning the Present State of Affairs*, 28.

[54] Ellys, *The Spiritual and Temporal Liberty of Subjects in England*, 120.

[55] Mackworth, *A Vindication of the Rights of the Commons of England*, 38.

[56] Frank O'Gorman, *Voters, Patrons, and Parties: The Unreformed Electoral System of Hanoverian England, 1734–1832* (Oxford: 1989), 179.

elections were uncompetitive and under the control of a landed "oligarchy."[57] However, in recent decades, historians have begun to push back – and to emphasize all the ways in which eighteenth-century parliamentary politics was in fact both lively and representative. Although elections were frequently uncontested, members of Parliament (MPs) only rarely possessed such security that they were not "anxious to be seen to be advancing the needs of the constituency," and they heartily defended local and regional interests in Parliament.[58] And although the *membership* of the House of Commons was dominated by landholders, the electorate was far more varied, while an array of pressure groups enabled commercial interests to influence parliamentary legislation.[59] Nor was it only economic interests that united to exert pressure on Parliament: so did dissenters, opponents of the slave trade, pacifists, and other social reformers.[60] This is not to overlook the powerful critiques of the eighteenth-century House of Commons that were expressed by eighteenth-century radicals and that would become a standard element of Victorian historiography.[61] However, there did exist real grounds for thinking of the House of Commons as a space in which a range of social and political perspectives were expressed, and in which decisions were arrived at through deliberation and persuasion.

Nor was parliamentary deliberation entirely in tension with popular political involvement, for one of the most important developments in eighteenth-century England was the growing entanglement of parliamentary politics and public opinion.[62] In 1771, it became legal for parliamentary debates to be recorded, enabling the public to be, in a sense, indirect participants in parliamentary deliberation, while the struggle between parties in Parliament increasingly came to be reflected at the constituency

---

[57] For a survey of the critical scholarship on the eighteenth-century House of Commons, see Clark, *English Society, 1688–1832*, 8–41. Importantly, this came from the discovery of a marked decline in the number of contested elections and the size of the electorate after 1715; see, e.g., Plumb, *The Growth of Political Stability in England*. Crucial as well was the turn to septennial elections in 1716.

[58] O'Gorman, *Voters, Patrons, and Parties*, 18, 240–252; H. T. Dickinson, *The Politics of the People in Eighteenth-Century Britain* (London: 1995), 50.

[59] Dickinson, *The Politics of the People in Eighteenth-Century Britain*, 33, 56–81. The working class was also able to exercise pressure on Parliament through petitions and popular disruptions. Ibid., 79–81.

[60] Ibid., 81–91.

[61] For the Victorian roots of twentieth-century critiques of the unreformed House of Commons, see Clark, *English Society, 1688–1832*, 13–14.

[62] For a study of the meaning of "public opinion" in the eighteenth century, see J. A. W. Gunn, *Beyond Liberty and Property: The Process of Self-Recognition in Eighteenth-Century Political Thought* (Montreal: 1983), 260–315.

level.[63] But the interplay between debates in Parliament and debates in the wider public sphere – and the argument that parliamentary politics stimulated popular politics – was long-standing. In 1743, Edward Spelman defended the practice of parliamentary deliberation because it enabled the people to ultimately judge between the competing sides. According to Spelman, a "real advantage, that accrues to the people" from the contest in the House of Commons, "is that each party, by appealing to them upon all occasions, constitutes them judges of every contest; and, indeed, to whom should they appeal, but to those, whose welfare is the design, or pretense, of every measure?"[64] The issues at stake within the House of Commons became the issues debated during general elections, making the electorate ultimately "judg[e] of every contest." This did not lead to the kind of popular control over Parliament that proponents of mandates desired, but the public was not uninvolved in parliamentary politics.

Controlling the Crown

As valuable as parliamentary deliberation was, eighteenth-century authors believed that the House of Commons' most important function was to control the executive. What fundamentally distinguished England from other European monarchies was that an English king depended upon Parliament for revenue and had ministers who were responsible to Parliament for their actions. By supervising the Crown, Parliament secured the unprecedented liberty of English subjects.

Because of the implications of parliamentary control over the Crown, a range of authors would break with Montesquieu's account of the English constitution. However, Montesquieu recognized the importance of this function. During his first visit to England in 1729, he wrote that "England is at present the freest nation in the world . . . because the prince does not have the power to do any imaginable wrong to anyone."[65] This would

---

[63] For discussions of parliamentary debate being recorded, see Christopher Reid, "Whose Parliament? Political Oratory and Print Culture in the Later 18th Century," *Language and Literature*, vol. 9, no. 2 (2000), 122–134; Peter D. G. Thomas, "The Beginning of Parliamentary Reporting in Newspapers, 1768–1774," *English Historical Review*, vol. 74, no. 293 (1953), 623–636. For the emerging partisan struggle to win over constituencies, see John Phillipson, *Electoral Behavior in Unreformed England: Plumpers, Splitters, and Straights* (Princeton: 1982).

[64] Edward Spelman, "Preface," in *A Fragment out of the Sixth Book of Polybius* (London: 1743), ix.

[65] Montesquieu, "Notes sur l'Angleterre," in *Oeuvres complètes de Montesquieu*, vol. 10, ed. Jean Ehrard, Gilles Bertrand, et al. (Paris: 2012), 505. A quite similar statement is expressed in Voltaire, *Lettres Philosophiques* (Amsterdam: 1733), 33. The translation of Montesquieu here is my own. This will be true in all cases where I quote from the original French version of a text rather than from a published translation.

continue to be a prominent theme in *The Spirit of the Laws*, in which Montesquieu argued, first, that the defining characteristic of a "free state" was that executive officials were "held accountable for their administration," and, second, that the only power able to accomplish this was the legislature.[66] "In a free state," he wrote, "legislative power . . . has the right and should have the faculty to examine the manner in which the laws it has made have been executed."[67]

Montesquieu claimed that this "right" and this "faculty" had never been properly instituted in "ancient republics."[68] In some republics, such as "Crete and Lacedemonia," there was no accountability at all for executive officials.[69] In Rome, by contrast, the constitution went too far in the opposite direction. The Tribunate could block executive actions just as it could block laws, depriving the executive of the discretion it needed in periods of crisis.[70] Montesquieu believed that England had found a middle path between these two extremes. Parliament could not directly block the Crown's actions; however, it judged and evaluated them retrospectively.

Montesquieu argued that Parliament's supervision of the executive rested on two specific powers. The first was the power of impeachment. While the king was inviolable, if any of his subordinate officers acted illegally, they could be removed from office and prosecuted.[71] The second and more important power was control over revenue. Should the Crown ever threaten the nation's rights, its funding would be taken away. Montesquieu claimed that the Crown's financial dependence on the House of Commons was absolutely essential to liberty.[72] "If the executive power enacts on the raising of public funds without the consent of the legislature," he wrote, "there will no longer be liberty."[73] There would likewise be an end to liberty "if the legislative power enacts, not from year to year, but forever, on the raising of public funds."[74]

---

[66] Montesquieu, *The Spirit of the Laws*, 162.   [67] Ibid.   [68] Ibid., 164.   [69] Ibid., 162.
[70] Ibid., 163.   [71] Ibid., 162.
[72] For modern scholarly arguments to this same effect, see Brewer, *The Sinews of Power*, 137– 166; Clayton Roberts, "The Constitutional Significance of the Financial Settlement of 1690," *Historical Journal*, vol. 20, no. 1 (1977), 59–76; Paul Seaward, "Parliament and the Idea of Political Accountability in Early Modern Britain," in *Realities of Representation: State Building in Early Modern Europe and European America*, ed. Maija Jannson (New York: 2007), 45–62. For a more skeptical take, see Clark, *Revolution and Rebellion*, 71–83.
[73] Montesquieu, *The Spirit of the Laws*, 164.
[74] Ibid. In addition to parliamentary supervision of the Crown, another distinctive feature of the English constitution for eighteenth-century authors such as Montesquieu, Smith, and de Lolme was its independent judiciary – this has recently been emphasized in Istvan Hont, *Politics in Commercial Society*, ed. Béla Kapossy and Michael Sonenscher (Cambridge, MA: 2015); Bourke, *Empire and Revolution*. However, this required parliamentary supervision of the government, for the public

Like the claim that Parliament was a uniquely deliberative assembly, this line of argument had long played an important role in English political thought – most obviously in the lead-up to the English Civil War, when the Crown's right to raise money without parliamentary consent was the crucial issue.[75] But it would become especially widespread during the eighteenth and nineteenth centuries. As the House of Commons' control over finances became increasingly uncontested, a range of authors would identify this power as the ultimate guarantee of political liberty. According to Adam Smith, an English king could not "maintain the government for one year" except through the permission of the House of Commons, "as he has no power of levying supplies."[76] It was "in this manner," Smith declared, that "a system of liberty has been established in England."[77] The House of Commons' supervision of the Crown "secure[d] the liberty of the subjects and establishe[d] those great rights which they have now obtained."[78] For Blackstone as well, "the liberty of the subject" was secured by the loss of the Crown's "ancient revenues," making it dependent upon taxes approved by the House of Commons.[79] "So reasonably jealous are the Commons of this valuable privilege," Blackstone noted, "they will not permit the least alteration or amendment to be made by the Lords."[80]

But if the House of Commons' control over revenue was crucial to its supervision of the Crown, many observers were convinced that it also made the House of Commons the dominant actor in English politics, upsetting any system of equal checks and balances. In particular, it radically undermined the Crown's formal check against the House of Commons: its veto. Should the monarch refuse his assent to a major piece of legislation passed by the House of Commons, the House of Commons

---

needed some recourse if the government chose to disregard the courts. In principle, any minister who acted in defiance of a court order would immediately lose his position. If he did not depart, the government would eventually collapse, as Parliament refused revenue.

[75] For the significance of control over revenue to seventeenth-century parliamentarian theorists during the Civil War, see Skinner, "A Third Concept of Liberty," 251–253. For the pervasiveness of this theme (and parliamentary control over the Crown more generally) in the seventeenth century, see Theodore Rabb, "The Role of the Commons," *Past and Present*, vol. 92 (1981), 55–78; Paul Seward and Pasi Ihaleinen, "Key Concepts for Parliament in Britain," in *Parliament and Parliamentarism*, 36–39.

[76] Smith, *Lectures on Jurisprudence*, 269.   [77] Ibid.   [78] Ibid., 272.

[79] William Blackstone, *Commentaries on the Laws of England*, vol. 1, ed. George Sharswood (Philadelphia: 1893), 306–308, 334.

[80] Ibid., 170. For the specific laws determining this, see *Journal of the House of Commons*, vol. 9 (London, 1802), 235, 509. The importance of these particular bills in assuring the supremacy of the House of Commons in matters of finance and revenue was discussed by Thomas Erskine May, the great nineteenth-century codifier of parliamentary procedure. See *A Practical Treatise on the Laws, Proceedings, and Usages of Parliament* (London: 1851), 405–412.

could threaten the government's revenue. At that point, what option would the monarch have but to give in?

In his *Essays Moral and Political*, one of the best-selling books of the eighteenth century, David Hume described at length this imbalance between the House of Commons and the Crown. "The principal weight of the Crown lies in the executive power," he wrote, while "the exercise of this power requires an immense expense; and the Commons have assumed to themselves the sole right of granting money."[81] He argued the Crown's dependence upon the House of Commons for revenue rendered its veto "plainly no proper check" and "little better than a form," for if the king ever exercised it, the House of Commons could respond by refusing to fund the government.[82] The monarch would then have no choice but to assent to the proposed law.

Hume was convinced not only that the House of Commons would triumph in any major confrontation with the Crown but also that if the House of Commons was ever sufficiently unified, it could utilize its control over revenue to "wrest from the Crown" all of its prerogatives, "one after another; by making every grant conditional."[83] To underline how radical the Crown's financial dependence upon the House of Commons was, Hume asked his reader to imagine the situation reversed. "Did the House of Commons depend in the same manner on the King, and had none of the members any property but from his gift, would not he command all their resolutions, and be from that moment absolute?"[84] Yet was this not exactly the position in which the monarch found himself? It was for this reason that Hume could write, "the share of power, allotted by our constitution to the House of Commons, is so great, that it absolutely commands all the other parts of the government."[85]

A crucial piece of evidence in favor of Hume's argument was the fact that the Crown did stop using its veto over the course of the eighteenth century. Although "Parliament hath sat every year since the beginning of this century, and though they have constantly enjoyed the most unlimited freedom both as to the subjects and the manner of their deliberation, and numberless proposals have in consequence been made," de Lolme noted that "the Crown has not been obliged during all that time to make use, even once, of its negative voice."[86] Adam Smith likewise emphasized that while "the king has ... the power of putting his assent or negative to a bill," this power "has gone into disuse. The king has always given his assent

---

[81] Hume, *Essays Moral and Political*, 44. [82] Ibid. [83] Ibid. [84] Ibid. [85] Ibid.
[86] De Lolme, *The Constitution of England*, 267.

to every bill since William III's time."[87] Smith's chronology was technically incorrect. The royal negative was used for the last time in 1708 by Queen Anne. But the significance of his statement remains unchanged. This was no longer a prerogative that the Crown exercised. To be clear, during this period, the House of Commons also never sought to undermine the Crown by denying appropriations – as it frequently did during the seventeenth century. Like the veto, this had become a power of last resort that was not to be used in normal politics. But Hume's point was that the House of Commons' power of last resort trumped the Crown's. If the Crown sought to veto legislation and the House of Commons responded by depriving the Crown of revenue, it was the Crown that would have to give way.

Authors committed to a balanced constitution feared that the House of Commons would exploit this situation to dominate or even destroy the other constitutional powers. Indeed, Montesquieu himself was one such author. From his first visit to England in 1729 through to the publication of *The Spirit of the Laws* nearly 20 years later, he repeatedly warned that the declining importance of the House of Lords and the growing power of the House of Commons had upset the delicate balance of English politics.[88] A devastating clash between the House of Commons and the Crown, like the one that occurred in the seventeenth century, was perhaps inevitable.[89] Its most likely consequence would be the House of Commons seizing total control of the executive power and exercising it without any of the limitations to which the Crown was subject, plunging England into despotism.[90] For although Montesquieu claimed that "England is at present the freest nation in the world . . . because the prince does not have the power to do any imaginable wrong to anyone," he warned that "if the House of Commons becomes master, its power would be unlimited and dangerous."[91] While currently the "executive power [is] in the king, where

[87] Smith, *Lectures on Jurisprudence*, 269.

[88] For a powerful discussion of this theme in Montesquieu, see Michael Sonenscher, *Before the Deluge: Public Debt, Inequality, and the Intellectual Origins of the French Revolution* (Princeton: 2007), 41–52.

[89] Montesquieu, "Notes sur l'Angleterre," 503–504.

[90] Ibid., 505. England's other potential fate was that the Crown would triumph over Parliament through corruption, a fear, we will see, which he shared with many other eighteenth-century authors (ibid., 501–503). While Montesquieu was somewhat more confident about England's future when he wrote *The Spirit of the Laws*, he remained convinced that the decline of the House of Lords had potentially doomed the English constitution, which would be destroyed by either corruption or a despotic House of Commons. See Montesquieu, *The Spirit of the Laws*, 18–19, 118, 166.

[91] Montesquieu, "Notes sur l'Angleterre," 505.

the power is limited," should the House of Commons seize command of it, there would be no such limitations.[92]

Proponents of the balanced constitution believed there were two ways this catastrophe could be prevented. The first was for the Crown to secure a source of revenue independent of parliamentary control, which would allow it to safely check Parliament through its veto. The second was for the Crown to secure a durable basis of popular support. That way, if Parliament *did* respond to the king's veto by denying revenue, it would face substantial popular opposition.

Blackstone argued that the Crown had a sufficiently independent source of revenue in the fund that was known as the Civil List. At the beginning of each monarch's reign, the House of Commons presented him with an allowance to live on for the rest of his life, which also financed much of the civil (i.e., nonmilitary) administration. These expenditures were largely unsupervised, and Blackstone believed that they would enable the monarch to survive a confrontation with the House of Commons.[93] But as well as the fact that the Civil List did not finance the vast majority of government expenditures, during the decades after Blackstone published his *Commentaries*, Parliament radically restructured the Civil List.[94] By the 1780s, it was far more strictly supervised by the House of Commons, depriving the monarch of any independence it had once provided.[95]

During the 1760s and 1770s, as Eric Nelson has recently emphasized, leading American colonists proposed a far more dramatic way for the king to escape the House of Commons' control over revenue.[96] Figures such as James Wilson, Benjamin Franklin, Alexander Hamilton, and John Adams argued that to solve the conflict between England and its American colonies, the American colonial assemblies should be raised onto an equal footing with the House of Commons. The result would have been an empire with a single independent monarch but multiple legislatures. These authors were aware that such a step would totally transform the Crown's relationship to Parliament. Because the monarch would have been able to turn to the American assemblies for revenue, he would no longer have

[92] Ibid.   [93] Blackstone, *Commentaries on the Laws of England*, vol. 1, 335–338.
[94] For a history of the reform of the Civil List, see Earl A. Reitan, *Politics, Finance and the People: Economical Reform in England in the Age of the American Revolution, 1770–1792* (Basingstroke: 2007).
[95] The profound implications of this change are explored in Earl A. Reitan, "The Civil List in Eighteenth-Century British Politics: Parliamentary Supremacy versus the Independence of the Crown," *Historical Journal*, vol. 9, no. 3 (1966), 318–337.
[96] Nelson, *The Royalist Revolution*, 29–65.

been completely dependent on the House of Commons and therefore might have safely exercised his veto – or any other prerogative. As Nelson has convincingly demonstrated, these Americans favored the strengthened monarchy that would have resulted, making the powerful presidency they created in 1787 far less mystifying.[97]

Montesquieu pursued the other strategy. He sought to find a basis of support for the Crown in public opinion and claimed that he had found one in the Crown's many employments. The large number of individuals who either held government positions or aspired to them would not abandon the Crown in a confrontation with the House of Commons.[98] Henry St. John, who was made Lord Bolingbroke in 1712 and would become one of the defining English political thinkers of the eighteenth century, offered exactly the opposite account of how the Crown might retain popular legitimacy in a struggle against Parliament. He argued that because Parliament was a large assembly, many of its members would inevitably be prone to corruption and faction, whereas a single virtuous king was sufficient to make the Crown a national symbol of virtue and patriotism. By standing for the general interest as opposed to personal and factional interests, a monarch who assumed the spirit of a *Patriot King* could maintain public support against a corrupt House of Commons.[99]

Bolingbroke wrote the *Idea of a Patriot King* during his 1730s campaign against Robert Walpole. His aim was to encourage Prince Frederick of Wales, the heir to George II, to remove Walpole and his allies from power, even if that required an open confrontation with Parliament.[100] But Bolingbroke had long believed there was another potential path to bringing down Walpole, which ran through Parliament. Because of its financial powers, the House of Commons was in a position where it could make the king remove any minister from power. Even if Walpole was never convicted of an impeachable offense, Bolingbroke argued that a new parliamentary majority could force him from office.

"Parliaments are not only, what they always were, essential parts of our constitution," Bolingbroke wrote; they were becoming "essential parts of

[97] Ibid., 30–38, 55–56.   [98] Montesquieu, *The Spirit of the Laws*, 325.
[99] Henry Bolingbroke, "The Idea of a Patriot King," in *Political Writings*, ed. David Armitage (Cambridge: 1997), 217–294.
[100] For perceptive discussions of the pamphlet's political context and argument, see David Armitage, "A Patriot for Whom? The Afterlives of Bolingbroke's Patriot King," *Journal of British Studies*, vol. 36, no. 4 (1997), 397–418; Christine Gerard, *The Patriot Opposition to Walpole: Politics, Poetry, and National Myth, 1725–1742* (Oxford: 1994).

our administration too."[101] "They do not claim the executive power. No. But the executive power cannot be exercised without their annual concurrence."[102] As a result, he argued that the House of Commons could subject the government to more strenuous oversight than ever before. "How few months, instead of years, have princes and ministers now, to pass without inspection and control," he declared.[103] "How easy therefore is it become to check every growing evil in the bud, to change every bad administration."[104] In the course of developing this strategy for unseating Walpole, Bolingbroke would help to articulate a new conception of political responsibility. Ministers did not merely need to avoid committing crimes to remain in office: they had to actively maintain the trust of the House of Commons.

Underlying Bolingbroke's argument was the premise that impeachment was insufficient. First, it required the agreement of the House of Lords. And, second, it was difficult to utilize against ministers who had not committed an obvious crime but were pursuing corrupt policies that went against the general interest. To create a new majority in the House of Commons that could force Walpole from power, Bolingbroke called for the formation of an organized parliamentary opposition that would systematically oppose all the government's actions and formulate its own alternative "system of conduct." "Every administration is a system of conduct," Bolingbroke wrote; "opposition, therefore, should be a system of conduct likewise."[105] What was needed was "a party who opposed, systematically, a wise to a silly, an honest to an iniquitous, scheme of government."[106] The opposition had to "contrast, on every occasion, that scheme of policy which the public interest requires to be followed, with that which is suited to no interest but the private interest of the prince or his ministers."[107] As soon as a majority of the House of Commons came to side with the opposition, the current government would be forced from power and a better one installed.

When Bolingbroke argued for this course of action in his 1736 essay *The Spirit of Patriotism*, no minister had ever left office because of a defeat in Parliament. However, his argument was that the role of Parliament had

---

[101] Bolingbroke, *The Spirit of Patriotism*, 206.   [102] Ibid.   [103] Ibid.   [104] Ibid.
[105] Ibid. Bolingbroke's pivotal role is emphasized in Archibald Foord's classic book on the emergence of a parliamentary opposition. See Archibald Foord, *His Majesty's Opposition: 1714–1830* (Oxford: 1964), 145–159. For a more skeptical take on Bolingbroke as a theorist of parliamentary opposition, see Caroline Robbins, "'Discordant Parties': A Study of the Acceptance of Party by Englishmen," *Political Science Quarterly*, vol. 73, no. 4 (1958), 523–525.
[106] Bolingbroke, *Spirit of Patriotism*, 216.   [107] Ibid.

fundamentally changed. Walpole's plan to raise the excise tax had recently been defeated through concerted public opposition.[108] Bolingbroke believed that further such efforts would make his position untenable. In 1741, Samuel Sandys introduced a historic motion in the House of Commons, declaring that Walpole had lost the public confidence and should be removed from office.[109] Importantly, Sandys' motion did not propose impeachment.[110] Rather it simply asked "his Majesty, that he would be graciously pleased to remove the Right Honorable Sir Robert Walpole ... from his Majesty's presence and councils."[111] Sandys' motion was defeated; however, a year later, Walpole resigned his office upon losing a vote in the House of Commons, the first prime minister to ever do so.[112]

It would be another century before the practice of cabinet responsibility was firmly entrenched in English politics. Until the late 1830s, monarchs regularly struggled to keep ministers in office, even when those ministers had lost the confidence of the House of Commons.[113] Yet a powerful precedent had been set by Walpole's departure. Denis Baranger argues that after 1742, "the revocation of a minister" following the loss of support in Parliament became "clearly distinguished from his punishment."[114] Three decades later, Edmund Burke penned the classic defense of this practice in his 1770 pamphlet *Thoughts on the Cause of the Present Discontents*. It would then attain a second major victory in 1782, when Lord North and his entire cabinet resigned following a vote of no confidence.[115] As we will

---

[108] Ibid., 201. For a discussion of that debate, see J. H. Plumb, *Sir Robert Walpole: The King's Minister* (Boston: 1961), 250–283.

[109] My discussion of Sandys' motion and its importance in the beginning of a parliamentary regime in England is indebted to Tapani Turkka, *The Origins of Parliamentarism: A Study of Sandys' Motion* (Baden-Baden: 2007).

[110] The significance of the turn away from impeachment (and other "penal forms of responsibility") in the formation of a parliamentary regime in England is explored in Denis Baranger, *Parlementarisme des origines: Essai sur les conditions de formation d'un exécutif responsable en Angleterre (des années 1740 au début de l'âge victorien)* (Paris: 1999), 254–290.

[111] Quoted from Turkka, *The Origins of Parliamentarism*, 35.

[112] For a discussion of this event, see Paul Langford, *A Polite and Commercial People: England, 1727–1783* (Oxford: 1989), 54. Baranger notes the disagreements among Walpole's opponents at this point over whether they needed to convict Walpole of a crime to get him removed or could merely show his revocation would conduce to "public utility" (Baranger, *Parlementarisme des origines*, 277–279).

[113] For an examination of how English monarchs attempted to exercise ministerial preferences between George I and Victoria, see Baranger, *Parlementarisme des origines*, 168–184 (Victoria was the first English monarch to give up this mode of political influence; ibid., 183). For another classic account of ministerial responsibility in the second half of the eighteenth century, see John Brewer, *Party, Ideology and Popular Politics in the Era of George III* (Cambridge: 1976), 112–136.

[114] Baranger, *Parlementarisme des origines*, 279.   [115] Ibid., 302, 352.

see in subsequent chapters, the principle that ministers should not serve without the confidence of the legislature would become central to parliamentary liberalism. Authors from Germaine de Staël and Benjamin Constant to Alexis de Tocqueville and John Stuart Mill would view this principle as the cornerstone of a liberal state, because it made the executive completely accountable to the assembly. For authors who remained committed to Montesquieu's account of the balanced constitution, by contrast, this principle signaled a further step toward a regime in which the legislature aggrandized all powers of government to itself.[116]

Jean Louis de Lolme and the Theory of Constitutional Monarchy

So far in this chapter, I have sketched a tension between the dominant eighteenth-century theory of the English constitution, which held that it was a system of three equally balanced powers, and the powerful position of the House of Commons. One response was to seek a contrivance that would restore constitutional balance and enable the Crown to safely veto legislation. But there was also a very different response. This was to embrace an English constitution that tilted in the direction of the House of Commons. The authors who pursued this approach believed not only that a powerful House of Commons was the greatest security for liberty but also that the nightmare scenario Montesquieu had sketched – in which the legislature aggrandized the executive power to itself and ruled arbitrarily – was not foreordained. Even if the House of Commons was increasingly the dominant constitutional power, certain mechanisms had emerged that would prevent it from becoming despotic.

A key author in the development of this alternative approach to the English constitution was Jean Louis de Lolme. Although de Lolme exercised a profound influence on eighteenth- and nineteenth-century political

---

[116] Bolingbroke's wider writings make clear that he generally fell within this latter camp. His ideal framework for the English constitution was not greater parliamentary control over the executive but rather a more independent executive (i.e., the liberation of the monarch from his corrupt ministers in parliament) and thus a system of checks and balances like that sketched by Montesquieu. See Henry Bolingbroke, *Dissertation upon Parties*, 96. This also underlay his argument for a Patriot King. Indeed, Montesquieu likely adopted much of his understanding of the British constitution from his acquaintance with Bolingbrok on which see Robert Shackleton, *Montesquieu: A Critical Biography* (Oxford: 1961), 297–301. However, within the political moment of the 1730s, Bolingbroke was willing to go in a different direction and advocate stricter parliamentary control over ministers.

thought, he was overlooked until very recently by scholars. For that reason, a general introduction to his life and thought is in order.[117]

De Lolme was born in Geneva in 1741. At the of age of 25, he was banished from his native city, eventually resettling in England. Prior to his banishment, de Lolme's great aspiration had been the regeneration of republican government in Geneva. He was a vocal critic of the oligarchs who dominated the city and supported Rousseau's campaign to restore power to the general citizens' assembly. But the failure of that effort, combined with his experiences in England, would lead him to abandon his republicanism. De Lolme was struck by the unprecedented liberty that the English monarchy granted its subjects. He was also impressed by the English public's extensive engagement in political affairs. In 1771, he published *The Constitution of England*, which contended that England offered a better model of a free state than any republic, ancient or modern.

Like so many eighteenth-century thinkers, de Lolme attributed the liberty of English subjects to the House of Commons' financial powers. "The right to grant subsidies to the Crown, possessed by the people of England, is the safeguard of all their other liberties, religious and civil," he wrote.[118] Because of the Crown's dependence on the House of Commons for revenue, that assembly was able to regularly monitor and "influenc[e] the motions of the executive power."[119] This was the decisive factor that distinguished England from an absolute monarchy like France:

> If we consider the extent of the prerogative of the King of England ... we shall find that it is no exaggeration to say, that he has power sufficient to be as arbitrary as the Kings of France, were it not for the right of taxation, which, in England, is possessed by the people; and the only constitutional difference between the French and English nations is, that the former can neither confer benefits on their sovereign, nor hinder his measures; while the latter, how extensive soever the prerogative of their King may be, can deny him the means of exerting it.[120]

De Lolme argued that if the House of Commons ever lost this power, the people would lose their liberty. "If, through unforeseen events, the Crown

---

[117] There has been a recent revival of interest in de Lolme. In 2007, a modern edition of *The Constitution of England* was published with an illuminating "Introduction" by David Lieberman (*The Constitution of England*, ix–xxii). Two other important recent discussions of de Lolme are Iain McDaniel, "Jean-Louis de Lolme and the Political Science of the English Empire," *Historical Journal*, vol. 55, no. 1 (2012), 21–44; Richard Whatmore, *Against War and Empire: Geneva, Britain, and France in the Eighteenth Century* (New Haven: 2012), 112–133.
[118] De Lolme, *The Constitution of England*, 327.   [119] Ibid.   [120] Ibid., 329.

could attain to be independent on the people in regard to its supplies," he wrote, "from that moment, all the means the people possess to vindicate their liberty would be annihilated."[121]

De Lolme agreed with Hume that because of the Crown's "depend-ence" on the House of Commons for revenue, that assembly had become unquestionably the dominant constitutional power. "In these days," he wrote, "when everything is rated by pecuniary estimation, when gold is become the great moving spring of affairs, it may be safely affirmed, that he who depends upon the will of other men, with regard to so important an article, is, whatever his power may be in other respects, in a state of real dependence."[122] Far from bemoaning this state of affairs, de Lolme cele-brated it. "To have too exactly completed the equilibrium between the power of the People, and that of the Crown," he contended, "would have been to sacrifice the end to the means, that is, to have endangered liberty with a view to strengthen the Government."[123] A "deficiency," he wrote, "ought to remain on the side of the Crown."[124] De Lolme's argument that liberty *required* the House of Commons to be predominant over the Crown signified a decisive break with Montesquieu's account of the English constitution.

This argument has been almost entirely overlooked by scholars. That may be because it appears so at odds with de Lolme's historical account of England, in which the crucial event was the Norman Conquest. In an era when other European nations were divided between competing feudal powers, de Lolme claimed that William the Conqueror was able to impose a unified government on England, creating one of the strongest monarch-ies in Europe. But for de Lolme, the significance of the powerful English monarchy was precisely that it inspired collective efforts at control. "It was the excessive power of the king which made England free, because it was this very excess that gave rise to the spirit of union, and concerted resistance."[125] According to de Lolme, "only by close and numerous confederacies" could English aristocrats resist the king, and "they were even compelled to associate the people in them, and to make them partners of public liberty."[126] Whereas in other European states, an absolute monarch came to seem attractive because of the power of feudal aristocrats, the strength of the medieval English monarchy inspired a

---

[121] Ibid., 327.   [122] Ibid., 64.   [123] Ibid., 143.   [124] Ibid.
[125] De Lolme, *The Constitution of England*, 31.   [126] Ibid.

widespread spirit of resistance.[127] The constrained English monarchy of the eighteenth century was an unintended consequence of the Norman Conquest.

As I have emphasized, de Lolme viewed this result with great satisfaction. He believed that justice lay entirely with the parliamentarian side during the English Civil War.[128] And he fiercely opposed the demands of the American colonists during the 1770s, fearing that their plan for an empire of multiple legislatures would end up unraveling the historic English achievement of parliamentary control over the Crown.[129] However, despite his conviction that the executive ought to be "deficient" vis-à-vis the legislature, de Lolme was by no means nonchalant about the danger of legislative overreach. To the contrary, he believed that the legislature could become an even greater threat to liberty than the executive. While it was "absolutely necessary, for securing the constitution of a state, to restrain the executive power;" de Lolme wrote, "it is still more necessary to restrain the legislature."[130] Because it exercised the state's coercive power, the executive posed the most immediate threat to liberty. But for the executive to overturn the rule of law and usurp all the other constitutional powers, a long train of actions was required. The legislature could accomplish this feat instantly. "The legislative power can change the constitution, as God created the light."[131]

Yet given the powers of the House of Commons, what could prevent legislative usurpation? De Lolme's answer was the institution of monarchy itself. His personal experience in Geneva and his study of ancient republics had convinced him that if usurpation were to occur, it would be led by an ambitious individual. Appealing to "what everyone knows of Pisistratus and Megacles, of Marius and Sylla, of Caesar and Pompey," de Lolme argued that the greatest danger posed by an assembly like the House of Commons was that it would come to be dominated by "some favorite whom the popular voice happens to raise."[132] That popular favorite would then use its powers to overthrow the other parts of government and rule arbitrarily.

De Lolme's contention was that the mere presence of a hereditary constitutional monarch greatly reduced this risk. Even if the House of Commons was the dominant constitutional power, no individual member

---

[127] For de Lolme's argument to this effect, see ibid., 23–54.   [128] Ibid., 48–50, 241.
[129] For discussions of this, see McDaniel, "Jean-Louis de Lolme and the Political Science of the English Empire," 39; Nelson, *The Royalist Revolution*, 50–51.
[130] De Lolme, *The Constitution of England*, 153.   [131] Ibid.   [132] Ibid., 141.

of the House of Commons – however eloquent or popular – could possibly hope to challenge the king. "The constitution has invested the man whom it has made the sole head of state, with all the personal privileges, all the pomp, all the majesty, of which human dignities are capable," he wrote.[133] An English monarch had "all that sort of strength that may result from the opinion and reverence of the people."[134] While Parliament could certainly play a dominant role in government, no member of Parliament, whatever "the greatness of his abilities and public services," could realistically expect to overthrow the monarch.[135] The effect of this was to profoundly limit the ambition of leading representatives and to make legislative usurpation close to unthinkable.

In classical republics, individuals "deeply versed in the management of public business" struggled to become the ultimate power in the state.[136] However, de Lolme argued that the English constitution was entirely different. It "render[ed] it impossible for any citizen even to rise to any dangerous greatness."[137] A representative who "acquired in a high degree the love of the people, and obtained a great influence in the House of Commons ... can hope neither for a dictatorship nor a consulship," and "the only door which the Constitution leaves open to his ambition, of whatever kind it may be, is a place in the administration, during the pleasure of the King."[138]

De Lolme's contention was that the imbalance in constitutional prerogatives between the Crown and House of Commons had been made up for through the monarch's symbolic authority. "The deficiency which ought to remain on the side of the Crown, has at least been in appearance made up, by conferring on the King all that sort of strength that may result from the opinion and reverence of the people," he wrote.[139] Unlike Bolingbroke, de Lolme did not believe that "the opinion and reverence of the people" would enable the king to engage in an equally matched struggle with Parliament. But it was sufficient to dissuade leading members of Parliament from considering usurpation. Because these were the figures who would push the assembly to overstep its position in the state, by moderating their ambition, constitutional monarchy indirectly moderated Parliament as a whole.

De Lolme argued that Parliament was also moderated by its division into two assemblies. However, he viewed the relationship between the House of Commons and House of Lords as parallel to that between the

---

[133] Ibid., 143.   [134] Ibid.   [135] Ibid., 144–149.   [136] Ibid., 173.   [137] Ibid., 144.
[138] Ibid., 145.   [139] Ibid., 143.

House of Commons and the Crown.[140] When it came to formal prerogatives, the Lords were no match for the Commons, which had the sole power to initiate all bills dealing with revenue and the budget. But like the Crown, the House of Lords "could at least in appearance" make up for this deficiency. "As the nobles, who form the second order of the legislature, bear, in point both of real weight and numbers, no proportion to the body of the people," de Lolme wrote, "they have received as a compensation, the advantage of personal honors and of an hereditary title."[141] In every way, "the established ceremonial" favored the Lords: their title was the "upper" house; the throne was placed in their assembly; and they were treated by the House of Commons as their superiors. De Lolme argued that through these conventions, "the inequalities in point of real strength" between the two Houses of Parliament "have been made up by the magic of dignity."[142]

Despite the key role that "the magic of dignity" played in de Lolme's constitutional theory, he did not believe an English monarch's position rested entirely on dignity. The king's actions were comprehensively supervised by Parliament – that is what made him a *constitutional* monarch – but he was still an "active power" in the state.[143] However, two other eighteenth-century writers were far more radical on this point than de Lolme. Thomas Gordon and John Trenchard were the authors of the famous series of essays *Cato's Letters*. They favored a monarch who played no role at all in political decisions and whose position in the state rested entirely on "opinion and reverence."

Unlike de Lolme, Gordon and Trenchard believed the most important characteristic of the English monarchy was not its control by the House of Commons but rather how the king *delegated* his powers to other individuals. According to Gordon and Trenchard, an English king did not directly exercise either legislative or executive functions. "The laws are chosen and recommended to him by his Parliament" and "executed by his judges, and other ministers of justice."[144] The king's "naval power is under the direction of his high admiral," while "acts of state and discretion are presumed to be done by the advice of his council."[145] Gordon and Trenchard argued that this placed the king above all political struggles so that he could be beloved by the entire nation. "All the subjects of such a

---

[140] Ibid., 153–159.   [141] Ibid., 157.   [142] Ibid.   [143] Ibid., 329.

[144] John Trenchard and Thomas Gordon, *Cato's Letters, or Essays on Liberty, Civil and Religious, and Other Important Subjects*, vol. 1 (New York: 1971), 92.

[145] Ibid.

prince highly honor, and almost worship, him."[146] This was a more durable source of authority than the actual exercise of power. An English king could not offend anyone, for he "has in his power all the means of doing good, and none of doing ill."[147] At the same time, he possessed "a vast revenue to support the splendor and magnificence of his court at home, and his royal dignity abroad ... all honors flow from him."[148] Through the monarch's political neutrality and extraordinary splendor, he could become the object of universal veneration.

The Constitution of England and *Cato's Letters* offered two very different visions of constitutional monarchy. For de Lolme, it was sufficient that the House of Commons supervise the monarch's actions. By contrast, *Cato* wanted the monarch not to really act at all. There is no question that de Lolme's account of the English monarchy was more accurate than *Cato's*. Although they claimed to depict an English king as he already was, Gordon and Trenchard were really making an argument about what the English monarchy might be – and, indeed, would be by the middle of the nineteenth century.[149] The question of which of these two models of constitutional monarchy to favor would be a central issue for nineteenth-century liberalism.

De Lolme has often been thought of as a follower of Montesquieu.[150] Yet we have seen how different their analyses of the English constitution really were. Unlike Montesquieu, de Lolme accepted a House of Commons that was the dominant constitutional power, and he argued that it was restrained not by the prerogatives of the king and House of Lords but rather by their symbolism and splendor. Specifically targeting his illustrious French predecessor, de Lolme bitingly declared that when it came to England, Montesquieu "rather tells us what he conjectured than what he saw."[151] In particular, de Lolme argued that the English constitution was significantly more durable than Montesquieu realized. So long as the Crown continued to depend on the House of Commons for revenue yet still served as an imposing obstacle to the ambition of its leading members,

---

[146] Ibid., 93–94.   [147] Ibid., 91.   [148] Ibid., 93–94.

[149] De Mably, who defended a monarch somewhat like the one proposed by Cato, claimed that such a figure was best approximated by "the King of Sweden" and "Doge of Venice." See Gabriel Bonnot de Mably, *Du gouvernement et des loix de la Pologne*, (Paris: 1781), 63.

[150] See David Lieberman, "Introduction," *The Constitution of England*, xiv–xv; F. T. H. Fletcher, *Montesquieu and English Politics: 1750–1800* (London: 1939). Iain McDaniel perceptively notes several of de Lolme's important breaks with Montesquieu and the influence of Hume on de Lolme. See McDaniel, "Jean-Louis de Lolme and the Political Science of the English Empire."

[151] De Lolme, *The Constitution of England*, 305.

there was no reason England would share the same fate as "Rome, Lacadaemon, and Carthage," as Montesquieu had predicted.[152]

Unlike England, these were republics rather than hereditary monarchies. They also were states in which the legislative power was held not by a representative body but by popular assemblies. De Lolme maintained that popular assemblies had significant disadvantages, especially when it came to controlling the executive. Put simply, they could not supervise executive officials like the House of Commons did:

> To render ineffectual the silent, powerful, and ever active conspiracy of those who govern, requires a degree of knowledge and a spirit of perseverance, which are not to be expected from the multitude. The greater part of those who compose this multitude, taken up with the care of providing for their subsistence, have neither sufficient leisure, nor even, in consequence of their more imperfect education, the degree of information requisite for functions of this kind.[153]

Only an assembly of elected representatives had the time and information to engage in this difficult task. "Even in the midst of quiet times," de Lolme contended, the members of the House of Commons were certain to "keep a watchful eye on the motions of Power."[154] They would be motivated by the rights they shared with the people as well as by their own *esprit de corps*. Inevitably, "a kind of rivalship between them and those who govern" would emerge, and "the jealousy which they will conceive against the latter, will give them an exquisite degree of sensibility on every increase of their authority."[155]

An *elected* legislature was therefore essential to the preservation of "general liberty."[156] But what about the point raised by radicals like James Burgh – that when compared with the popular assembly of an ancient republic, an elected assembly like the House of Commons led to insufficient popular involvement in lawmaking? De Lolme denied there was any such trade-off. Although the people were not directly involved in lawmaking, he argued that they were involved indirectly through the press. An English individual's right "to give his opinion on all public matters, and by thus influencing the sentiments of the nation, to influence those of the legislature" was itself "a sort of legislative authority."[157] De Lolme claimed that this was "of a much more efficacious and beneficial nature than any

---

[152] Ibid., 304.
[153] Ibid., 171. According to de Lolme, institutions such as the Roman Tribunate and Spartan Ephori had proven entirely insufficient as checks on the executive as well. At best, they were overruled before the assembly by the more popular consuls and at worst, they joined with the aristocrats out of their own ambition for power and glory. This is a major theme in ibid., 178–192.
[154] Ibid., 177.   [155] Ibid.   [156] Ibid., 80.   [157] Ibid., 279.

formal right ... of voting by a mere *yea* or *nay*, upon general propositions suddenly offered to him."[158] This right could be exercised collectively as well as individually. De Lolme noted the "numerous and irregular meetings" that took place in England to discuss political events, and that enabled individuals without the skill to write a pamphlet to take an

> active part for procuring the success of those public steps which they wish to see pursued: they may frame petitions to be delivered to the Crown, or to both Houses, either to procure the repeal of measures already entered upon by government, or to prevent the passing of such as are under consideration, or to obtain the enacting of new regulations of any kind.[159]

Like Ellys, de Lolme believed that parliamentary deliberation was a form of political education. Through an issue being debated *pro et contra*, "all matters of fact are, at length, made clear; and, through the conflict of different answers and replies, nothing at last remains, but the sound part of the arguments."[160] The press therefore extended the benefit of this political education to the public, by keeping it "acquainted with the nature of the subjects that have been deliberated upon in the assembly of their representatives; – they are informed by whom the different motions were made, – by whom they were supported; and the manner in which the suffrages are delivered."[161] The result was that "a whole nation as it were holds a council, and deliberates."[162] Through parliamentary rule, the English people were no less meaningfully involved in public affairs than the citizens of a classical republic, even as they gained crucial safeguards against usurpation and the abuse of executive power that had been neglected by classical republicanism.

Ministers in the Legislature

Through his account of the English monarchy, de Lolme offered a powerful argument that the House of Commons would not emerge as a threat to political stability, even as it became the most powerful constitutional actor. A second argument to this effect was derived from a different practice: the presence of the Crown's ministers in Parliament. Across the eighteenth century, ministers were regularly drawn from the House of Commons, and they fulfilled their executive duties while serving simultaneously in the legislature. This practice, which would become a core practice of parliamentarism, was never mentioned by Montesquieu. Nor, for that matter,

---

[158] Ibid., 279–280.   [159] Ibid., 284, 285.   [160] Ibid.   [161] Ibid., 210.   [162] Ibid., 209.

was it analyzed by de Lolme in *The Constitution of England*.[163] However, for a range of other authors, the presence of ministers in the House of Commons was the crucial means through which the Crown prevented that assembly from overreaching. As early as 1701, one author wrote:

> whoever considers the number of a discontented party among ourselves . . . joined with those who are against all kings, and with others who are and will always be against all governments . . . cannot but conclude (if true to his country) that his majesty should not be depriv'd of any friends in the House of Commons, but that his hands ought by all possible means to be strengthened.[164]

In addition to defending the Crown's interests in Parliament, it was widely argued that ministers improved the quality of parliamentary deliberation. They contributed knowledge and experience to parliamentary debate and smoothed over any disagreement that arose between the Crown and Parliament. This led to "good counsels" within Parliament and "harmony" between the different parts of the English constitution.[165] But the presence of ministers in Parliament was far from uncontroversial. Some critics worried that rather than strengthening the monarch's hand in Parliament, this practice actually weakened it, for it left the king even more under the control of representatives. The ministers who led his government had as much loyalty to Parliament as they did to him, and their aim was not only to serve the monarch but also to aid their party.[166]

However, the greatest controversy that arose from this practice stemmed from the opposite fear: that it undermined the House of Commons. The ground for this fear was that ministers were not the only administrative officers who sat in the House of Commons. It has been calculated that at the turn of the eighteenth century, a quarter of MPs were employees of the Crown – a percentage that would only grow over the following decades.[167] Customs offices, postal offices, and positions in the king's many palaces were distributed to members of the House of Commons. Many of these offices were for non-existent jobs; they existed for no other reason than to

---

[163] De Lolme was the likely author of a pamphlet published during the 1780s debate over parliamentary reform that strongly defended the ministry's influence in the House of Commons. See *An Essay on Constitutional Liberty: Wherein the Necessity of Frequent Elections of Parliament Is Shewn to Be Superseded by the Unity of the Executive Power* (London: 1780).

[164] Anon., *Officers Good Members: Or the Late Act of Settlement Consider'd* (London: 1701), 1.

[165] Abel Boyer, *An Essay Towards the History of the Last Ministry and Parliament* (London: 1710), 43.

[166] This concern was at the heart of Bolingbroke's argument for a "patriot king," discussed earlier in this chapter, who would act without being beholden to the parties in Parliament (Bolingbroke, *The Idea of a Patriot King*).

[167] See Holmes, *British Politics in the Age of Anne*, 354.

establish influence over representatives.[168] In addition to its patronage in Parliament, the Crown also exercised enormous influence over elections. Approximately 1 in 10 seats in the House of Commons was directly determined by the Crown, while many more were influenced by the Crown's electoral expenditures.[169]

Critics argued that this undermined the House of Commons' control over government. How could it possibly fulfill that function when so many of its members depended on the government for their livelihood? Patronage also seemed to corrupt the House of Commons as a deliberative assembly: it encouraged representatives to cast votes in exchange for offices and favors rather than to reflect on which measure would lead to the general good.[170] In the first decade after the Glorious Revolution, the widespread animus against corruption seemed like it might bring an end to the presence of ministers in Parliament.[171] The Act of Settlement included a prohibition against government employees serving in Parliament, which would have applied to ministers – though it was repealed before it ever went into effect. Following the failure of this measure, opponents of patronage stopped seeking the total exclusion of officeholders from the legislature and instead fought for more specific exclusions, which would spare the king's ministers.[172] The presence of ministers in Parliament was thus no longer directly implicated in the debate over corruption. But it continued to be indirectly implicated, for patronage was a crucial tool that ministers made use of. It was questionable whether they could adequately

[168] The classic account of the unreformed Parliament and the forms of influence predominant in it is Lewis Namier, *The Structure of Politics at the Accession of George III* (London: 1957), 11–42, 211–221. See as well P. G. Richards, *Patronage in British Government* (London: 1963), 19–62; Phillip Harling, "Rethinking 'Old Corruption,'" *Past and Present*, vol. 147, no. 1 (1995), 127–158.

[169] See Namier, *The Structure of Politics at the Accession of George III*, 139–142, 194–211. The smaller English boroughs were particularly amenable to government influence (ibid., 76–77).

[170] For these two different arguments against parliamentary corruption, the one that it would undermine political virtue and the common good, the other that it would undermine parliamentary control of the Crown and liberty, and their different histories, see David Hayton, "The Reorientation of Place Legislation in England in the 1690s," *Parliaments, Estates and Representation*, vol. 5, no. 2 (1985), 103–108.

[171] The campaign against patronage at the turn of the eighteenth century, which also targeted the emerging structure of parliamentary government, is discussed in Dennis Rubini, *Court and Country, 1688–1702* (London: 1968), 100–117; Caroline Robbins, *The Eighteenth-Century Commonwealthman: Studies in the Transmission, Development and Circumstance of English Liberal Thought from the Restoration of Charles II until the War with the Thirteen Colonies* (Cambridge: 1959), 8, 110–11; Holmes, *British Politics in the Age of Anne*, 130–144.

[172] For discussions of this turn away from "general exclusion," see Holmes, *British Politics in the Age of Anne*, 131–132; Rubini, *Court and Country*, 36–37, 172–177; Gunn, *Beyond Liberty and Property*, 62–65. Hayton is skeptical that a general exclusion was ever seriously a possibility during this period. See Hayton, "The Reorientation of Place Legislation in England in the 1690s."

defend the Crown's interests, let alone play a leading role in shaping Parliament's agenda, unless they were assured a degree of parliamentary support through patronage.

These issues would come to a head during the ministry of Robert Walpole, which lasted from 1721–1742. Walpole was, in Paul Langford's words, the first prime minister to gain close to "a monopoly of parliamentary patronage," and in large part because of that achievement, he played an unprecedented leadership role within the House of Commons.[173] Before Walpole, no prime minister had actively made use of patronage to build a parliamentary majority and ensure the predominance of his party in Parliament, but nearly every eighteenth-century prime minister who followed Walpole would seek to imitate these feats.[174] Walpole's opponents, however, would castigate him for corruption.

Scholars have construed the debate between Walpole and his critics as a clash between virtue and interest. While opponents of patronage appealed to a classic ideal of virtue, its defenders supposedly embraced the modern politics of self-interest.[175] As an account of Walpole's critics, this interpretation is often accurate, but for his defenders, it is wholly inadequate. Walpole's supporters did not deny the importance of virtue or public spirit among parliamentary representatives. Indeed, they trumpeted "the virtue and penetration of the majority of our representatives" and claimed that electors must set their minds to "choosing men of greater integrity" to serve in Parliament.[176] What Walpole's supporters denied was that there existed any contradiction between holding one of the Crown's offices and displaying virtue. They believed ministers could appeal to both publicly

---

[173] Langford, *A Polite and Commercial People*, 21. Langford notes that Walpole did not have complete control over offices as later prime ministers would. He had little say in either ecclesiastical or military appointments. But his control over fiscal and revenue offices was nonetheless unparalleled in previous English history (ibid., 20–21). For a further discussion of Walpole's administrative skill and his use of it to build a political majority, see Plumb, *Sir Robert Walpole*, 233–248. Part of Walpole's significance was that he was a member of the House of Commons whereas most previous ministers had been Lords, and he recognized that the power of the English constitution was increasingly centered in the lower house. On this point, see Paul Langford, "Swift and Walpole," in *Politics and Literature in the Age of Swift*, 65.

[174] For an account of how ministers acted before Walpole, see Holmes, *British Politics in the Age of Anne*, 345–381.

[175] The classic account of the debate in these terms is J. G. A. Pocock, *The Machiavellian Moment* (Princeton: 2003). For other such treatments, see Gunn, *Beyond Liberty and Property*, 10–42; Robbins, *The Eighteenth-Century Commonwealthman*, 271–378; Isaac Kramnick, *Bolingbroke and His Circle: The Politics of Nostalgia in the Age of Walpole* (Cambridge: 1968); Eric Nelson, *The Greek Tradition in Republican Thought* (Cambridge: 2004), 129–154.

[176] Anon., *An Enquiry into the Danger of Multiplying Incapacities on the Gentlemen of England to Fit in Parliament* (London: 1739), 39; Anon, *A Letter to a Member of Parliament. Concerning the Present State of Affairs at Home and Abroad* (London: 1740) 27–28.

spirited arguments and private interests in order to win over parliamentary representatives.[177]

What was most striking about Walpole's defenders was not their appeal to interest but rather their attempt to articulate the role of ministerial leadership in Parliament and to defend this as a fundamental element of the English political system. They made three striking claims, which would redound over the rest of the eighteenth century and profoundly influence the theory of parliamentarism:

> They claimed that it was essential for ministers to be in the House of Commons so they could defend the government's position within that assembly.
>
> They claimed that the presence of ministers in the House of Commons improved its deliberations and brought about a degree of harmony between otherwise opposing constitutional powers.
>
> Most controversially, they contended that no ministry would be able to remain in power and achieve these objectives without patronage.

The most famous of Walpole's defenders was David Hume. Earlier in this chapter, I emphasized Hume's belief that the House of Commons' control over revenue had made it the most powerful part of the English constitution.[178] While this would motivate de Lolme to develop his theory of constitutional monarchy, Hume argued that the real moderating influence on the House of Commons lay in Walpole's use of patronage to defend the government's vital interests. "The Crown has so many offices at its disposal," he argued, that "when assisted by the honest and disinterested part of the House, it will always command the resolutions of the whole so far, at least, as to preserve the ancient constitution from danger."[179] "We may, therefore, give to this influence what name we please;" he wrote, "we may call it by the invidious appellations of *corruption* and *dependence*; but some degree and some kind of it are inseparable from the very nature of the constitution, and necessary to the preservation of our mixed government."[180]

I noted earlier how Montesquieu also came to believe that the Crown's offices were "necessary to the preservation of mixed government." But his argument was quite different. Whereas Hume defended patronage because a true constitutional balance was impossible, Montesquieu thought that

---

[177] See, for instance, Anon., *A Second Letter to a Member of Parliament*, 40–41.
[178] Hume, *Essays Moral and Political*, 44.   [179] Ibid., 45.   [180] Ibid.

the Crown's offices helped to uphold constitutional balance.[181] They ensured that large swaths of the public were financially dependent upon the Crown and would side with the monarch should an open confrontation with Parliament occur. Importantly, Montesquieu's argument did not require the Crown to use its offices to influence elections or win over members of Parliament (which was exactly what Hume emphasized) and Montesquieu believed those practices constituted a dangerous form of corruption.[182] While Montesquieu argued that the growing size of the English administrative state helped to maintain constitutional balance, he never defended parliamentary patronage.

Many of Walpole's allies agreed with Hume that parliamentary patronage was necessary to restrain the House of Commons.[183] However, they also made a different argument in favor of this practice. This was that ministers had to make use of patronage not only as a defensive weapon against Parliament but also constructively, so that they could build a stable parliamentary majority. If patronage were eliminated, the immediate result would be not legislative usurpation (as Hume feared) but cabinet instability. As one of Walpole's pamphleteers wrote, "the administration, in whatever hands it is, must have a strong dependence upon the Commons, and must cultivate a good understanding with them, by the best methods they can devise."[184] "Whatever ways, whatever arts, whatever means, such as are in the administration, and their friends use, to maintain this interest in the Commons, and therefore to keep the government in a steady, settled course," were appropriate and necessary.[185] Walpole's enemies might call these methods "ministerial influence."[186] But they were really part of a broad arrangement of "ministerial dependence," as they arose from the fact that ministers needed support in Parliament to be efficacious.[187] This

---

[181] The desire for financial gain associated with the Crown would balance Parliament's "natural trust in the people" and the fears of arbitrary power it stirred up; this balance of psychological motivation is obviously parallel to the balances of prerogatives between the two constitutional powers. See Montesquieu, *Spirit of the Laws*, 326.

[182] Montesquieu's famousl argument in *The Spirit of the Laws* was that corruption of the legislature would bring down the English constitution (ibid., 166). He was no less critical of parliamentary corruption in his earlier "Notes sur l'Angleterre" (501–503). While he would later write that this fate might be postponed by the English people's political virtue and commercial spirit, that was not a license for encouraging legislative patronage but rather a hope that the worst extent of the damage might be avoided. See Montesquieu, *My Thoughts (Mes Pensées)*, tr. Henry Clark (Indianapolis: 2012), 593–596.

[183] For a survey of the influence of this set of claims, see J. A. W. Gunn, "Influence, Parties and the Constitution: Changing Attitudes, 1783–1832," *Historical Journal*, vol. 17, no. 2 (1974), 301–328.

[184] Anon., *A Second Letter to a Member of Parliament*, 60.   [185] Ibid.   [186] Ibid., 61.

[187] Ibid.

writer lamented that Walpole's opponents were able to recognize the value of only a political *opposition*. They failed to recognize the equal value of a steady *administration* and the difficulty an administration faced in maintaining support in Parliament. While he acknowledged that "an opposition is everlastingly necessary to preserve our liberties," it was also true that "the government must subsist; for otherwise, I think our liberties would be hardly worth preserving. If you admit this, you must allow them the means of subsisting; and these are no other than such an interest ... as may, in some measure, balance the power of a continual opposition" in Parliament.[188]

Walpole also emphasized how difficult it was for ministers to maintain a government. "It will be granted," he declared in a speech to the House of Commons, "that no government could support itself, or answer any of the ends of government, if the majority of this house consisted of such as were its declared enemies."[189] But it was inevitable that parties would emerge in Parliament to oppose every government. Some members would disagree with the principles of the ministers, while others would be envious of their power. "In every free country there are different parties," Walpole declared, and "all these sorts of men, the discontented, the disappointed, the jacobites, the republicans, will always be ready to condemn and oppose the measures of the administration ... and by their arguments they will often be able to prevail with some well-meaning and unthinking men."[190] Walpole denied that patronage alone could maintain a ministry against so many opponents. "Our administration has no defense against this formidable union of parties, but by the wisdom of their measures," he declared.[191] But if patronage was a secondary tool, it was nonetheless an important one. "A bad government can never, by this way, gain many friends," he argued, but "a title of honor, or a lucrative post or employment, may be of some service in prevailing with a gentleman to judge favorably of the government's measures, in all cases where he is wavering in his opinion."[192]

Walpole and his defenders claimed that when ministers were able to win the support of a majority of the House of Commons, they achieved a crucial constitutional value: *harmony* between the executive and the legislature. "There is certainly nothing more apparent in our political system,"

[188] Ibid., 59.
[189] Robert Walpole, "Debate in the Commons on the Place Bill," in *The Parliamentary History of England*, vol. 11 (London: 1812), 366.
[190] Ibid.   [191] Ibid.   [192] Ibid.

one author wrote, "than that the health of our government consists in the union of its several branches."[193] This same author went on to contend that a reduction in patronage would "create everlasting jealousies between the legislative and executive powers."[194] Another defender of Walpole insisted that just as to Parliament "must be trusted the making of laws" so "to the members thereof must be committed the execution of them."[195] In the words of an earlier writer:

> In our political constitution, if the springs or the ministerial part of the government do not exactly agree with the wheels or Parliament, nothing can be expected from them but continual jars and misunderstandings, each contending to put the other in the wrong, and obstructing what the other moves for the public good: whereas, on the contrary, when both concur in opinion and designs, all good counsels, prosperity and success, attend so excellent an harmony.[196]

As these passages make clear, Walpole and his defenders had a more concrete view of constitutional harmony than Montesquieu. For Montesquieu, a well-structured constitution was one in which the different powers "move in concert," without any individual consciously directing them.[197] Blackstone, ever Montesquieu's follower, described the different powers of the English constitution as "like three distinct powers in mechanics, they jointly impel the machine of government in a direction different from what either, acting by itself, would have done."[198] For Walpole and his supporters, this was insufficient. Harmony required that the executive be in concrete agreement with a majority of the legislature about the agenda of government, and this required a ministry that could consciously direct both powers in unison. This conception of constitutional harmony would profoundly influence later theorists of parliamentarism, beginning with Edmund Burke and Jacques Necker.

Walpole's defense of patronage would also persist long after he left office. During the great debate over parliamentary reform that occurred in the 1780s, a pamphlet entitled *A Dialogue on the Actual State of Parliament* would powerfully reiterate the argument that patronage had become the crucial control on the House of Commons. The pamphlet's anonymous author agreed with Hume and de Lolme that a "great

---

[193] Anon, *A Letter to a Member of Parliament*, 20.   [194] Ibid., 86.
[195] Anon., *An Enquiry into the Danger of Multiplying Incapacities*, 38.
[196] Boyer, *An Essay Towards the History of the Last Ministry and Parliament*, 43.
[197] Montesquieu, *The Spirit of the Laws*, 164. For a discussion of this dimension of Montesquieu's thought, see Craiutu, *A Virtue for Courageous Minds*, 39–51.
[198] Blackstone, *Commentaries on the Laws of England*, 158.

revolution" in British politics "has made the balance preponderate in favor of the House of Commons."[199] "The power of the House of Commons . . . seems to be transcendent."[200] He also noted that the king's veto "has fallen into disuse" and cannot "ever be revived, to any great effect, without setting the Crown at variance with . . . the legislature."[201] The Crown's "influence" within the House of Commons had thus become its major check on the assembly.[202] Importantly, the author claimed that this was true not only of the Crown but also of the House of Lords, which likewise shaped British politics more through its members' networks of patronage in the House of Commons than through its formal powers.[203] As opposed to the old balance that had obtained *between* constitutional powers, *A Dialogue on the Actual State of Parliament* contended that a new balance had been created *within* the House of Commons itself.

According to this pamphlet, "the peculiar excellence of the constitution" lay in the way that all three parts of the constitution had been "mixed and blended together" within the House of Commons.[204] The virtue of this system was that each constitutional power could challenge the other's actions without causing a stalemate that brought government to a halt. The struggle between the different parts of the constitution blended seamlessly into the regular practice of parliamentary deliberation, and any decision made in the House of Commons reflected the unified assent of all three branches. "It is upon the harmony, not the dissention," of constitutional powers, "upon the close and intimate connection, not upon the opposition, of them; that depend the beauty and efficacy of the British constitution."[205]

A year after the publication of this pamphlet, Soame Jenyns (a writer best known for his earlier criticisms of the American colonists) would reiterate several of its arguments against reducing the Crown's influence. He forthrightly declared that "parliaments have ever been influenced, and by that means our constitution has so long subsisted."[206] Jenyns especially emphasized the risk of cabinet instability. Reflecting on the membership of a large representative assembly, he argued that among the representatives,

---

[199] Anon., *A Dialogue on the Actual State of Parliament* (London: 1783), 28.   [200] Ibid.
[201] Ibid., 9–10.   [202] Ibid., 44–45.
[203] Ibid., 6. This innovation is also noted in Gunn's illuminating discussion of the pamphlet; see Gunn, "Influence, Parties and the Constitution," 309. A similar statement has been made succinctly by J. C. D. Clark, who notes that "the English peerage . . . had an institutionalized share in the political process via the House of Lords, and an even more important informal share through its stake in the Commons." See *English Society, 1660–1832* (Cambridge: 2000), 219.
[204] Anon., *A Dialogue on the Actual State of Parliament*, 7.   [205] Ibid.
[206] Soame Jenyns. *Thoughts on a Parliamentary Reform* (London: 1784), 26.

"there must be some who have judgment, others who have conscience, and some who have neither."[207] Unless ministers could appeal to "self-interest," Jenyns warned that that the third group "will have no star to steer by, but must sail without a compass, just as the gales of favor, or resentment, or popular absurdity, or their own, shall direct them."[208] For Jenyns, this implied the absolute necessity of patronage. "A minister therefore must be possessed of some attractive influence, to enable him to draw together these discordant particles and unite them in a firm and solid majority, without which he can pursue no measures of public utility with steadiness or success."[209]

This whole tradition of argument would receive its best summation in William Paley's 1785 treatise *The Principles of Moral and Political Philosophy*:

> For when we reflect upon the power of the House of Commons to extort a compliance with its resolutions from the other parts of the legislature or put to death the constitution by a refusal of the annual grants of money to the support of the necessary functions of government – when we reflect also what motives there are, which, in the vicissitudes of political interests and passions, may one day arm and point this power against the executive magistrate; when we attend to these considerations, we shall be led perhaps to acknowledge, that there is not more of paradox than of truth in that important, but much decried apophthegm, "that an independent parliament is incompatible with the existence of the monarchy."[210]

At the heart of the emerging theory of a parliamentary government was the notion that ministers had to struggle to defend the Crown's position within parliamentary deliberation. As Paley's remarks make clear, this was felt necessary because of the Crown's weakened position in the English constitution. As it effectively could no longer block legislation, its leading officials should at least be given the opportunity to persuade representatives about what course of action to take. But the paradox was that if ministers were successful at doing this, then the Crown might find itself in a stronger position than ever before. Should a sufficient number of parliamentary representatives become disposed to always side with the reigning ministry, then the House of Commons' superior prerogatives would effectually belong to the Crown, and liberty would be lost. The dominant position of the House of Commons might result, ironically, in a vastly strengthened monarch.

---

[207] Ibid., 23–24.   [208] Ibid., 24.   [209] Ibid., 25.
[210] William Paley, *The Principles of Moral and Political Philosophy* (Indianapolis: 2002), 351.

It was this fear that motivated the opponents of patronage, for that was the most obvious means through which ministers might permanently capture a majority of Parliament. Defenders of patronage, on the other hand, had to assure their readers (and themselves) that its influence would not reach such a level that the House of Commons was entirely subservient to ministers or unable to decisively defend the people's liberties against the Crown. The author of *A Dialogue on the Actual State of Parliament* wrote that "the patronage of the crown" was beneficial only so long as it "affects the House of Commons ... to induce a general support of public measures, and a bias towards the system that is pursued, not a blind confidence in, or prostituted devotion to, a minister."[211] A similar statement was offered by Adam Ferguson, who wished that "the king has influence enough in Parliament to obtain the necessary supports of his government, though never, I hope, to obtain the smallest resignation of the people's right."[212]

Should Parliament become corrupted, Walpole professed himself confident that public opinion would regenerate it. If "the court" was actually "making any encroachments upon the rights of the people, a proper spirit would no doubt arise in the nation; and in such a case I am persuaded that none, or very few ... electors could be induced to vote for the court candidate."[213] The absence of such an event implied that ministers were not using their powers illicitly and that the House of Commons' control over government had not been put in jeopardy by patronage.[214]

Walpole's opponents were unconvinced by his reassurances. They believed that the patronage not only undermined the House of Common's capacity to control the Crown but also corrupted the people, so that *pace* Walpole they might not have "the proper spirit" to rise up when the government began making "encroachments." "By the corruption of Parliament," Bolingbroke declared, "we return into that state, to deliver or secure us from which Parliaments were instituted" – a state in which there was no control upon the government's exercise of power.[215] He warned that if the House of Commons were corrupt and unwilling to control the Crown, and if electors were corrupt and unwilling to force their representatives to perform that role, then the English people "are really governed by

[211] Anon., *A Dialogue on the Actual State of Parliament*, 47.
[212] Adam Ferguson, *Remarks on a Pamphlet Lately Published by Dr. Price* (London: 1776), 16.
[213] Robert Walpole, *The Celebrated Speech of Sir Robert Walpole, against Short Parliaments; to Shew That a Parliamentary Reform Is Both Unnecessary and Dangerous*, ed. Henry Dundas (London: 1793), 57.
[214] Ibid., 58.   [215] Bolingbroke, *Dissertation upon Parties*, 94.

the arbitrary will of one man."[216] While there were other "securities to liberty," Bolingbroke argued that "the freedom and the independency of Parliament, is the key-stone that keeps the whole together."[217] The corruption of Parliament therefore led straight to despotism. "For Parliaments to establish tyranny, there is no need therefore to repeal Magna Carta, or any other of the great supports of our liberty. It is enough, if they put themselves corruptly and servilely under the influence of such a prince, or such a minister."[218]

In eighteenth-century England, *patronage* therefore had two radically contradictory meanings. For Walpole's opponents, such as Bolingbroke, it was an instrument of corruption that enabled the Crown to evade parliamentary control and supervision, while for Walpole and his supporters, it was inconceivable that ministers could play a leading role in Parliament without patronage. With the decline in the monarch's ability to veto legislation, this was the only way for the Crown to have any influence on the legislative process. Patronage was at once essential to the emerging structure of parliamentary government yet potentially debilitating to parliamentary control over the executive.

This quandary would persist long into the nineteenth century. So would each of the other themes that this chapter has surveyed: the ideal of Parliament as a representative and deliberative assembly, the demand for ministers to be strictly responsible to Parliament for their positions, the fear that Parliament's powers tended made it the dominant actor in the state, and the conviction that a constitutional monarch and a parliamentary government could moderate Parliament without making the monarch its equal. They would become the defining elements of the classical theory of parliamentarism, and the next chapter will examine one of the first authors to bring them together into a coherent whole.

---

[216] Ibid.   [217] Ibid.   [218] Ibid., 95.

CHAPTER 2

Edmund Burke's Theory of Parliamentary Politics

In 1925, the German legal theorist Carl Schmitt made the following statement about the intellectual foundations of European parliamentarism:

> Like every great institution, parliament presupposes certain characteristic ideas. Whoever wants to find out what these are will be forced to return to Burke, Bentham, Guizot, and John Stuart Mill. He will then be forced to admit that after them, since about 1848, there have certainly been many new practical considerations but no new principled arguments ... Therefore one has to concern oneself with those "moldy" greats ... because what is specific to parliamentarism can only be gleaned from their thought.[1]

This passage could well have served as an epigraph for this book. One of its most intriguing aspects, however, is the role Schmitt assigns to Edmund Burke. He suggests that in one crucial domain, Burke was the great precursor to nineteenth-century liberals such as François Guizot and John Stuart Mill. This was Burke's analysis of *parliament.*

Despite the ever-growing interest in Schmitt, his brilliant historical analysis of parliamentarism has not been followed up by scholars.[2] Nor have scholars emphasized Burke's role as a theorist of parliamentarism, as Schmitt did.[3] If the aim of this book is to recover parliamentarism's central place in modern political thought, the contention of this chapter is that it

---

[1] Schmitt, "On the Contradiction between Parliamentarism and Democracy," 2.

[2] Schmitt's critique of parliamentary liberalism is discussed in Wolfgang Mommsen, *Max Weber and German Politics 1890–1920*, tr. Michael Steinberg (Chicago: 1990), 332–390; John McCormick, *Carl Schmitt's Critique of Liberalism: Against Politics as Technology* (Cambridge: 1999), 175–206; Dominique Leydet, "Pluralism and the Crisis of Parliamentary Democracy," in *Law as Politics: Carl Schmitt's Critique of Liberalism*, ed. David Dyzenhaus (Durham: 1998), 109–130; Nadia Urbinati, "Schmitt's Critique of Liberalism," *Cardozo Law Review*, vol. 21 (2000), 1645–1651. But scholarship on eighteenth- and nineteenth-century thought has rarely used Schmitt's ideas as a resource.

[3] See, however, the classic essay by Caroline Robbins, "Edmund Burke's Rationale of Cabinet Government," *Burke Newsletter*, vol. 7, no. 1 (1965), 457–465. As for Schmitt, it is worth noting that that he was most interested in Burke's influence on German theorists such as Gentz and Bluntschli as opposed to the French and British authors examined in this book. Schmitt believed this

is impossible to accomplish this without a significant reevaluation of Burke – the first major author who brought together all the different threads of argument examined in Chapter 1. Burke defended a powerful House of Commons that strictly controlled the executive and deliberated over the common good. To restrain that assembly, he turned not to the Crown's veto but rather to a dignified constitutional monarch and ministers who served in Parliament.

Burke thought that since 1688, this had been the fundamental arrangement of English politics. He also became convinced, at two crucial moments in his political career, that it was under dramatic assault. The first was in the late 1760s, when he feared that George III wanted to restore the Crown's power and autonomy. It was in response to this perceived threat that he wrote *Thoughts on the Cause of the Present Discontents*, his most important account of the English constitution. The second such moment was the French Revolution. Among France's most devastating mistakes, Burke contended, was its complete disregard of the constitutional order that had arisen across the Channel – and that was defined by a powerful House of Commons, the presence of a dignified constitutional monarch, and the involvement of responsible ministers in Parliament. Not only was the French monarch deprived of his dignity, members of the National Assembly were expressly prohibited from serving in ministerial office – indeed, ministers could not even attend the Assembly's meetings.[4] The National Assembly inscribed into the constitution it was writing, the eventual Constitution of 1791, a similar prohibition on ministers serving in the legislature.[5] Burke warned that France would have a constitution in which the legislature was subject to no restraint, and he predicted that the result would be usurpation and despotism. However, I will contend that the standard by which he judged the Constitution of 1791 deficient was not Montesquieu's theory of equal checks and balances but was rather his own account of parliamentary government and limited constitutional monarchy, which he had laid out in *Thoughts on the Present Discontents*.

Burke's argument that the National Assembly erred decisively by rejecting English parliamentarism would be among his great legacies to

---

influence to be profound. See Schmitt, *Constitutional Theory*, 338; Schmitt, "On the Contradiction between Parliamentarism and Democracy," 5.

[4] See "Suite de la discussion de la motion de M. comte de Mirabeau relative à l'entrée des ministres dans l'Assemblée," in *Archives Parlementaires*, ser. 1, t. 9 (Paris: 1877), 715–718.

[5] See Léon Duguit and Henry Monnier, *Les constitutions et les principales lois politiques de la France depuis 1789: collationnées sur les textes officiels, précédées des notices historiques et suivies d'une table analytique détaillée* (Paris: 1908), 10, 17.

the nineteenth century. Another crucial legacy, as Emily Jones has recently underscored, was his theory of political parties.[6] Burke believed that the establishment of competing parties in Parliament ensured that an energetic opposition would always be present – but one sufficiently organized to itself become the government, should it force the current ministers from office. Burke also thought that political parties were the best antidote to parliamentary corruption, which he recognized as the defining pathology of the English constitution. Parties would not eliminate the need for ministers to distribute patronage in Parliament, Burke acknowledged, but he was convinced that they would limit the worst effects of patronage – though, as we will see, he was not always satisfied by this as a solution.

This chapter will proceed as follows. I will begin by systematically examining Burke's constitutional theory. I will then consider the challenge that parliamentary corruption posed to his ideal of the English constitution, and I will show how his famous account of political parties came out of his long-standing effort to wrestle with the Crown's "influence" in Parliament. Finally, I will turn to Burke's reflections on the French Revolution.

Parliament and Parliamentary Government

Burke's constitutional ideas came out of the intellectual currents I explored in Chapter 1. He agreed with Smith and De Lolme that what distinguished England from an absolute monarchy was the House of Commons' control over the Crown. He also cherished the House of Commons' role as a "deliberative assembly" – famously rejecting binding electoral mandates because they would interfere with Parliament's capacity to freely discuss political issues.[7]

What enabled the House of Commons to perform these functions was its distinctive capacity to *represent* the people. Burke argued that the House of Commons could "feel with a more tender and nearer interest everything that concerned the people" than the other branches of government.[8] In

---

[6] Emily Jones, *Edmund Burke and the Invention of Modern Conservatism, 1830–1914: An Intellectual History* (Oxford: 2017), 16–33.

[7] Edmund Burke, "Speech at Conclusion of the Poll," *Writings and Speeches of Edmund Burke*, vol. 3, ed. Warren Elofson and John Woods (Oxford: 1996), 70. Discussions of Burke's famous attack upon mandates include Hannah Pitkin, *The Concept of Representation* (Berkeley: 1967), 168–189; James Conniff, "Burke, Bristol, and the Concept of Representation," *Western Political Quarterly*, vol. 30, no. 3 (1977), 329–341; Bourke, *Empire and Revolution*, 376–390.

[8] Edmund Burke, *Thoughts on the Cause of the Present Discontents, Writings and Speeches of Edmund Burke*, vol. 2, 292.

Thoughts on the Present Discontents, he wrote that "the virtue, spirit, and essence of a House of Commons consists in it being the *express image* of the feelings of the nation."[9] Nearly 15 years later, he would similarly instruct the king that "the collective sense of his people, His Majesty is to receive from his Commons in Parliament assembled."[10]

Burke argued that there could not be a "free constitution" without a representative assembly that represented the people's interests and opinions, deliberated over their grievances, and challenged those "abuses" that "must accumulate in every monarchy not under the constant inspection of a popular representative."[11] Following the authors I examined in Chapter 1, Burke held that control over finances – "Parliament['s] ancient, hereditary, inherent right of controlling and checking the public expenditure" – was the crucial power that enabled Parliament to supervise the Crown.[12] One of Burke's great projects in Parliament was to bring the Civil List – a fund of money traditionally spent at the Crown's discretion – under thorough parliamentary oversight.[13] He achieved that goal with the passage of his economic reform bill in 1782, an act that greatly expanded Parliament's supervision of government expenditures.[14]

Like Bolingbroke, Burke believed that the power of the purse was necessary but not sufficient for securing parliamentary control over the executive. He argued that the House of Commons must additionally have the right to reject any minister it found unsuitable. It was "the first duty of Parliament," he wrote, "to refuse to support Government, until power was in the hands of persons who were acceptable to the people."[15] No ministry should hold office without the express confidence of the House of Commons.

---

[9] Ibid. Eric Nelson points out that Burke was inconsistent in how he understood the representative function of the House of Commons. At certain moments, like in this passage, Burke argued that "all parts" of the British government were equally representatives of the people but nonetheless that the *virtue* of the House of Commons was to have a special "sympathy" with the people's "opinions and feelings" that none of the other branches was capable of possessing. At other moments, however, Burke makes the much stronger argument that the other branches of the British government are not even representatives of the people at all – only the House of Commons is. For this important observation see Nelson, *The Royalist Revolution*, 279.

[10] Edmund Burke, "Representation to His Majesty," *Writings and Speeches*, vol. 4, ed. P. J. Marshall and Donald Bryant (Oxford: 2015), 192.

[11] Edmund Burke, *Reflections on the Revolution in France*, *Writings and Speeches*, vol. 8, ed. L. G. Mitchell (Oxford: 1989), 175.

[12] Edmund Burke, "Speech on Economical Reform Bill," *Writings and Speeches of Edmund Burke*, vol. 4, 50; Burke, *Thoughts on the Present Discontents*, 279.

[13] Burke's effort to bring accountability to the Civil List is a major theme in Earl A. Reitan's definitive book on this topic. See *Politics, Finance and the People*, 95–110.

[14] Ibid.   [15] Burke, *Thoughts on the Present Discontents*, 278.

Burke argued that this principle had enabled eighteenth-century England to possess "all the good effects of popular election ... without the mischiefs attending on perpetual intrigue, and a distinct canvass for every particular office throughout the body of the people."[16] Without the disorder of popular elections, the English people could be confident that "their executory system" was oriented toward the public interest.[17] As I noted in Chapter 1, this stricter conception of ministerial responsibility would be contested into the nineteenth century. But Burke believed it was indispensable. He contended that ministers would necessarily have some autonomy in how they chose to enforce the laws. Unless they were continually accountable to Parliament for their actions, neither liberty nor the public interest would be secure:

> The laws reach but a very little way. Constitute government how you please, infinitely the greater part of it must depend upon the exercise of the powers which are left at large to the prudence and uprightness of ministers of state. Even all the use and potency of the laws depends upon them. Without them, your commonwealth is no better than a scheme upon paper ... It is possible, that through negligence, or ignorance, or design artfully conducted, ministers may suffer one part of government to languish, another to be perverted from its purposes, and every valuable interest of the country to fall into ruin and decay, without possibility of fixing any single act on which a criminal prosecution can be justly grounded.[18]

By requiring ministers to always possess the confidence of the House of Commons, that body could ensure that "the discretionary powers which are necessarily vested in the Monarch, whether for the execution of the laws, or for the nomination to magistracy and office, or for conducting the affairs of peace and war, or for ordering the revenue," would "all be exercised upon public principles and national grounds" – not according to "the likings or prejudices, the intrigues or policies, of a Court."[19] It was the strict responsibility of ministers to the House of Commons that "kept ministers in awe of Parliaments."[20]

Burke recognized that the set of vital functions he expected the House of Commons to perform – its control over the "public expenditure" of the state; its right to veto any minister selected by the monarch; its claim to *represent* the English people; its capacity to freely deliberate without direct control by the electorate – tended to augment its power at the expense of the other parts of the constitution. He was convinced, as were Hume and de Lolme, that the natural tendency of English politics after 1688 was

---

[16] Ibid., 278–279. [17] Ibid., 278. [18] Ibid., 277. [19] Ibid. [20] Ibid.

toward the increasing supremacy of the House of Commons. "Since the Revolution at least," Burke declared, "the power of the nation has flowed with a full tide into the House of Commons. The power of the state nearly melted down into this house."[21] As I have argued, Burke saw great value in a powerful representative assembly. But he also foresaw potential danger. He claimed that "because the House of Commons . . . is the most powerful [it] is the most corruptible part of the whole constitution," and that "abuse in this house" was effectively no different than "the abuse of the whole."[22] "The distempers of monarchy were the great subjects of apprehension and redress in the last century," Burke wrote; "in this [century], the distempers of Parliament."[23]

Burke recognized that the Crown's traditional check on Parliament lay in its veto. However, he was greatly relieved that this prerogative had gone out of use and strongly opposed its resuscitation.[24] As he emphasized in his *Letter to the Sheriffs of Bristol*, there was no doubt that Parliament had passed several laws that were mistaken or even harmful. But even in such a circumstance, the monarch should not use his negative. "The exercise itself is wisely forborne."[25] Except in a crisis of the highest order, where the very existence of constitution was at stake, Burke was opposed to the Crown vetoing legislation.[26]

According to Burke, it was through ministers serving in Parliament that England had moderated a powerful representative assembly. After 1688, "the Crown, deprived, for the ends of the Revolution itself, of many prerogatives, was found too weak to struggle against all the difficulties which pressed so new and unsettled a Government," he wrote.[27] It therefore decided to "delegate a part of its powers" to "the leaders of Whigs or Tories, men of talents to conciliate the people, and engage to their confidence."[28] As the king's ministers, these figures could use the Crown's extensive patronage to secure their own powerful position in Parliament. In exchange, they protected the Crown's vital interests.[29] By the time Burke entered the House of Commons in 1765, this original "connection" between William III and the Whigs of the 1690s was slowly evolving into a modern parliamentary government.[30]

---

[21] Burke, "Speech on Parliamentary Incapacitation," 234.   [22] Ibid.
[23] Burke, *Thoughts on the Present Discontents*, 311–312.
[24] See Burke, "Representation to His Majesty," 195.
[25] Edmund Burke, "Letter to the Sheriffs of Bristol," in *The Works of the Right Honorable Edmund Burke*, vol. 2 (London: 1887), 225.
[26] Ibid., 226.   [27] Burke, *Thoughts on the Present Discontents*, 259.   [28] Ibid., 259, 261.
[29] Ibid., 258–259.   [30] Ibid., 269.

Burke realized that this arrangement was far from perfect, and he grappled with its tendency toward corruption. But he was among its greatest defenders. Like Walpole, he believed that the presence of ministers in Parliament enabled harmony between the executive and legislature. "Nothing, indeed, will appear more certain," he wrote, "than that every sort of government ought to have its administration correspondent to its legislature. If it should be otherwise, things must fall into a hideous disorder."[31] The selection of the Crown's ministers from among the leading members of Parliament ensured this indispensable "correspondence." It placed "the great strong holds of government in well-united hands" and helped "secure the predominance of right and uniform principles."[32] For Burke, as for Walpole, it was necessary to unite "the capital offices of deliberation and execution" in the hands of a single group, "who can deliberate with mutual confidence, and who will execute what is resolved with firmness and fidelity."[33]

Most importantly, this practice gave the king a way to act within the legislature that was consistent with his limited constitutional role. Because his ministers were drawn from among the leading members of Parliament, they were certain to have a political agenda and an importance in the state that were separate from their position under him. As his decisions came to be guided by these figures, and as his patronage came to be distributed through their hands, the weight of the monarchy was divided between "the Court and the leaders of parties."[34] In many cases, it was even transformed into an "accessory to the popular rather than to the royal scale."[35] This was all in addition to the House of Commons' right to reject any minister whom it did not wish to see in office.

Burke's conception of constitutional monarchy was similar to de Lolme's. He agreed with his Swiss-born contemporary (whose classic treatise on the English constitution came out the year after *Thoughts on the Present Discontents*) that an English monarch was "a real King," whose "direct power is considerable," but that even more important was the monarch's "indirect power. He stands in need of nothing towards dignity; of nothing towards splendour; of nothing towards authority."[36] Like de Lolme, Burke claimed that an English monarch lost no *real* authority as a

---

[31] Ibid., 278.
[32] Edmund Burke, *Observations on a Late State of the Nation, Writings and Speeches of Edmund Burke*, vol. 2, 210.
[33] Ibid.   [34] Burke, *Thoughts on the Present Discontents*, 259.   [35] Ibid.
[36] Edmund Burke, "A Letter to a Member of the National Assembly," in *Further Reflections on the Revolution in France*, ed. Daniel Ritchie (Indianapolis: 1992), 68.

result of his dependence on Parliament. "A wise prince," he argued, "will not think" that the "restraint" of parliamentary control "implies a condition of servility."[37] The reign of George II suggested that governing through ministers acceptable to Parliament only augmented the monarch's dignity. "In times full of doubt and danger to his person and family, George the Second maintained the dignity of his Crown connected with the liberty of his people, not only unimpaired, but improved, for the space of thirty-three years. He carried the glory, the power, the commerce of England, to a height unknown."[38]

Burke was not only a theorist of Parliament but also was among the great parliamentary statesmen of the eighteenth century. Born in 1729, he entered the House of Commons in 1765, after an uneven career in law and letters, and he served in Parliament for nearly three decades, retiring in 1794. For much of that period, he was convinced that British politics had entered an era of profound upheaval because of the actions of George III. During the previous reigns of George I and George II, the Whig party had maintained a steady hold on ministerial office. From 1721 to 1742, Robert Walpole had been prime minister. He was succeeded by his protégé Henry Pelham, who was prime minister between 1743 and 1754. Following Pelham's death, the dominant figure in Parliament was his brother the Duke of Newcastle. Even William Pitt, the most popular and eloquent statesman of the period, could not hold onto power without Newcastle's support. However, with George III's ascension to the throne in 1760, the monopoly of the Whigs came to an end.[39] In 1762, the king dismissed Newcastle's ministry, leading to sustained cabinet instability for the rest of the 1760s.[40] As Burke declared in horror at the end of the decade, "no less than seven prime ministers of state" had recently held office.[41]

In 1770, Lord North became prime minister and the cabinet instability came to an end. However, for Burke, this constituted little improvement.

---

[37] Burke, *Thoughts on the Present Discontents*, 267.　　[38] Ibid., 266–267.

[39] J. C. D. Clark persuasively traces the "disintegration of the *Old Corps*" as Parliament's ruling power further back to the 1750s and to the weakening of the conventional Whig and Tory parties during that period. See J. C. D. Clark, *The Dynamics of Change: The Crisis of the 1750s and English Party Systems* (Cambridge: 1982). In contrast with Clark, Burke saw the crucial event as George III's ascent to the throne.

[40] The history leading up to this event is recounted in Lewis Namier, *England in the Age of the American Revolution* (London: 1930), 51–262, 331–485.

[41] Edmund Burke, "Speech on London Remonstrance," *Writings and Speeches of Edmund Burke*, vol. 2, 240. Scholarly discussions of the parliamentary instability of the 1760s include Richard Pares, *King George III and the Politicians* (Oxford: 1953), 61–118; Paul Langford, *The First Rockingham Administration, 1765–1766* (Oxford: 1973), 1–108, 199–263; Baranger, *Parlementarisme des origines*, 91.

George III put the full weight of his influence behind North's ministry, even though it was one of the greatest disasters in British history. The fact that North was able to remain in office for 12 years (longer than any prime minister since Walpole) was a sign to Burke that the system was not working properly. When North's administration fell in 1782, Burke's party finally entered power. However, it would exit after less than a year, following the death of its leader Lord Rockingham. This set the stage for the next great constitutional crisis. In 1783, Burke's party (now under the leadership of Charles James Fox) formed a government with North. George III responded by dismissing the government and appointing William Pitt Jr. as prime minister. Because Pitt did not have majority support in Parliament, the king dissolved the House of Commons and called an election – correctly judging that the nation would return a majority for Pitt.[42]

Burke thought that George III's actions made effective leadership in Parliament impossible. The result was substantial political turmoil – not only in England but also across the entire British empire. However, during the late 1760s, Burke became convinced that more was at stake even than this. He believed that the king's refusal to govern with the Whigs evinced a secret plot to restore the Crown's power and independence. The supposed inspiration for this project was Bolingbroke's "Patriot King."[43] Edmund Burke published *Thoughts on the Cause of the Present Discontents* in 1770 to expose this plot to the nation and defend the English constitution.

The argument of the pamphlet was not that George III was openly contesting parliamentary control. Such a course of action would be sure to arouse substantial opposition, so instead, Burke argued, the king had decided to achieve greater independence surreptitiously. At the beginning of his reign, he picked a close personal acquaintance with no prior importance in Parliament to be prime minister – the infamous Earl of Bute.[44] When Bute left office, the king adopted an even more dangerous strategy: a double cabinet. While ministerial positions were still held by prominent members of Parliament, Burke claimed that most government

---

[42] For an analysis of this series of events, see John Cannon, *The Fox-North Coalition: Crisis of the Constitution 1782–1784* (Cambridge: 1970).

[43] For the dialogue between Burke and Bolingbroke that played out in Burke's criticisms of George III, see Harvey Mansfield, *Statesmanship and Party Statesmanship and Party Government: A Study of Burke and Bolingbroke* (Chicago: 1965).

[44] Burke, *Thoughts on the Present Discontents*, 260. For an analysis of Bute's role in the political thought of this period and of the wider discourse that Burke was contributing to in making this argument, see John Brewer, "The Misfortunes of Lord Bute: A Case-Study in Eighteenth-Century Political Argument and Public Opinion," *Historical Journal*, vol. 16, no. 1 (1973), 3–43.

offices were being filled with George III's handpicked men, who were acting in collusion with the Court behind the backs of the House of Commons. "By this operation, two systems of administration were to be formed," Burke warned.[45] That of the ministers was "merely ostensible;" the real "executory duties of government" were being performed by the king's minions.[46] Through a double cabinet, the king had figured out how he might govern independently of Parliament.

While Burke warned that this project would lead to the destruction of liberty, he argued that its most immediate effect had been the unprecedented cabinet instability of the 1760s. By distributing government offices to his own favorites rather than to allies of the ministry in power, George III deprived each successive ministry of support in Parliament and unraveled the unified exercise of legislative and executive power. "The control of Parliament upon the executory power is lost," Burke lamented, even as "government" became "in all its grand operations languid, uncertain, ineffective."[47] A double cabinet led to "neither the security of a free government, nor the energy of a monarchy that is absolute."[48] Burke was almost certainly incorrect about George III's intentions – it is close to inconceivable that he was actually governing through a double cabinet.[49] But if the double cabinet was entirely imaginary, it was also the perfect foil against which Burke could posit his own ideal of the English constitution – in which a limited monarch governed through responsible ministers in Parliament.

Corruption and Party Government

Several of Burke's most perceptive readers have traced his political ideas back to Montesquieu.[50] While it is true that, like Montesquieu, Burke conceived of the English constitution as a system with numerous balances and counterweights, and even cited Montesquieu to that effect, it should

---

[45] Burke, *Thoughts on the Present Discontents*, 260.

[46] Ibid. As was the convention, Burke did not attribute these actions directly to the king but instead to nefarious figures in his court.

[47] Burke, *Thoughts on the Present Discontents*, 283, 294.   [48] Ibid., 283.

[49] This was a widely expressed fear during this period, even if it was almost certainly incorrect. For a judicious summary of the debate among scholars over George III's actual intentions, see H. T. Dickinson, "George III and Parliament," *Parliamentary History*, vol. 30, no. 3 (2011), 395–413.

[50] For studies of Burke that make Montesquieu central to understanding his thought, see Bourke, *Empire and Revolution*; Daniel O'Neill, *The Burke-Wollstonecraft Debate: Savagery, Civilization, and Democracy* (University Park: 2007); F. P. Lock, *Edmund Burke, volume II: 1784–1797* (Oxford: 2006).

be clear by now that Burke also departed from Montesquieu on several fundamental points.[51] Whereas Montesquieu claimed that the House of Commons was checked by an independent executive armed with the power to veto legislation, Burke was skeptical of both an independent executive and the veto power. He argued that the highest executive officials should be members of Parliament, and that Parliament should have a decisive say over their appointments. Because of his faith in the emerging practice of parliamentary government – which Montesquieu never even mentioned – Burke believed that constitutional liberty could still be preserved, even if the balance of constitutional prerogatives tilted decisively in the direction of the House of Commons.

As a strong defender of the presence of ministers in Parliament, Burke had no choice but to grapple with the issue of patronage. His position on this issue was quite complex. Following in the tradition of Walpole, he did not believe stable ministries were possible, unless ministers distributed patronage to their allies in Parliament. This was why George III's supposed double cabinet was creating such ministerial instability: the offices that ministers should have been giving to their followers were instead being distributed to "the King's men." But even though Burke accepted parliamentary patronage as an inescapable element of English politics, he displayed genuine concern that it was corrupting English politics. There were moments when he feared that it threatened the House of Commons' control over the crown – even as he saw no way for the English constitution to function without it.

In *Thoughts on the Present Discontents*, Burke made clear his basic acceptance of patronage.[52] "It were better, undoubtedly, that no influence at all could affect the mind of a member of Parliament," he wrote.[53] "But of all modes of influence, in my opinion, a place under the Government is the least disgraceful to the man who holds it, and by far the most safe to the country."[54] This kind of "influence ... is open and visible," and it is "connected with the dignity and the service of the state."[55] Burke distinguished patronage from more secret forms of corruption like "bribery,"

---

[51] For examples of his invocations of Montesquieu and for the strongest case that Burke was a follower of Montesquieu, see Bourke, *Empire and Revolution*, 19–26.

[52] Burke's opposition to a place bill is also discussed in David Bromwich, *The Intellectual Life of Edmund Burke: From the Sublime and the Beautiful to American Independence* (Cambridge, MA: 2014), 171–172; Frank O'Gorman, *Edmund Burke: His Political Philosophy* (Bloomington: 1973), 49–50. For an interpretation of Burke that draws him much closer to Bolingbroke and the country party tradition, see W. M. Elofson, *The Rockingham Connection and the Second Founding of the Whig party, 1768–1773* (Montreal: 1996).

[53] Burke, *Thoughts on the Present Discontents*, 311.   [54] Ibid.   [55] Ibid.

which ministries might turn to if patronage was prohibited.[56] He also accepted that a large administrative state was a permanent feature of English politics and thus deserving of a voice in Parliament. "A great official, a great professional, a great military and naval interest, all necessarily comprehending many people of the first weight, ability, wealth, and spirit, has been gradually formed in the kingdom. These new interests must be let into a share of representation."[57] Finally, Burke expressed confidence that Parliament could still hold ministers responsible, even as those ministers were distributing "places under Government" to parliamentary representatives. He argued that "an inquisitive and distinguishing Parliament" would withdraw its confidence from any ministry that used jobs and favors to pursue illicit action.[58] "In such a Parliament," he declared, if ministers "act ill, they know that no intrigue can protect them."[59]

Burke's confidence that ministers could not evade accountability through patronage would become especially evident during his effort to reform British rule in India. The East India reform bill that Burke supported in 1783 would have placed the East India Company entirely under the control of two commissions appointed by Parliament. While one of the commissions would have been limited to making political decisions, the other would have appointed all the company's officers. Burke strenuously supported the bill, even though it was opening up an enormous new field for political patronage. There would have existed nothing to prevent ministers from appointing their political supporters to the most lucrative positions in the East India Company.

Burke felt that this price would have been worth paying, if it meant reforming British rule in India. However, he also argued, even more explicitly than in *Thoughts on the Present Discontents*, that it was appropriate for a minister to appoint "friends" and "persons of his own party" to administrative positions. As long as this was done openly rather than "clandestine[ly]," and so long as the minister was accountable to Parliament, there was no cause for complaint.[60] If a minister "proposes for his own ends" that an individual be placed in administrative office who is defective with respect to "character, ability, or knowledge," Burke reminded the assembly, "he is in an independent House of Commons; in a House of Commons which has, by its own virtue, destroyed the

[56] Ibid., 310.   [57] Ibid., 311.   [58] Ibid.   [59] Ibid.
[60] Edmund Burke, "Fox's India Bill," *Writings and Speeches*, vol. 5, ed. P. J. Marshall (Oxford: 1981), 445.

instruments of parliamentary subservience."[61] The House of Commons "would not endure" such corruption, Burke argued, and the minister "would perish by the means which he is supposed to pursue for the security of his power."[62]

Burke's confidence that patronage would not prevent the House of Commons from vigilantly supervising ministers rested, above all, on his faith in *political parties*. The parties that existed in Parliament were united by bonds of friendship and principle. They also had their own independent networks of patronage, which were based in the wealth and electoral influence of aristocrats.[63] Because of the loyalty of parliamentary representatives to their respective parties, Burke believed that they could not be bribed to support just any ministry. They would remain steadfast in opposition when their party was out of power.[64]

As well as ensuring that there would always be groups of representatives who refused to accept offices from the current government, political parties ensured that those offices were given out in a manner that was not corrupting. When ministers distributed the Crown's patronage to the members of their party, their intention was not to bribe representatives to forsake their principles but rather to reward political allies who shared their principles. It was because of his commitment to party government that Burke could make the striking claim that Walpole was not at all "a prodigal and corrupt minister" and that "the charge of systematic corruption is less applicable to him, perhaps, than to any minister who ever served the crown for so great a length of time."[65] According to Burke, Walpole was "a sound Whig" who "governed by party attachments."[66] In Burke's mind, the crucial distinction was between "systematic corruption" and "party attachments." So long as patronage was distributed to members of Parliament who shared the ministry's principles – and who would loyally enter opposition once the ministry left office – it was not a force for corruption. Party attachments enabled the House of Commons to continue to serve as the control on the executive, even as executive officials made use of patronage in the House of Commons to fortify their positions.

[61] Ibid.   [62] Ibid.   [63] Burke, *Thoughts on the Present Discontents*, 264.

[64] Edmund Burke to Charles O'Hara (September 30, 1772), in *Correspondence of Edmund Burke*, vol. 2, ed. Lucy Sutherland (Cambridge: 1960), 336.

[65] Edmund Burke, *Appeal from the New to the Old Whigs*, *Works of Edmund Burke*, vol. 3 (London: 1854), 50.

[66] Ibid.

Burke has long been read as a pioneering theorist of party govern-ment.[67] He believed that without political parties, which governed according to their conception of the common good and then loyally opposed the government upon losing power, a free constitution was impossible. However, within the eighteenth-century English constitution, the great benefit of parties was that they moderated the corrupting effect of patronage. Burke thought that there was no way to prevent the Crown's employments from being *a* support for government. Parties ensured that they were not the only support – and kept alive a parliamentary opposition that was not bribable.

Should parties fail at this function and should Parliament become so corrupt that it no longer vigilantly contested the government's actions, Burke thought that hope was still not lost, for at that point, the task of opposing government would be taken up by the English people. Despite his well-known fears about popular political participation, Burke argued that the role of controlling ministers involved the public as well as the House of Commons. When the king made a serious mistake in his choice of ministers, and Parliament was unwilling to force them out, "the people must on their part show themselves sensible of their own value. Their whole importance, in the first instance, and afterwards their whole free-dom, is at stake."[68] "The natural strength of the kingdom must interpose, to rescue their Prince, themselves, and their posterity."[69] While Burke was famously opposed to electoral mandates and expanding the suffrage, he defended meetings, petitions, and even the occasional disruptive protest as a way for the public to show its discontent with those in power. Through these means, a corrupt ministry that had managed to subdue the House of Commons could be forced from office – once the depth of public discon-tent was revealed.[70]

Because of the counterposing forces of *party attachment* and *public opinion*, Burke believed that minsters who strengthened their adminis-tration through patronage would remain under the control of the House of Commons. "Influence" would only threaten the values of deliberation and responsible government if it was distributed in excess – and outside normal parliamentary oversight. That is why Burke was so concerned about the Civil List, the Crown's one fund of revenue during the eighteenth century

---

[67] Classic accounts of Burke on parties include Nancy Rosenblum, *On the Side of the Angels: An Appreciation of Parties and Partisanship* (Princeton: 2008), 108–126; Mansfield, *Statesmanship and Party Government.*
[68] Burke, *Thoughts on the Present Discontents*, 282.   [69] Ibid.   [70] Ibid., 313–314.

that was spent outside the supervision of the House of Commons. He was convinced that George III was making use of it to surreptitiously corrupt Parliament – indeed, the very idea of the king creating a double cabinet was inconceivable without the many positions that were appointed through the Civil List. As I noted earlier in the chapter, Burke devoted substantial effort to reducing the offices the king could fill through the Civil List and bringing its expenditures under parliamentary supervision.

Burke's fundamental position was that patronage in a parliamentary government was both necessary and legitimate. However, there were moments in his career when he felt extraordinary ambivalence about this position – especially during the North administration. As I discussed earlier, North became prime minister in 1770, and he remained in power for 12 years despite an astonishingly poor performance. North brought England into an unnecessary war first with its American colonies, then with France, and finally with Spain. He so badly mismanaged these wars that England was nearly invaded. Catastrophic military defeats were suffered by British forces in America, and there was a near-revolution in Ireland.[71] Yet still, North remained in office. As Burke angrily declared to the House of Commons in 1779, "you see the same men, in the same power, sitting undisturbed before you, though thirteen colonies have been lost."[72]

Throughout the North administration, Burke lamented that the House of Commons had abdicated its role of controlling the government. Although the ministry's policies did not have "the smallest degree of common sense," the House of Commons stood in the "most perfect repose," he wrote.[73] "Scarcely one can be found ... who will take a step towards putting our affairs in a better condition by endeavoring a change of hands or an alteration of counsels."[74] Despite his manifest errors, North was able to "carry on administration with the most perfect success and perfect Tranquility."[75] Nor did Burke believe that the English people had performed any better. In 1779, a popular movement finally emerged to

---

[71] Burke summarizes the litany of North's failures and mistakes in the articles of impeachment against North that he drafted in 1779 – though they were never brought forward. See Edmund Burke, "Articles of Impeachment," *Writings and Speeches of Edmund Burke*, vol. 3, 454–463.

[72] Edmund Burke, "Speech on Public Expenses," *Writings and Speeches of Edmund Burke*, vol. 3, 472.

[73] Edmund Burke to Charles O'Hara (August 17, 1775), in *Correspondence of Edmund Burke*, vol. 3, ed. George Guttride (Cambridge: 1961), 518; Edmund Burke to Charles Lee (February 1, 1774), *Correspondence of Edmund Burke*, vol. 2, 518.

[74] Burke to O'Hara (August 17, 1775), 518.

[75] Edmund Burke to Charles O'Hara (December 11, 1773), *Correspondence of Edmund Burke*, vol. 2, 496.

challenge North's administration. But over the prior decade, Burke repeatedly lamented the English's public's failure to be at all "jealous" and "inquisitive" of those who were in office, and he feared that acquiescence to North signaled a real deterioration in political character:

> As to the good people of England, they seem to partake every day more and more of the character of that administration which they have been induced to tolerate. I am satisfied, that within a few years there has been a great change in the national character. We seem no longer the eager, inquisitive, jealous, fiery people, which we have been formerly, and which we have been, a very short time ago.[76]

As the English people fell into "a sort of heavy lumpish acquiescence" to North's administration, Burke lost his earlier confidence that they would intervene against a nefarious ministry when Parliament failed.[77]

Like the "country party" that had opposed Walpole a half-century earlier, Burke argued that patronage had deprived the House of Commons and the English people of their public spirit.[78] It was "to this cause," he told Parliament, that "I attribute that nearly general indifference to all public interests ... for some years."[79] Indeed, his remarks against parliamentary corruption during the North administration go beyond a desire for Parliament to exercise greater supervision over the Civil List. He declared to the House of Commons in 1781 that the use of "places, pensions, and honors" to stay in office he "considered as pernicious to freedom as open force."[80] "When virtue which was the spirit of commonwealths and of all free states, was gone," Burke contended, "liberty could not survive."[81] The only legitimate "influence" a minister could rely on in order to stay in power was that of "superior wisdom and virtue;" the "influence" of patronage "he must ever deny to be either necessary or justifiable."[82]

Because of statements like these, it is possible to read Burke as carrying on the "country party" legacy.[83] And there is no question that the length of North's administration pushed him in that direction. Yet Burke never abandoned his commitment to a Whig administration that maintained itself in power partly through distributing patronage to its political allies,

---

[76] Edmund Burke to Lord Rockingham (August 22–23, 1775), *Correspondence of Edmund Burke*, vol. 3, 190.

[77] Edmund Burke to Charles Fox (October 8, 1777), *Correspondence of Edmund Burke*, vol. 3, 382.

[78] Burke, "Speech on Public Expenses," 471.   [79] Ibid.

[80] Burke, "Speech on Economical Reform Bill," 63.   [81] Ibid.   [82] Ibid., 62.

[83] For the most sophisticated example of this, see Elofson, *The Rockingham Connection and the Second Founding of the Whig party*.

just as Walpole and his successors had done prior to George III. Burke labored to bring the distribution of patronage under parliamentary supervision and to eliminate useless jobs that existed purely for corruption. However, he could never conceptualize the political order that had emerged in England during the eighteenth century without patronage. The best he could offer was a system of political parties, which would at least prevent patronage from *completely* undermining parliamentary politics.

Burke and the French National Assembly

During the 1760s, Burke feared that George III would manage to escape the control of the House of Commons. However, in the defining moment of his political career, it was exactly the opposite event that occurred. Not a monarch but a representative assembly would reject the constitutional order that had emerged in England during the eighteenth century. That representative assembly was the French National Assembly, which formed in June of 1789 out of the Estates General. Over the next two years and led by such illustrious figures as Emmanuel Sieyès, the Marquis de Lafayette, and the Comte de Mirabeau, the National Assembly would set about rewriting the fundamental laws of France.

Edmund Burke's *Reflections on the Revolution in France* is arguably the most famous and influential account of the National Assembly's actions ever written. However, scholars have generally overlooked how significant that body is to the structure of Burke's argument. The first time in the pamphlet that Burke discusses events in France is to analyze the National Assembly's membership and social composition – and compare it with that of the House of Commons.[84] The account of the French Revolution that Burke goes on to offer is almost entirely centered on two decisions taken by the National Assembly: its decision to move with the Royal Family from Versailles to Paris and its decision to confiscate Church land in order to pay off France's debt. Burke concludes the pamphlet by analyzing the Assembly's great project, the Constitution of 1791. At bottom, *Reflections on the Revolution in France* is a pamphlet about the actions of a *representative assembly*.

Burke believed that the members of the National Assembly completely surrendered their legitimacy when they disbanded the Estates General. "I can never consider this Assembly as anything else than a voluntary association of men who have availed themselves of circumstances to seize upon

---

[84] Burke, *Reflections on the Revolution in France*, 91.

the power of the state," he declared.[85] "They have not the sanction and authority of the character under which they first met," having "completely altered and inverted all the relations in which they originally stood."[86] However, Burke's argument against the National Assembly extended to more than just its illegitimacy. On repeated occasions, he contended that it had failed as a *deliberative* body. The National Assembly was not "possessed of any real deliberative capacity," he argued in an early letter concerning events in France.[87] It paid no homage whatsoever to "prudence, deliberation, and foresight," he declared in *Reflections*.[88] With the Parisian populace standing in the galleries, "the Assembly ... acts before them the farce of deliberation with as little decency as liberty."[89] There is "a compelled appearance of deliberation," but not the actuality, since the members all "vote under the domination of a stern necessity."[90]

"Who is it that admires, and from the heart is attached to national representative assemblies," Burke wrote, "must turn with horror and disgust from such a[n] ... abominable perversion of that sacred institute."[91] He predicted that the Constitution of 1791 would contain an assembly no different than the current one. It too would be "a body without fundamental laws, without established maxims, without respected rules of proceeding, which nothing can keep firm to any system whatsoever."[92] "The future is to be in most respects like the present assembly."[93]

Burke described the French Revolution as an unprecedented event, "the most astonishing that has hitherto happened in the world."[94] He depicted its egalitarian ideology, embodied in the Declaration of the Rights of Man and Citizen, as a willful, even satanic revolt against nature and history. But when we focus on the fact that *Reflections on the Revolution in France* is fundamentally a pamphlet about a representative assembly, striking continuities with his earlier political career become apparent.

The most important is his commitment to a parliamentary government. While Burke had called the presence of responsible ministers in Parliament "the most noble and refined part of our constitution," the National Assembly rejected this practice entirely. As I noted at the beginning of the chapter, it not only prohibited its own members from being ministers but also inscribed into the Constitution of 1791 a strict ban on ministers serving in the legislature. In the final part of *Reflections*, Burke stridently

---

[85] Ibid., 213.   [86] Ibid.

[87] Edmund Burke to William Wyndham (September 15, 1789), in *Correspondence of Edmund Burke*, vol. 6, ed. Alfred Cobban and Robert Smith (Cambridge: 1967), 25.

[88] Burke, *Reflections on the Revolution in France*, 216.   [89] Ibid., 119.   [90] Ibid., 118.

[91] Ibid., 119.   [92] Ibid., 245.   [93] Ibid.   [94] Ibid., 60.

attacked the separation between legislative and executive officials instituted by the National Assembly, expressing many of the same arguments he had made two decades earlier in *Thoughts on the Present Discontents*.

His broader argument in this section of the pamphlet was that the Constitution of 1791 contained a dangerously weak executive. While this was partly due to the king's not being given specific prerogatives, such as "the right of peace and war," Burke criticized the National Assembly far more extensively for not integrating the executive into the other parts of the constitution.[95] "The higher parts of the judicature" would no longer be held by the Crown, Burke noted, and the failure of integration was equally manifest when it came to the legislature.[96] "I see nothing in the executive force (I cannot call it authority) ... that has the smallest degree of just correspondence or symmetry, or even amicable relation, with the supreme power, as it now exists, or as it is planned for the future government," he wrote.[97] By the "supreme power as it now exists," he meant, of course, the National Assembly.

The reason the French monarch failed to have any "correspondence or symmetry" with the National Assembly was that his ministers were not allowed to participate. "The ministers of state in France are the only persons in that country who are incapable of a share in the national councils," Burke thundered. "What ministers! What councils! What a nation!"[98] The result was frightening disunity. "Your supreme government [i.e., the National Assembly] cannot harmonize with its executory system," he warned, and with ministers absent from the assembly, the monarch would have no way of shaping its decisions – "not so much as ... a single vote by himself or his ministers, or by any one whom he can possibly influence."[99]

Although Burke's target in *Reflections on the Revolution in France* was an unrestrained assembly rather than an uncontrolled monarch, his criticism of the National Assembly remarkably paralleled his attack on George III's double cabinet 20 years earlier.[100] In Burke's mind, George III and the

[95] Ibid., 251. This line of argument reiterated Burke's fears about Pitt's Regency bill during George III's madness a year and a half earlier, which Burke argued would give the Prince of Wales a truncated executive power. See Edmund Burke, "Debate in the Commons on the Regency Bill," in *The Parliamentary History of England*, vol. 27 (London: 1816), 1171–1177.

[96] Burke, *Reflections on the Revolution in France*, 246.   [97] Ibid., 250.   [98] Ibid., 249.

[99] Ibid., 248, 250.

[100] Strikingly, Burke even reverted to the language of a double cabinet. "You have settled, by an economy as perverted as the policy, two establishments of government – one real, one fictitious," he wrote when describing how the true executive power would be controlled in "the committees of the Assembly." Ibid., 248).

National Assembly both wanted an executive who was more independent of the legislature than the eighteenth-century English constitution allowed. Whereas George III disdained the "control" the House of Commons was able to exercise over his ministers, the National Assembly sought to be rid of any "influence" the king's ministers might exercise within the legislature.

Burke's warning in *Reflections on the Revolution in France* was that without this influence, the king of France would have no way of shaping the legislature's decisions and would quickly lose all authority. Nor, under the Constitution of 1791, would ministers themselves be able to maintain any authority. "Competitors of the ministers are enabled by your constitution to attack them in their vital parts, whilst they have not the means of repelling their charges," Burke wrote.[101] Although ministers were to be appointed entirely at the monarch's discretion, Burke charged that they would live in perpetual terror of the Legislative Assembly, for they would have no connection to that body and no opportunity to defend their actions there. While "in all other countries, the office of ministers of state is of the highest dignity," Burke argued, "in France it is full of peril and incapable of glory."[102] With characteristically unmatchable prose, he portrayed the French ministers who were unable to participate in the ruling assemblies: "they are to execute, without power; they are to be responsible, without discretion; they are to deliberate, without choice."[103]

Although in *Reflections on the Revolution in France*, Burke emphasized the danger of an unrestrained legislature, he made clear throughout the text that this institution was essential to a free state. At the beginning of the pamphlet, he argued that the most valuable consequence of the Revolution of 1688 was that "the whole government" had come to be "under the constant inspection and active control" of the House of Commons, calling this a "security" not only "against the vices of administration" but for "constitutional liberty."[104] He lamented that there was no such institution in pre-Revolutionary France. "Your government in France, though usually, and I think justly, reputed the best of the unqualified or ill-qualified monarchies, was still full of abuses. These abuses accumulated in a length of time, as they must accumulate in every monarchy, not under the constant inspection of a popular representative."[105] It was for this reason that "the French monarchy" was "by no means a free, and therefore by no means a good constitution" – even if it

[101] Ibid., 249.   [102] Ibid.   [103] Ibid., 252.   [104] Ibid.   [105] Ibid., 175.

was better than what the National Assembly had created in its stead.[106] Burke never gave up his commitment to a monarch who was controlled by Parliament, and just like in *Thoughts on the Present Discontents*, his great example of such a monarch was George II. "When George the Second took Mr. Pitt, who certainly was not agreeable to him, into his councils, he did nothing which could humble a wise sovereign."[107]

The Fall of the Constitution of 1791

The prohibition on ministers serving in the legislature was far from the only flaw in the new French constitution. Burke was stunned that the Assembly "have forgot to constitute a Senate," and that France would thus have a unicameral legislative body.[108] "Never before this time," he wrote, "was a body politic composed of one legislative and active assembly" only.[109] Burke claimed that a higher and more elevated "council" brought stability and consistency to government.[110] It was "something to which, in the ordinary detail of government, the people could look up; something which might give a bias and steadiness, and preserve something like consistency in the proceedings of state."[111]

Burke also attacked the Constitution of 1791's system of election. Instead of directly electing the members of the Legislative Assembly, citizens elected representatives to intermediate assemblies – those assemblies then selected the national legislature. Despite the National Assembly's stated commitment to political equality and popular sovereignty, Burke noted that "the member who goes to the . . . assembly is not chosen by the people, nor accountable to them. There are three elections before he is chosen: two sets of magistracy intervene between him and the primary assembly."[112] As a result, "there is little, or rather no, connection between the last representative and the first constituent."[113] Finally, Burke attacked the term limits to which legislative representatives would be subject. "Just as these magistrates begin to learn their trade," he wrote, "they are disqualified for exercising it."[114]

In an important continuity with his earlier writings on England, Burke predicted widespread corruption within the National Assembly. He argued that the representatives from the Third Estate in particular "must *join* (if their capacity did not permit them to *lead*) in any project . . . which could lay open to them those innumerable lucrative jobs which follow in the

---

[106] Ibid., 176. [107] Ibid., 248. [108] Ibid., 245. [109] Ibid. [110] Ibid. [111] Ibid.
[112] Ibid., 235. [113] Ibid. [114] Ibid., 236.

train of all great convulsions and revolutions."[115] In a pamphlet written the year after *Reflections*, Burke would make this accusation even more dramatically. The "National Assembly," he wrote, "holds out the highest object of ambition to vast multitudes as, in an unexampled measure, to widen the bottom of a new species of interest merely political, and wholly unconnected with birth or property."[116] What made the Assembly so susceptible to patronage was its social composition. It was made up of third-rate lawyers and "dealers in stocks and funds." For such men, attaining administrative office would be an unprecedented opportunity:

> Whilst they sit in the Assembly they are denied offices of trust and profit – but their short duration makes this no restraint – during their probation and apprenticeship they are salaried with an income to the greatest part of them immense; and after they have passed the novitiate, those who take any sort of lead are placed in very lucrative offices, according to their influence and credit, or appoint those who divide their profits.[117]

Burke emphasized that under the Constitution of 1791, the offices available to legislative representatives would no longer be distributed by the monarch. While he expected tremendous corruption, its consequence would not be a legislature subjected to the Crown but rather a legislature dominated by the nation's financial interests.[118] This formed yet another of Burke's criticisms of the National Assembly. He lamented that under the Constitution of 1791, a French monarch could no longer give out even "the vainest and most trivial title" – let alone "a pension," or "a permanent office."[119] The king would have none of the "dignity, authority, and consideration" that Burke, like de Lolme, was convinced a constitutional monarch must possess to maintain his position in the state.[120] The king's inability to be "the foundation of honor" and distribute titles, honors, offices, and pensions greatly contributed to his weakness vis-à-vis the legislature.[121]

Burke's critics immediately recognized that his account of the French Revolution hinged on his evaluation of the National Assembly. James Mackintosh devoted the second chapter of *Vindiciae Gallicae* to defending "the Composition and Character of the National Assembly." Even though he thought "the character of the National Assembly is of secondary importance," he felt forced to defend it, "as Mr. Burke has expended so

---

[115] Ibid., 94.
[116] Edmund Burke, *Thoughts on French Affairs, Writings and Speeches of Edmund Burke*, vol. 8, 365.
[117] Ibid., 366.   [118] Burke, *Reflections on the Revolution in France*, 242.   [119] Ibid., 247.
[120] Ibid.   [121] Ibid.

much invective against that body."[122] Thomas Paine similarly offered an account of what he called "the happy situation the National Assembly were placed in," while Mary Wollstonecraft and Burke's friend Phillip Francis both claimed that his critique of the National Assembly was self-contradictory: how could that body be so omnipotent, yet also completely subservient, as Burke argued, to the people of Paris?[123]

Indeed, many of Burke's claims about the composition and corruption of the National Assembly are unpersuasive. Because he was unwilling to admit there were real ideological differences between the different factions in the Assembly, all he could see was a corrupt mob lusting after profit. But Burke's argument regarding the presence of ministers in the Assembly was more compelling. In *Vindicae Gallicae*, Mackintosh (who would later emerge as an important theorist of parliamentary government in his own right) acknowledged that the National Assembly should have allowed ministers to sit in the legislature.[124] This part of Burke's argument would also be quickly confirmed by historical events. The Constitution of 1791 collapsed less than a year after it went into effect, following explosive conflicts between Louis XVI and the Legislative Assembly. Because this series of events is important not only for evaluating Burke's argument but also for understanding many of the subsequent authors in this book, it is worth outlining it in some depth.

One set of conflicts was over the king's use of his veto. In a pamphlet written a year after *Reflections* and shortly before the Constitution of 1791 went into effect, Burke described the suspensive veto given to Louis XVI as a "mischievous" and "dreadful prerogative," which it would be "impossible for the king to show even the desire of exerting," lest he put his life at risk.[125] Burke's judgment would quickly be confirmed. The Legislative Assembly opened on October 1, 1791, and within two months, Louis XVI had already vetoed two different bills. The first threatened France's *emigres* with death and confiscation; the second required priests who had not sworn an oath to the new constitution to do so within eight days. In May, Louis XVI vetoed another measure targeting the non-juring

---

[122] James Mackintosh, *Vindiciae Gallicae*, ed. Donald Winch (Indianapolis: 2006), 57–58.

[123] Thomas Paine, "The Rights of Man," in *Political Writings*, ed. Bruce Kuklick (Cambridge: 2000), 107; Mary Wollstonecraft, *Vindication of the Rights of Men and a Vindication of the Rights of Women*, ed. Sylvana Tomaselli (Cambridge: 1995), 63; Phillip Francis to Edmund Burke (November 3/4, 1790), *Correspondence of Edmund Burke*, vol. 6, 154.

[124] Mackintosh, *Vindiciae Gallicae*, 118.

[125] Burke, *Thoughts on French Affairs*, 378. In *Reflections*, Burke seems to have mistakenly believed that the king had lost his veto permanently (Burke, *Reflections on the Revolution in France*, 247).

priests as well as a bill to gather the new National Guard in Paris – though with the latter bill, his veto was flatly ignored.

Meanwhile, another set of conflicts had broken out over the king's appointment of ministers. In March, the king dismissed his hawkish minister of war, the Comte de Narbonne. The Legislative Assembly responded first with a vote of confidence in Narbonne's favor and then with the impeachment and criminal indictment of Louis XVI's minister of foreign affairs, Claude de Lessart. By the middle of March, the king had acceded to the Assembly and appointed a ministry acceptable to its majority – only to dismiss it two months later. With tension at a fever pitch, on August 9, 1792, Jérôme Pétion proposed a motion to the Legislative Assembly calling for the king to be removed. The motion was rejected, leading the *sections* of Paris and the members of the National Guard who had gathered to rise up in arms. The next day, the Legislative Assembly reversed its position, and voted for Louis XVI to be suspended and jailed. A new constitutional convention was called to create a republic, setting in motion the chain of events that would lead to the Terror.[126]

Although the framework of the Constitution of 1791 was only one factor in this dramatic series of events, nineteenth-century authors reflecting on the French Revolution would view it as among the most important. For British writers, the collapse of the Constitution of 1791 confirmed the value of the political framework that was developing in eighteenth-century Britain, as it moderated the House of Common, without requiring that the Crown exercise its veto or otherwise openly confront Parliament. In France, this set of events would motivate political theorists to reconsider their nation's opposition to the British parliamentary model. As they did, they would turn frequently to Edmund Burke. The constitutional ideal Burke articulated – a limited monarch governing through responsible ministers in Parliament – was never achieved to his satisfaction while he was in politics. But it would be his great legacy to the nineteenth century.

---

[126] For scholarly treatments of the dramatic events in France during the course of 1791 and 1792 (discussed in the previous two paragraphs), see François Furet, *Revolutionary France 1770–1880*, tr. Antonia Nevill (Malden: 1995), 101–116; Michel Vovelle, *The Fall of the French Monarchy: 1787–1792*, tr. Susan Burke (Cambridge: 1984), 210–232; C. J. Mitchell, *The French Legislative Assembly of 1791* (Leiden: 1988), 103–220. For an attempt to use intellectual history to account for the events of this period, see Michael Sonenscher, *Sans-Culottes: An Eighteenth-Century Emblem in the French Revolution* (Princeton: 2008).

CHAPTER 3

The French Revolution and the Liberal Parliamentary Turn

Republicanism. Socialism. Democracy. Human Rights. These are the ideological traditions we now associate with the French Revolution. But for much of the nineteenth century, the most important ideological legacy of the French Revolution was the victory of an entirely different tradition – the one explored in this book. It was the French Revolution that made *parliamentarism* the dominant paradigm of a free state across Europe.

This was by no means an intended result. In Chapters 1 and 2 of this book, I showed how each of the crucial elements of parliamentarism – a powerful representative assembly; ministers who served in and were responsible to the assembly; a system of political parties; a limited constitutional monarch whose authority came from moral (or financial) influence rather than his veto – emerged in eighteenth-century England. Of these four elements, a powerful representative assembly was introduced at the beginning of the French Revolution and widely viewed as the key institution of a free state. But the involvement of ministers in the assembly was rejected in 1789 by practically all sides, while the French monarchy was stripped of much of its influence and later overthrown. Nor was the legitimacy of political parties accepted.[1] While France experimented with numerous political frameworks during the 1790s, all sought to achieve parliamentary rule – but without the practices that would come to be associated with parliamentarism.

By 1814, when Napoleon fell from power, everything had changed. France immediately adopted a constitution modeled on England, and it contained (at least in embryonic form) all the crucial elements of parliamentarism. It was also defended by a range of authors – including

---

[1] For the tendency to reject parties in the Revolutionary period (and a discussion of certain key exceptional figures), see Gunn, *When the French Tried to Be British*, 11–62. For another classic discussion, which emphasizes the ideological context that made the legitimacy of parties difficult to accept, see Lynn Hunt, *Politics, Culture, and Class in the French Revolution* (Berkeley: 1986), 19–51.

Benjamin Constant, Simonde de Sismondi, François Guizot, Destutt de Tracy, Germaine de Staël, and Chateaubriand.[2] To a greater degree than the authors examined in Chapters 1 and 2, who had generally viewed themselves as defending the English constitution or a particular interpretation of it, these figures were self-conscious about the fact that they were defending a distinct form of government, which any nation could adopt according to its circumstances. It is not a coincidence that a term for *parliamentary government* first appeared during this period in France.[3]

In this chapter and the following one, I will argue that it was through the constitutional debates of the French Revolution that parliamentarism came to be articulated as a coherent political alternative for modern states. This chapter will focus on Jacques Necker and Germaine de Staël while the next one takes up Benjamin Constant. I will situate them among a range of French authors but also with respect to developments in Britain. The "Coppet Circle" – as de Staël, Necker, Constant, and their intellectual acquaintances are known – was remarkably intertwined with a similar British group that also argued with increasing self-consciousness for parliamentarism at the dawn of the liberal era. Known as the "Edinburgh Whigs" because of its association with the University of Edinburgh and the *Edinburgh Review*, this British circle included such authors as Dugald Stewart, John Millar, Francis Jeffrey, James Mackintosh, and Henry Brougham.

I will begin this chapter with an examination of the early years of the French Revolution, a period in which France decisively rejected the English constitutional model. I will then consider Jacques Necker, the great champion of a parliamentary government during the 1790s, as well as his daughter Germaine de Staël. Although de Staël preferred monarchy, I will show that during the 1790s, she tried to sketch a republic that would approximate all the advantages of the English parliamentary system – the first of many figures to do so. This led her to place special emphasis on the interplay between parliament and public opinion, a theme that would later be taken up by Constant. I will conclude the chapter with the Edinburgh Whigs and point out the parallels between their writings and those of Necker and de Staël.

---

[2] For discussions of the turn to English institutions in 1814, see Alain Laquièze, "La Charte de 1814 et la question du gouvernement parlementaire," *Jus Politicum*, vol. 13 (2014), 1–13; Rosanvallon, *La monarchie impossible*, 15–55; Gunn, *When the French Tried to Be British*.
[3] Laquièze, "La Charte de 1814 et la question du gouvernement parlementaire."

1789 and the Rejection of the Parliamentary Model

The representative assembly was the defining political institution of the French Revolution. It was the formation of a National Assembly that first initiated the Revolution, and for a great many of the Revolution's actors, this was the institution that would make France a free state. That conviction was also widely held by the French people. Summarizing the contents of the *cahiers de doléances*, Stanislas de Clermont-Tonnerre noted to the National Assembly that both the *cahiers* "desiring a new constitution" and those favoring "the existing constitution" were in agreement about the need for a permanent legislature that could represent the public, ensure that "agents of authority are responsible," and offer the public's consent to taxation and the budget.[4]

In England, these functions had long been exercised by the House of Commons. But the representative assemblies of the French Revolution would differ from the House of Commons in a fundamental respect. While the House of Commons was classically viewed as the only part of the English constitution capable of representing the *people*, there existed a separate representation for the aristocracy – the House of Lords. When the Estates General was abolished, that model of representation collapsed with it. The National Assembly represented not simply the people but the *whole nation*. It was *une représentation nationale*.[5]

This difference is especially apparent in the 1789 writings of Emmanuel Sieyès, who was instrumental in the formation of the National Assembly. According to Sieyès, the formation of a National Assembly would enable the "*nation*" to "exercise the full extent of the legislative power."[6] "After beginning by setting all taxation under its safeguard," he wrote, "it can then, if it so wills, deliberate on and legislate in the most entire freedom for whatever it judges to be useful to the nation."[7] Because France's new constitution was likely to contain a similar body – which controlled all revenue and represented the *nation* – the members of the National

---

[4] Stanislas de Clermont-Tonnerre, "Rapport par M. le comte Stanislas de Clermont-Tonnerre contenant le résumé des cahiers au point de vue de la Constitution," *Archives parlementaires*, ser. 1, t. 8 (Paris: 1875), 283–284.

[5] For this important characteristic of the National Assembly, see Marcel Gauchet, *La Révolution des droits de l'homme* (Paris: 1989), 13–59; and Marcel Gauchet, *La Révolution des pouvoirs. La souveraineté, le peuple et la représentation (1789–1799)* (Paris: 1995), 55–121.

[6] Emmanuel Joseph Sieyès, "Views of the Executive Means," in *Political Writings*, ed. Michael Sonenscher (Indianapolis: 2003), 8.

[7] Ibid., 43. On this issue, see as well, Emmanuel Joseph Sieyès, "Bases de l'ordre social," in *Sieyès et l'invention de la constitution en France*, ed. Pasquale Pasquino (Paris: 1995), 185.

Assembly faced a profound challenge: to ensure that the legislative assembly they were creating would not become a threat to liberty.[8]

In the first year of the Revolution, two different approaches to containing the legislature were articulated before the National Assembly. The first was essentially that of Montesquieu. The Monarchien party, which was founded by Jean Joseph Mounier, argued for a bicameral legislature (preferably with the upper chamber being hereditary) and for a king who could veto legislation.[9] Montesquieu's account of England in *The Spirit of the Laws* was Mounier's model, and he was especially committed to the king's veto being *absolute* – so that no dangerous law could be passed.[10]

A second and more novel constitutional paradigm was proposed by Sieyès. Rather than a system of checks and balances, he defended a structure in which each power was strictly limited to its particular function. The goal was not for arbitrary actions to be blocked but for no power to be able to act arbitrarily in the first place. Toward this end, executive officials were to play no role in the legislative process, and a distinction was also to be drawn between two different kinds of legislatures.[11] While regular laws would be passed in the normal "legislative assembly," when changes had to be made to the constitution itself, an entirely separate "constituent assembly" would be formed with the power to alter the constitution.[12]

Sieyès argued that this structure rendered the king's veto unnecessary, as a legislature that could neither control the executive power nor exercise the constituent power was incapable of acting arbitrarily. Such a strict separation of powers did not exist "in England," he noted, where "one has not distinguished the constituent power from the legislative power; so the British Parliament, unlimited in its operations, is capable of attacking the royal prerogative."[13] This was why the English Crown needed a veto. But so long

---

[8] The centrality of this issue is noted in Pasquino, *Sieyès et l'invention de la constitution en France*, 15–29. My treatment of the conflict between Sieyès and the Monarchiens largely parallels Pasquino's.

[9] See Jean Joseph Mounier, "Présentation par M. Mounier du projet contenant les premiers articles de la Constitution," *Archives parlementaires*, ser. 1, t. 8, 285–288, and "Rapport fait par M. Mounier contenant les articles concernant l'organisation du pouvoir législatif," *Archives parlementaires*, ser.1, t. 8, 522–527.

[10] See Jean Joseph Mounier, "Suite de la discussion relative à la sanction royale. Rapport de M. Mounier sur la nécessité de cette sanction," *Archives parlementaires*, ser. 1, t. 8, 554–564, and "Suite de la discussion sur la permanence et l'organisation du pouvoir législatif et sur la sanction royale," *Archives parlementaires*, ser. 1, t. 8, 585–587.

[11] Emmanuel Joseph Sieyès, "Reprise de la discussion sur l'organisation du pouvoir législatif et la sanction royale," *Archives parlementaires*, ser. 1, t. 8, 592–597.

[12] Ibid., 595.   [13] Ibid.

as France did not follow England's dangerous conflation of powers, checks and balances were unnecessary. "We have as a fundamental and constitutional principle," Sieyès declared, "that the ordinary legislature will not have the exercise of the constituent power" nor "of the executive power."[14]

Sieyès' commitment to a strict separation of powers led him to reject the veto power entirely.[15] It also led him to oppose the emerging English practice of parliamentary government. Prior to the formation of the National Assembly, he demanded that the king's ministers not be present at its meetings and that representatives be prohibited from holding ministerial office.[16] Imitating this English practice, he argued, would violate the separation of powers, corrupt the spirit of deliberation, and prevent the formation of a national will.[17] Sieyès was far from the only figure in 1789 who rejected parliamentary government. In an early meeting of the Assembly, Lanjuinais reminded the other representatives that "we have desired to separate the powers," and he warned that creating any relations between the ministry and the National Assembly would "join the legislative power to the executive power in the hands of the ministers."[18] This same argument would also be expressed regarding the Legislative Assembly of 1791. Robespierre warned that the presence of ministers in the Legislative Assembly would create a situation in which "the executive power and the legislative power are confounded," violating one of "the first principles of the Constitution."[19] Simply having ministers present at legislative sessions, he argued, would bring an end to free deliberation.[20] "It would be wise of the National Assembly to oppose all sorts of barriers to the influence of the executive power over the deliberations of the legislative body."[21] That last point was reiterated by Lanjuinais, who was a strident opponent of ministers serving in the Legislative Assembly as well as the National Assembly.[22]

---

[14] Ibid.
[15] Ibid., 592–597. See as well, Sieyès, "Représentation et élections," in *Sieyès et l'invention de la constitution en France*, 171–173. Sieyès was capable of shifting his position on this issue for practical purposes, and he ultimately came to defend the Constitution of 1791 despite the King's suspensive veto. See "Controversy between Mr. Paine and M. Emmanuel Sieyès," in *Political Writings*, 165–173.
[16] See Sieyès, "Views of the Executive Means," 34–35.   [17] Ibid.
[18] Jean-Denis Lanjuinais, "Suite de la discussion de la motion de M. comte de Mirabeau relative à l'entrée des ministres dans l'Assemblée," *Archives parlementaires*, ser. 1, t. 9, 716.
[19] Maximilien Robespierre, "Suite de la discussion du projet de Constitution – Discussion de l'article 10," in *Archives parlementaires*, ser. 1, t. 29 (Paris: 1888), 445.
[20] Ibid.   [21] Ibid.
[22] Jean-Denis Lanjuinais, "Suite de la discussion du projet de Constitution – Discussion de l'article 10," *Archives parlementaires*, ser. 1, t. 29, 446.

Despite his admiration for England, Mounier never tried to convince the National Assembly that ministers should serve in the legislature. Indeed, there was another element of the English political system that he did not merely overlook but actively opposed. This was the strict responsibility of ministers to Parliament – which Burke had so eloquently defended in *Thoughts on the Present Discontents*. Mounier called the House of Commons' control over the selection of ministers "one of the greatest abuses of the English Parliament, and one of the causes of the greatest outrages," both "in the constitution" and "in the ministry."[23] He warned that imitating this practice in France would threaten "the liberty and the power" of the king.[24] "It is necessary to prevent the joining of powers," he declared, and for that reason "it is necessary that the National Assembly not confound the legislative and executive powers."[25] "It is not the nation's function to have influence over the choice of ministers."[26] Like Montesquieu, Mounier's overriding concern was that the monarch be equal to the legislature, so he rejected the stronger form of ministerial responsibility that had been defended by Burke and Bolingbroke.

The Constitution of 1791 was an unstable compromise between Sieyès and Mounier's proposals. There was no second chamber or absolute veto, as Mounier had demanded, and ministers were prohibited from serving in the legislature. But the monarch did have the power to temporarily veto laws, so checks and balances were not completely eliminated.[27] As I discussed in Chapter 2, the Constitution of 1791 survived less than a year. It collapsed following severe conflicts between Louis XVI and the Legislative Assembly – primarily over the king's appointment of ministers and exercise of his veto.

French political thinkers would respond to this calamity in two different ways. The first was to hold on to the original constitutional paradigm of either Sieyès or Mounier and insist that it had not been implemented properly. Because neither Sieyès nor Mounier's original proposal was strictly followed in 1791, it was plausible that either might have worked. As Adam Lebovitz has shown, a range of French authors responded to the Terror by trying to revive Mounier's vision of an executive who truly

---

[23] Jean Joseph Mounier, "Discussion de diverses motions relatives au renvoi des ministres et au rappel de M. Necker," *Archives parlementaires*, ser.1, t. 8, 242.
[24] Ibid.   [25] Ibid., 243.   [26] Ibid.
[27] As Pasquale Pasquino has shown, the two figures who dominated the assembly during the writing of the constitution, Barnave and Thouret were followers of Montesquieu: they insisted that the king have some capacity to stop laws from going into operation without his consent. See Pasquino, *Sieyès et l'invention de la constitution en France*, 84.

balanced the legislature.[28] By contrast, the constitution that France ultimately instituted in 1795 was closer to Sieyès' version.[29] The executive, a five-person committee titled *the Directory*, was appointed by a bicameral legislature and had purely executive and administrative powers. The Directory could neither veto nor initiate legislation, and its ministers were prohibited from serving in the assembly. It also could not dissolve the assembly. The Constitution of 1795 approximated the complete separation of executive and legislative power that Sieyès had proposed in 1789.[30]

A second way of responding to the collapse of the Constitution of 1791 was to seek an entirely different constitutional paradigm. One example of this – which has become increasingly important in recent political theory – was the Girondin Constitution of 1793, which was written by the Marquis de Condorcet. What was so radical about Condorcet's proposal was the extraordinary degree of popular participation he envisioned. The Girondin Constitution allowed the people to formally censure any law under discussion and to sanction any political official. It also contained a procedure whereby the people could vote directly on legislation, and it called for recurrent conventions to revise the constitution, which would then be subject to popular referenda.[31]

I will be examining a different set of authors who found the original paradigms of Sieyès and Mounier unsatisfactory. Jacques Necker, Germaine de Staël, and Benjamin Constant all thought that Sieyès' strict separation of executive and legislative functions was mistaken. But they also rejected Condorcet's call for an unprecedented expansion of popular participation as well as Mounier's argument for a powerful independent executive. While they were appalled by the actions of France's legislative assemblies, they did not think the answer was to create an executive on par with the legislature. Rather they sought a constitutional structure that

---

[28] By this point, however, defenders of a rebalanced constitution were turning to John Adams and the United States, rather than to Montesquieu and England. See Adam Lebovitz, *The Colossus: Constitutional Theory in America and France, 1776–1799*, Ph.D. dissertation (Harvard: 2018).

[29] This thesis is argued in Michel Troper, *Terminer la Révolution: la Constitution de 1795* (Paris: 2006), 141–147.

[30] For the French Constitution of 1795, see Duguit and Monnier, *Les constitutions et les principales lois politiques de la France*, 95. A range of essays on its significance are found in *La Constitution de l'an III: Boissy d'Anglas et la naissance du libéralisme constitutionnel*, ed. Gérard Conac, Jean-Pierre Machelon (Paris: 1999).

[31] For the details of the Girondin Constitution, see Marquis de Condorcet, "Projet de constitution française," *Oeuvres complètes*, t. 12 (Paris: 1847), 436–437. For broader discussions of Condorcet's constitutional design and its significance, see Uribinati, *Representative Democracy*, 172–222; Rosanvallon, *La démocratie inachevée*, 59–74.

would restrain the legislature without necessarily reducing its constitutional importance – and while enhancing its capacity to deliberate and govern. Toward this end, they turned to the theories of the English constitution that I explored in Chapters 1 and 2. Their answer to the constitutional crises of the French Revolution was *parliamentarism*.[32]

Over the course of the 1790s, Sieyès and Mounier would each take hesitating steps down this path as well. Sieyès' final constitutional proposal – which he argued for just following the coup d'état that brought Napoleon to power in 1799 – called for a "government" that submitted legislation to the assembly and was appointed by a quasi-constitutional monarch entitled the *Grand Elector*. The Grand Elector was elected for life, selected the members of the government, and "represent[ed] the majesty of the people."[33] In a formulation reminiscent of de Lolme's English monarch, Sieyès claimed that "by his mere existence," the Grand Elector "prevents or neutralizes any dangerous ambition."[34] This argument – and the distinction Sieyès drew between a monarchical figure and the government – would lay crucial groundwork for Constant's conception of constitutional monarchy. But what Sieyès could never accept about the English constitution was the presence of ministers in the legislature – the *sine qua non* of a parliamentary government. Because of his attachment to the separation of powers, he always supported a strict division between executive and legislative offices.[35]

Ironically, this was the very element of a parliamentary government that Mounier would come to advocate. Following the collapse of the Constitution of 1791, he became increasingly open about the value of having ministers (and their employees) in the legislature.[36] But his deepest

---

[32] An even earlier defender of parliamentary government in the National Assembly had been Mirabeau and had he survived, such a government might have been instituted much earlier. See Comte de Mirabeau, "Discussion de diverses motions relatives au renvoi des ministres et au rappel de M. Necker," *Archives parlementaires*, ser. 1, t. 8, 242–243; as well as Comte de Mirabeau, "Motion concernant : 1* les subistances; 2* la création d'une banque nationale; 3* l'entrée des ministres dans l'Assemblée," *Archives parlementaires*, ser. 1, t. 9, 710–711.

[33] Emmanuel Sieyès, "Constitutional Observations," in *Emmanuel Joseph Sieyès: The Essential Political Writings*, ed. Oliver W. Lembcke and Florian Weber (Leiden and Boston: 2014), 193.

[34] Ibid.

[35] This is strongly emphasized in Oliver Lembcke and Floria Weber, "Introduction to Sieyès' Political Theory," in *Emmanuel Joseph Sieyès*, 32, 41.

[36] See Jean Joseph Mounier, *Recherches sur les causes qui ont empêché les Français de devenir libres, et sur les moyens, qui leur restent pour acquérir la liberté*, vol. 1 (Paris: 1792), 62. Although never expressly stated, there are some signs that Mounier had always expected this to occur in France. In the constitutional proposal he made in 1789, the only restriction upon a member of the legislature taking an office or pension from the Crown was that he needed to then run for election again. This regulation had manifestly not stopped the development of the Crown's influence in England, nor

commitment was to the king's absolute veto. What he wanted was the system of equal checks and balances that Montesquieu had sketched in Chapter 11 of *The Spirit of the Laws,* and like Montesquieu, Mounier recognized how difficult this system was to achieve once the legislature could control revenue and claim to represent the people.[37] Attaining parity between the executive and legislature required a monarch who regularly exercised his veto, appointed ministers without any interference or control by the legislature, and distributed considerable patronage.[38] Montesquieu is often hailed as the progenitor of European liberal constitutionalism. But Mounier's proposals – which so closely followed the logic of Montesquieu's account of the English constitution – would be rejected by nineteenth-century liberals beginning with the Coppet Circle.

Jacques Necker and Germaine de Staël

By the middle of the 1790s, Jacques Necker and Germaine de Staël were two of the most famous individuals in Europe. Though originally of Swiss descent, Necker served as France's director of finance from 1776 to 1783 and again from 1788 to 1790.[39] He was considered one of the greatest financial minds of his time, and his writings on trade, commerce, and administration were read throughout the world.[40] He retired from active political life just as de Staël (born in 1766) was beginning to be recognized for her genius. She was one of the last polymath intellectuals of the Enlightenment – a novelist, philosopher, literary critic, social theorist, and constitutional innovator. Unlike her father and Burke, de Staël

---

would it in France under the July Monarchy. See Mounier, "Rapport fait par M. Mounier contenant les articles concernant l'organisation du pouvoir législatif," 525.

[37] Mounier was utterly preoccupied with the constitutional dominance that the legislature acquired through its control over revenue and the budget – a power that he recognized was impossible to take away from the legislature. See Jean Joseph Mounier, *Considérations sur les gouvernements et principalement sur celui qui convient à la France* (Paris: 1789), 31.

[38] While it is tempting to think that Mounier merely wanted such a powerful monarch for France, he also believed that the House of Commons had become far too powerful in England. See Jean Joseph Mounier, *Recherches sur les causes qui ont empêché les Français de devenir libres, et sur les moyens, qui leur restent pour acquérir la liberté,* vol. 2 (Paris: 1792), 271. The claim that Mounier actually rejected much of the English constitutional experience is also made in François Burdeau and Marcel Morabito, "Les expériences étrangères et la première constitution française," *Pouvoirs,* vol. 50 (1989), 97–112.

[39] For an account of Necker's life as financial director, see Henri Grange, *Les idées de Necker* (Paris: 1974), 21–52.

[40] A discussion of Necker's economic and political thought prior to the Revolution is found in Sonenscher, *Before the Deluge,* 302–310. For a discussion of Necker's influence, see Donald Swanson and Andrew Trout, "Alexander Hamilton, 'the Celebrated Mr. Neckar,' and Public Credit," *William and Mary Quarterly,* vol. 47, no. 3 (1990), 422–430.

strongly defended the social transformations of the French Revolution. She wanted a government that was based in reason rather than prejudice and led by a "natural aristocracy" as opposed to a hereditary one.[41] For much of the 1790s, she was also an ardent republican.[42]

For both Necker and de Staël, the great lesson of the French Revolution was the danger of an unrestrained legislature. But each was convinced of this institution's fundamental value. Necker's appreciation of representative assemblies came from his comparative observation of France and England. While serving in Louis XVI's administration, he was fascinated by "the great power of public opinion" and noted the increasing alienation of the French government from public opinion.[43] The "power of public opinion" was equally manifest in England. However, there it was not estranged from the government because it was represented in "the House of Commons," which "like every assembly represents or at least symbolizes the general will."[44] The House of Commons served as a space where the public mind (including its most "impassioned elements") could be expressed.[45] The lack of such an institution in France was what caused the revolutionary outburst of 1789. It also meant a lack of protection for "civil and political liberty," and the absence of genuine public deliberation.[46] "In free nations, like England," Necker wrote, "new laws are discussed in an assembly of national deputies; the people are enlightened, or at least held to be, at the moment these laws are determined; and each individual can know the laws' motivations by reading the record of parliamentary debates."[47]

De Staël was even more emphatic than her father about the value of representative assemblies. She argued that this institution was the best approximation of a classical republic in the modern world. Where the people could not rule directly, it was essential that at least "their opinion presides."[48] An elected assembly achieved this function. It served as a

---

[41] See, for instance, Germaine de Staël, *Des circonstances actuelles qui peuvent terminer la Révolution et des principes qui doivent fonder la république de France*, *Oeuvres complètes*, ser. 3, t. 1, ed. Lucia Omacini (Paris: 2009), 294–296, 300, 325–327.

[42] Biancamaria Fontana has stressed de Staël's still earlier commitment to the project of constitutional monarchy. See Biancamaria Fontana, *Germaine de Staël: A Political Portrait* (Princeton: 2016), 11–60.

[43] Jacques Necker, *De la révolution françoise*, vol. 1, *Oeuvres complètes*, t. 9, ed. Auguste de Staël (Paris: 1821), 7.

[44] Jacques Necker, *Du pouvoir exécutif dans les grands états*, *Oeuvres complètes*, t. 8, ed. Auguste de Staël (Paris: 1821), 51.

[45] Ibid.   [46] Ibid., 266.

[47] Jacques Necker, *De l'administration des finances de la France*, *Oeuvres complètes*, t. 4, ed. Auguste de Staël (Paris: 1821), 60.

[48] De Staël, *Des circonstances actuelles qui peuvent terminer la Révolution*, 373.

"picture in miniature" of "the *grand ensemble* of public opinion" and as a space in which "the distinct interests in society [can] be represented."[49] The absence of such a body was equivalent to despotism.[50] "The object of the representative system," she wrote, "is that the will of the people, otherwise called the interest of the nation, be always defended and protected as if the nation itself could … gather in the public square."[51]

The question for both Necker and de Staël was how to achieve the benefits of a representative assembly while avoiding the devastating events of 1792 and 1793. Necker's answer can be found in a series of treatises he published across the 1790s. Like Mounier, he believed that England offered the best model for moderating a powerful assembly. Yet whereas the lesson Mounier drew from England was that the French king needed a stronger veto power, Necker believed that the most important constitutional lesson to be derived from England was that the veto was of secondary importance. He wrote that an English monarch's "right of opposition to bills in parliament is reduced, as a matter of fact, to a sort of royal pomp."[52] It was impossible to cite "a single example" of the veto being used.[53] Moreover, should the monarch ever decide to veto a bill, he would have no choice but to relent if the House of Commons persisted in its position in order "to prevent the refusal of revenue."[54]

The real way an English monarch influenced the legislative process was through the presence of his ministers in Parliament. In England, Necker wrote, "the true participation of the government in legislating does not consist in … the agreement of the monarch to bills of parliament, but in the engagement of ministers in the deliberations which proceed the laws."[55] This enabled the government to influence the course of legislation well before a law arrived for his signature. "Habitual discussion between the ministers and all the other members of parliament," Necker argued, "serves effectively to prevent the Monarch refusing his sanction to multiple resolutions passed by the legislature."[56] Because the veto was "a circumstance of great explosiveness … which easily becomes the origin of a spirit of disunion among the two powers," the presence of ministers in Parliament was indispensable to the English constitution.[57]

Necker argued that by giving Louis XVI only a veto to oppose the Legislative Assembly and not allowing ministers to participate as legislative

---

[49] Ibid., 381.　　[50] Ibid., 299.　　[51] Ibid., 381.

[52] Jacques Necker, *Sur l'administration de M. Necker*, *Oeuvres complètes*, t. 6, ed. Auguste de Staël (Paris: 1821), 155.

[53] Ibid.　　[54] Ibid.　　[55] Necker, *Du pouvoir exécutif dans les grands états*, 162–163.　　[56] Ibid.

[57] Ibid., 163.

representatives, the National Assembly had set in motion "the debasement of the ministers" and the "invasion" of the monarchy.[58] He thought "the different constitution of the ministry in France and England" had, "more than any other circumstance," brought about the overthrow of the French monarchy and "the union of all authority in the hands of the Assembly."[59] Necker's preference for the king to influence the legislature through the presence of his ministers accounts for his nonchalance in 1789 about whether the veto would be absolute or merely temporary.[60] By contrast, Mounier was insistent that it be absolute, and he later criticized Necker for not giving the veto sufficient attention, professing himself stunned that the latter had referred to the English monarch's negative as "a simple decoration ... of which the King of England could not make use."[61] "If one only knows a single refusal [of legislation] under George III," Mounier wrote in response to Necker, "one can cite many instances under the preceding reigns."[62] It is not clear how Mounier reached this conclusion given that neither George II nor George I used their negative either. Put simply, Necker had a more accurate sense of eighteenth-century English politics than Mounier. He viewed the emerging structure of parliamentary government not as an additional influence that English kings used in addition to their veto but as a superior substitute for it.[63]

Necker also argued that the regular involvement of ministers in Parliament enhanced the quality of deliberation, and he denied that it interfered with Parliament's role as the control on the executive.[64] Representatives could still contest the executive's actions, he noted, but rather than this leading to a struggle between independent powers – which might tear the constitution apart – it was interwoven into the very process of parliamentary deliberation. "The ministers of England are attacked in the middle of parliament but it is peer to peer," he wrote.[65] "In the contestation which one engages in ... it is always to *the honorable member of parliament* that one makes one's address," while, metaphorically speaking, "the king's minister disappears from the arena."[66] Although Necker expected that ministers would face regular contestation in the legislature, he agreed with Burke and Walpole that their presence made possible a greater degree of constitutional harmony. While ministers were chosen at the discretion of

---

[58] Ibid., 167, 169.   [59] Ibid., 166–167, 169.
[60] Jacques Necker, "Mémoire de M. Necker sur la sanction royale," *Archives parlementaires*, ser. 1, t. 8 (Paris: 1875), 612–615.
[61] Mounier, *Recherches sur les causes qui ont empêché les Français de devenir libres*, vol. 2, 81.
[62] Ibid., 82.   [63] Necker, *Du pouvoir exécutif dans les grands états*, 163.   [64] Ibid., 160.
[65] Ibid., 165.   [66] Ibid.

the monarch, their position depended upon their having "the confidence" of Parliament and broadly executing its agenda.[67] As the ministry won support from both the monarch and the legislature, it became the crucial link between both powers. According to Necker, "the habitual presence of ministers in parliament, their title as representatives of the people," was "necessary . . . to establish between the legislative body and administration that harmony without lethargy, absolutely necessary for the regular action of government."[68] Necker has recently been recovered as a formative theorist of executive leadership.[69] But like Walpole, the kind of executive leadership he held highest – and believed most characteristic of a free polity – was leadership within a representative assembly, by a minister who defended his actions through "the art of persuasion" and maintained his majority in the face of a real parliamentary opposition.[70]

Necker argued that because of their obsession with "the separation of powers" and "checks and balances," the members of the National Assembly had neglected the importance of ministerial leadership within the legislature. They had focused entirely on creating distinctions and rivalries between the executive and legislature and overlooked the necessity of harmony – which could be brought about only by enabling ministers to hold executive and legislative offices simultaneously.[71] As de Staël later put it, by "mixing harmoniously the individuals who are in power, without ceasing to distinguish the powers themselves, you would achieve harmony of government . . . instead of creating two armed camps."[72] Necker believed that the National Assembly's devotion to the "separation of powers" and unwillingness to follow the English parliamentary model was what doomed the Constitution of 1791.[73] He would make a similar argument about the Constitution of 1795 – which likewise prohibited ministers from serving in the legislature – writing that "the essential tendency of the republican constitution given to France in 1795; the capital tendency which could place order or liberty in peril, is the complete and absolute separation of the two primary authorities: the one which makes the laws, and the other which directs and monitors their execution."[74] Necker placed the Constitution of 1795 at the "other extreme"

---

[67] Ibid., 164; also Necker, *De l'administration des finances de la France*, 20.
[68] Necker, *Du pouvoir exécutif dans les grands états*, 161.
[69] This is especially emphasized in Rosanvallon, *Le bon gouvernement*, 156.
[70] Necker, *De l'administration des finances de la France*, 20.   [71] Ibid.
[72] De Staël, *Des circonstances actuelles qui peuvent terminer la Révolution*, 397.
[73] Necker, *Du pouvoir exécutif dans les grands états*, 168–169.
[74] Necker, *De la révolution françoise*, 122.

from the "National Convention," which had "united, confounded all powers in a monstrous organization."[75] The Constitution of 1795 attempted "an absolute separation between the two supreme powers."[76] Unlike the Constitution of 1791, the Constitution of 1795 was ultimately brought down by the executive rather the legislature. But Necker believed that this equally confirmed his argument. Rather than submit to a dominating legislature, the weak executive staged a coup. As de Staël later wrote, the Directory ended up with "too much arbitrary power" because it had "too little legal power."[77]

Like Burke and de Lolme, Necker was convinced that the English parliamentary model was impossible without a hereditary monarch who displayed the trappings of royalty.[78] He strongly criticized the National Assembly for depriving Louis XVI of "the majesty of the chief of state," which was one of "the principle advantages attached . . . to a monarchical government."[79] The monarch's dignity was essential "for the maintaining of public order, and for the peaceable exercise of administration."[80] Echoing de Lolme in particular, Necker argued that in England, the dignity of the king and House of Lords made up for the superior prerogatives of the House of Commons:

> The House of Commons in England, the same House that makes kings and proscribes their conditions, the same House that would with a sure hand effortlessly repress the slightest attack on national liberties, goes to the House of Lords to listen while standing, and in the humblest countenance, to the speech that monarch addresses to his parliament from the height of his throne.[81]

---

[75] Ibid.   [76] Ibid., 124.

[77] Germaine de Staël, *Considerations on the Principal Events of the French Revolution* (Indianapolis: 2008), 396. She notes how her critique of the Directory was indebted to Necker (*De la révolution françoise*, 390–391). For discussions of each of their criticisms of the Constitution of 1795, see Lucien Jaume, "Necker: examen critique de la Constitution de l'an III," in *La Constitution de l'an III*, 167–182; Henri Grange, "Mme de Staël et la Constitution de l'an III: avant et après," in *La Constitution de l'an III*, 183–200.

[78] Foreshadowing Tocqueville's argument four decades later, Necker believed that the United States could make do without monarchy because its circumstances allowed a weaker and less active government than France (*Du pouvoir exécutif dans les grands états*, 221–241). Necker praised the American constitution as appropriate for these circumstances; however, he characteristically emphasized the ways in which it nonetheless approximated the English parliamentary model. He claimed that by making the Senate determine cabinet officials, ambassadors, and treaties, and by giving the vice president a tie-breaking vote in the Senate, the American Constitution "associates" to the executive, and "unites to its interests one of the two chambers of which the American Congress is composed" (ibid., 352).

[79] Ibid., 213.   [80] Ibid., 56.   [81] Ibid., 201.

As this passage makes clear, even in England (let alone Revolutionary France) Necker doubted that the monarch's prerogatives could be equal to those of a representative assembly. Along with the presence of ministers in the House of Commons, it was because of the English monarch's majesty and dignity that parliamentary rule had led to liberty – rather than disaster.

Parliamentary Republicanism

While Necker followed Burke in defending monarchy and aristocracy, his daughter would wrestle, over the course of the 1790s, with how to institute the English parliamentary model in a republic of equal citizens. She believed this could be accomplished through an improved version of the Constitution of 1795. An executive committee would still be appointed by a bicameral assembly, but unlike the Directory, the committee's ministers would serve in the legislature, and they would hold their positions only so long as a majority supported them. "In England," she noted admiringly, "when the minister no longer has a majority in Parliament, he leaves his position."[82] "There is never an instance," this meant, "of the king preserving a minister who has lost the majority in the chamber."[83]

De Staël argued not only that the executive committee's ministers should resign when opposed by the legislature but that in such a circumstance, the committee itself should resign as well. This would ensure that "there never arrives something which cannot reasonably exist: a supreme authority executing a decision it reproves."[84] The executive's other option was to dissolve the legislature and call an election. "In a free government," according to de Staël, "public opinion in all its force can alone force one of the powers to cede to the other, if by misfortune they differ."[85] By dissolving the legislature, the executive committee was gambling that public opinion was on their side. If a legislature friendlier to their position was elected, they could stay in office – but should the electorate return a legislature still at odds with them, they would have no choice but to resign.

De Staël's argument that public opinion should determine which government held power was her distinctive contribution to the theory of a parliamentary constitution. Neither Burke nor Necker would have

---

[82] De Staël, *Des circonstances actuelles qui peuvent terminer la Révolution*, 387.
[83] Germaine de Staël, *Réflexions sur la paix intérieure, Oeuvres complètes*, ser. 3, t. 1, 152.
[84] De Staël, *Des circonstances actuelles qui peuvent terminer la Révolution*, 387.   [85] Ibid., 388.

accepted this notion, let alone that dissolving Parliament should be a means for regularly determining where public opinion stood.[86] Burke was famously aghast when George III dissolved Parliament in 1783 because he wanted a majority more aligned with his preferred ministers, but for de Staël, this was paradigmatic of how parliamentary government was supposed to function. Having turned away from constitutional monarchy, she viewed dissolution as indispensable for containing the legislature. What made a representative assembly so powerful was its claim to represent the people, and while that claim could not be contested in principle, it was possible to contest whether *this present legislature* really represented popular sentiment. Through dissolution, the executive could appeal beyond the legislature to the people it claimed to represent and call for a new legislature to come into being. But should public opinion side with the existing assembly, the executive left office.

While de Staël supported the executive being able to veto legislation, this was under the expectation that use of the veto power would lead to dissolution and new elections, so public opinion could determine between the two sides.[87] A less explosive way for the executive to influence the legislative process was through the presence of its ministers. De Staël was critical of the "absurd decree" in the Constitution of 1791 that prohibited ministers from serving in the legislature, and she was convinced the Constitution of 1795 would meet a similar fate unless it adopted a parliamentary government.[88] She attributed all the same advantages to this framework that her father had. It enabled the executive to influence the legislature as it was still deliberating, reducing the occasions in which the veto was necessary and enabling clashes between the legislature and executive to be seamlessly integrated into the regular process of parliamentary debate. Far from parliamentary control over the executive being weakened by this practice, it was actually strengthened. In *Des circonstances actuelles qui peuvent terminer la Révolution*, her most important text arguing for a parliamentary republic, de Staël expounded upon these advantages at length:

> It seems to me that we would evade all these inconveniences ... by permitting it [i.e., the Directory] to choose its ministers from among the deputies. They would discuss then in the heart of the council itself, the

---

[86] The importance of this argument in de Staël's thought is also noted in Gauchet, *La Révolution des pouvoirs*, 206.
[87] De Staël, *Des circonstances actuelles qui peuvent terminer la Révolution*, 387–388.
[88] De Staël, *Considerations on the Principal Events of the French Revolution*, 232.

decrees required by the administration, while bringing the knowledge that the exercise of government alone can give. They would be more easily attacked if they are in the wrong, since it would not be necessary to denounce them … it would be sufficient to respond to them. Yet they would more easily exonerate themselves if they are in the right, since, each day, they can explain and justify their conduct.[89]

By exercising legislative and executive functions simultaneously, ministers brought about unity between the two powers. It was by "mixing together the individuals, without ceasing to distinguish the powers," she wrote, that "harmony in government" was possible.[90] "To confound … the necessary separation of functions with a division of powers that forcefully renders them enemies of one another" was a serious mistake.[91]

Because of her rejection of hereditary monarchy, de Staël grappled with the question of how a government under genuine parliamentary control would not be overwhelmed by the assembly. Her answer was that parliament's legitimacy came from representing public opinion, which could be questioned by the government. By dissolving the legislature and calling new elections, the executive committee tested whether the existing assembly really was aligned with the nation. If it was not, then a new assembly might form that was willing to maintain the executive officials in power.

The Challenge of Corruption

The argument that France could have avoided the disasters of the Revolution by adopting the English parliamentary model would have an extraordinary influence on European thought. In Chapter 4, we will see it taken up by Constant and Guizot, while during the era of the 1848 Revolution – more than a half century after Necker and de Staël's initial writings – figures such as Prosper de Barante and Duvergier de Hauranne would continue to attack the National Assembly for rejecting English parliamentarism.[92] This argument would find its way into many of the classic works of nineteenth-century political thought.[93] Writing in the 1880s, A. V. Dicey specifically traced the National Assembly's mistake back to Montesquieu. "Montesquieu misunderstood … the principles and practices of the English constitution," he wrote, "and his doctrine was in turn, if not

---

[89] De Staël, *Des circonstances actuelles qui peuvent terminer la Révolution*, 396–397. [90] Ibid., 397.
[91] Ibid., 385.
[92] See Prosper de Barante, *Questions constitutionnelles* (Paris: 1849), 66–67; Duvergier de Hauranne, *De la réforme parlementaire et de la réforme électorale* (Paris: 1847), 138–139.
[93] See, for instance, James Bryce, *The American Commonwealth* (New York: 1908), vol. 1, 320–321.

misunderstood, exaggerated and misapplied by the French statesmen of the Revolution."[94] A generation later, the jurist Léon Duguit likewise attacked "the system that the authors of the Constitution of 1791 believed they had found in England and in *The Spirit of the Laws*. They wished to institute it in France; we know what contradictions were the price, and what was the result."[95]

Although Necker and de Staël were the first great champions of a French parliamentary government, they recognized the long-standing association between parliamentary government and corruption. One might have expected that Necker, with his insistence on preserving the strength and dignity of the throne, would have defended the English practice of parliamentary patronage. Yet he was deeply critical of it. Within the Coppet Circle, it was de Staël who offered the strongest defense of the Crown's legislative and electoral "influence."

One of the few errors that Henri Grange makes in his magisterial study of Necker is his claim that Necker agreed with Hume about the benefits of the Crown's patronage in Parliament.[96] All the evidence suggests that Necker was quite opposed to this practice. At the very least, he was more ambivalent about it than even Burke. Necker acknowledged that "corruption … can stand in, with certain governments, for a lack of proportion between the different established powers."[97] But he then immediately rejected this strategy. Even "leaving to the side for a moment its immorality," he argued that corruption was highly corroding, and once unleashed in a political system, it was impossible to predict where it would end.[98] "It is by the prudent accord of all the parts of the constitution … that one prevents the abuse of power," he wrote, "it is never by its abuse that one should assure political harmony."[99] In place of corruption, Necker put his trust entirely in a dignified constitutional monarch. The "majesty" of the king sustained his ministers' influence in Parliament and his own influence across the nation.[100]

---

[94] A. V. Dicey, *Introduction to the Study of the Law of the Constitution*, ed. E. C. S. Wade (London and New York: 1961), 338.

[95] Léon Duguit, *Manuel de droit constitutionnel: théorie génerale de l'état – organisation politique* (Paris: 1907), 395.

[96] Grange, *Les idées de Necker*, 318–321.   [97] Necker, *Du pouvoir exécutif dans les grands états*, 64.

[98] Ibid.   [99] Ibid., 65.

[100] Ibid., 60; also Necker, *De la révolution françoise*, 295. While Necker recognized that this majesty was based on the Crown's appointments (which the National Assembly had taken away from the French monarch), he never advocated the use of appointments to maintain support within the legislature. In this way, he was like Montesquieu, who similarly supported the use of appointments to maintain the Crown's popularity in the English nation while always frowning on parliamentary and electoral patronage.

Because of its tendency toward corruption, Necker decisively changed his mind in the late 1790s about the merits of a parliamentary government. This reversal has to be distinguished from another shift in his thinking that has been documented by Marcel Gauchet: his judgment that it was impossible to rebuild the French monarchy.[101] In his last major political work, *Dernières vues de politique et de finance*, Necker not only admitted the greater convenience of a republic in post-Revolutionary France but also argued that even if it were possible to recreate monarchy, France should not imitate England.[102] The reason was corruption. In particular, Necker asked how English monarchs could reliably ensure the individuals they wanted as ministers were also members of Parliament. The answer, he acknowledged, was the Crown' influence in elections. "The monarch, by his influence in the diverse borough of the realm, is sure to make his ministers enter into the popular chamber with the title of 'deputies of the people.'"[103] It was through "boroughs dependent on the Crown, or proprietors who are devoted to him" that "the prince has certain means to make his ministers enter into the popular chamber."[104] Necker never reversed his position that it was advantageous for ministers to serve in Parliament.[105] But he had come to think that these advantages were not worth a corrupt electoral system like England's.[106] The "diminution in the influence of the prince over the popular chamber" that he acknowledged would follow from ministers not participating as representatives "would not be a sufficient reason for imitating the English system of elections."[107] And without the Crown's influence over elections, it would be dangerous to introduce parliamentary government, as the king's choice of ministers would be entirely dependent on the whims of the electorate.[108] Insofar as Necker acknowledged that parliamentarism might require corruption, he was willing to reject it entirely.

This was not true of de Staël. By the end of the Napoleonic period, she had given up her earlier republicanism. "After such a revolution as that of France," she wrote, "constitutional monarchy is the only peace, the only treaty of Westphalia, if we may use the expression, which can be concluded between . . . society and hereditary interests," and she called for France to

---

[101] See Marcel Gauchet, "Necker, une lecture politique de la Révolution française," in *La condition politique*, 274–276.

[102] Jacques Necker, *Dernières vues de politique et de finance offertes á la nation françoise, Oeuvres complètes*, t. 11, ed. Auguste de Staël (Paris: 1821), 203–205, 223.

[103] Ibid., 203.   [104] Ibid., 205.   [105] Ibid., 203–204.   [106] Ibid., 203, 205.

[107] Ibid., 204.   [108] Ibid., 207.

imitate the English constitution from top to bottom.[109] Though she did not give up her strong belief in an elected assembly that represented popular opinion, she acknowledged that introducing monarchy required the establishment of a hereditary assembly.[110] She also acknowledged the great dilemma of the English constitution: that it was unclear whether ministers could preserve their position in Parliament without the support provided by electoral and legislative corruption. "We may reckon, in the number of the prerogatives of the Crown," she wrote "the right of introducing by its influence sixty or eighty members into the House of Commons out of the six hundred and fifty-eight who compose it," and she also noted the Crown's extensive patronage within Parliament.[111] Although she referred to the Crown's electoral influence as "an abuse," she maintained that this abuse "has not, down to the latest times, altered the strength and independence of the English Parliament."[112] More startlingly, she openly praised the distribution of patronage to parliamentary representatives. "The favors at the disposal of the Crown form a part of the prerogative of the king, and consequently of the constitution. This influence is one of the weights in the balance so wisely combined."[113]

De Staël was convinced that parliamentary politics thrived on the exchange of opinion. Why did she accept, indeed praise, ministers distributing "favors" to representatives in exchange for political support? Her reasons, I will argue, were the same as Burke's. Like Burke, she believed that the corrupting influence of patronage was blunted by party connections, which meant that representatives were unwilling to accept favors from just any ministry. "For nearly half a century the members of the opposition have been in place only three or four years," she noted, "yet party fidelity has not been shaken among them."[114] De Staël claimed that while visiting England, she saw individuals loyal to the opposition "refuse places of 7 or 8000 livres a year."[115] Because of political parties, patronage was distributed not to bribe representatives to change their principles but rather to solidify bonds among representatives who already shared the same principles. "If tomorrow the ministers go out of office," she wrote, "those who voted with them and to whom they have given places quit those places along with them. A man would be dishonored in England were he to separate himself from his political friends for his own particular interest."[116] A system of parliamentary parties kept the Crown's influence from

[109] De Staël, *Considerations on the Principal Events of the French Revolution*, 724.
[110] Ibid., 726–727.   [111] Ibid. 669.   [112] Ibid.   [113] Ibid., 668.   [114] Ibid., 667.
[115] Ibid.   [116] Ibid., 666–667.

being distributed in a manner that corrupted Parliament, and it created a vibrant struggle between ministry and opposition:

> The existence of a ministerial and opposition party, although it cannot be prescribed by law, is an essential support of liberty ... In every country where you see an assembly of men constantly in accord, be assured that despotism exists, or that despotism, if not the cause, will be the result of unanimity. Now, as power and the favors at the disposal of power possess attraction for men, liberty could not exist but with this fidelity to party, which introduces, if we may use the phrase, a discipline of honor into the ranks of members enrolled under different banners.[117]

Should patronage get out of hand and Parliament be entirely corrupted, de Staël was convinced, like Burke, that it would be rescued by the public. "The enemies of the English constitution ... are incessantly repeating that it will perish by the corruption of Parliament, and that ministerial influence will increase to such a point as to annihilate liberty," she wrote.[118] "Nothing of the kind is to be dreaded. The English Parliament always obeys national opinion, and that opinion cannot be corrupted."[119] Despite the "influence" at its disposal, "never would [a] ministry have either the power or the idea of making any change in what regards the constitutional liberties of England. Public opinion presents in that respect an invincible barrier."[120] Put simply, "the corrupt elements that enter into the composition of the national representation do not prevent it from proceeding under the eye of public opinion."[121]

As I showed earlier in this chapter, de Staël's conception of the rule of public opinion was considerably more expansive than Burke's. Public opinion did more than bring issues to parliament's attention and prevent parliament from becoming corrupt: it was the final arbiter for determining which ministry held power. Although she first argued for this view when envisioning a parliamentary republic, it infused her later account of the English constitution. She argued that the different parties in the House of Commons competed, first, to win over the considerable number of representatives who were neutral or undecided, and, second, to convince the public. "Public opinion bears the sway in England, and it is public opinion that constitutes the liberty of the country."[122] Whereas Burke saw George III's dissolution of the House of Commons in 1783 and Pitt's victory against the reigning coalition as a threat to the independence of the House of Commons, de Staël saw it as an example of the system working exactly

---

[117] Ibid., 667.   [118] Ibid., 718.   [119] Ibid.   [120] Ibid., 666.   [121] Ibid., 669.
[122] Ibid., 668.

as it should. "Mr. Pitt," she wrote, "was enabled to keep his place because public opinion ... was in his favor."[123]

In subsequent chapters of this book, we will see de Staël's account of the interaction between the parliamentary competition and public opinion taken up by authors such as Benjamin Constant, Alexis de Tocqueville, and Walter Bagehot. They would make use of it to argue that patronage was unnecessary in the English constitutional model: national opinion was a sufficient force to create stable governments in Parliament. Yet it is notable that de Staël came to the opposite conclusion. Far from being a reason to eliminate corruption, the rule of public opinion was a reason not to worry about corruption. The corrupt "elements that enter into the composition of the national representation do not prevent it from proceeding under the eye of public opinion."[124]

The Edinburgh Whigs and the Theory of Parliamentary Government

Scholars have analyzed de Staël and Necker's political thought in one of two ways. The first, recently exemplified by Aurelian Craiutu, is to depict them as followers of Montesquieu. Although Craiutu is aware that their formulations differ from Montesquieu's, he argues that a single commitment to moderation and constitutional balance links Montesquieu, Mounier, and the Coppet Circle.[125] The second approach, which has been followed by scholars such as Henri Grange and Alain Laquièze, is exactly the opposite. These interpreters emphasize how different Necker's account of England was from Montesquieu's – and draw the far-reaching conclusion that Necker invented the modern theory of the English constitution. If parliamentarism first came to be practiced in England, it was first theorized in Coppet, Switzerland.[126]

My interpretation of the Coppet Circle differs from both these approaches. Necker and de Staël were not followers of Montesquieu. And although I have suggested that the constitutional debates of the French Revolution led them to defend parliamentarism with greater self-consciousness than previous authors and to view it as a unified system that could be adopted by a nation other than England or accommodated to the

---

[123] Ibid.   [124] Ibid., 669.

[125] See Craiutu, *A Virtue for Courageous Minds*, 32, 53, 109, 150, 153.

[126] See Alain Laquièze, "Le modèle anglais et la responsabilité ministérielle selon le Groupe de Coppet," in *Coppet, creuset de l'esprit libéral: les idées politiques et constitutionnelles du Groupe de Madame de Staël*, ed. Lucien Jaume (Paris: 2000), 166–168; Grange, *Les idées de Necker*, 335–349.

circumstances of a republic, in making this argument, they drew heavily on earlier interpretations of the English constitution. Necker's attack on the French Constitution of 1791 clearly followed Burke, as did de Staël's account of patronage and party government.[127] Another crucial source for both Necker and de Staël was de Lolme.[128]

The best evidence that the ideas of the Coppet Circle were continuous with eighteenth-century British thought was the simultaneous emergence in Britain of a very similar group: the Edinburgh Whigs. Edinburgh became an important center of British political thought for two reasons. The first was Edinburgh University, which had influential professors such as Dugald Stewart. The second was the *Edinburgh Review*, which was founded in 1802 by four graduates of Edinburgh University (Francis Jeffrey, Francis Horner, Sydney Smith, and Henry Brougham). For the next half century, this journal would serve as one of the major organs of the Whig party.[129]

The *Edinburgh Review*'s initial objective was to chart a middle path in British politics. Contributors such as Jeffrey, Brougham, James Mackintosh, and Thomas Macaulay rejected universal suffrage and abhorred the radical doctrines that flourished in the aftermath of the French Revolution. But these "first Edinburgh Reviewers," as Walter Bagehot would later call them, also acknowledged that Britain's political structures were out of step with an emerging modern society.[130] Major cities and classes went unrepresented in Parliament while elections across the country were determined nakedly by corruption. The "first Edinburgh reviewers" sought to find a *juste milieu* between the status quo and democracy.

---

[127] Grange compares Necker's constitutional thought with that of Montesquieu, Blackstone, de Lolme, and the Monarchiens – yet not to Burke (*Les idées de Necker*, 335–349.) Craiutu does note one commonality between Necker and Burke, namely that both saw the French revolutionaries as committed to abstract theory rather than to prudence and moderation (Craiutu, *A Virtue for Courageous Minds*, 122, 130).

[128] I have already discussed de Lolme's influence on Necker; however, his influence on de Staël was no less important. In the notes she wrote in preparation for her book *Des circonstances actuelles qui peuvent terminer la Révolution*, she included a three-page summary of de Lolme. See Germaine de Staël, "Notes de Germaine de Staël pour la préparation de son livre," *Oeuvres complètes*, ser. 3, t. 1, 534–536. Such esteem did de Staël have for de Lolme that her notes on him are placed alongside her notes on Machiavelli, Plato, Aristotle, and Montesquieu (ibid., 521–536).

[129] For broad surveys of the thought of the Edinburgh Whigs and their legacy, see Biancamaria Fontana, *Rethinking the Politics of Commercial Society: The Edinburgh Review 1802–1832* (Cambridge: 1985); Stefan Collini, Donald Winch, and John Burrow, *That Noble Science of Politics: A Study in Nineteenth-Century Intellectual History* (Cambridge: 1983).

[130] Walter Bagehot, "The First Edinburgh Reviewers," *The Collected Works of Walter Bagehot*, vol. 1, ed. Norman St. John-Stevas (Cambridge, MA: 1965), 308–341.

The Coppet Circle could, of course, sympathize with this aim, and they formed an array of connections with the Edinburgh Whigs. Benjamin Constant studied at Edinburgh University, where he began a lifelong friendship with James Mackintosh, and in 1815, Mackintosh praised Constant as "unquestionably the first political writer of the Continent, and apparently the ablest man in France."[131] Francis Jeffrey similarly called de Staël "the most powerful writer that her country has produced since the time of Voltaire and Rousseau."[132] As well as being a close friend of Constant, Mackintosh was also the brother-in-law of Simonde de Sismondi.

The connection between Coppet and Edinburgh that I want to specifically highlight regards the constitutional theories that were put forward in each context. An obvious figure with whom to begin is Dugald Stewart, as he instructed many of "the first Edinburgh Reviewers" when they were studying at Edinburgh University.[133] Stewart was an academic polymath who wrote on an endless number of subjects, including mathematics, the organization of scientific knowledge, and moral philosophy. He played an important role in popularizing the study of political economy and was the first person to teach it to undergraduates.[134] One of his duties as an instructor of political economy was to lecture on constitutional theory. The final part of his "Lectures on Political Economy" was about "The Theory of Government," and it included an extended discussion of the English constitution.

In his lectures on the English constitution, Stewart took great pains to explain to his students that "the theoretical accounts of our government, to be found not only in Montesquieu, but in Blackstone," were deeply mistaken when "applied to the actual state of our political establishment."[135] He lamented that those accounts, especially Montesquieu's, had caused a serious misunderstanding of the English constitution to

---

[131] James Mackintosh, "France," *Edinburgh Review*, vol. 24, no. 48 (1815), 530.

[132] Francis Jeffrey, "Mad. de Staël sur la Revolution Françoise," *Edinburgh Review*, vol. 30, no. 60 (1818), 275. For a somewhat less sympathetic portrayal of de Staël (and her father) by Jeffrey, see Francis Jeffrey, "Germaine de Staël," *Edinburgh Review*, vol. 36, no. 71 (1822), 54–82.

[133] For an analysis of Stewart's profound influence, see Donald Winch et al., "The System of the North: Dugald Stewart and His Pupils," in *That Noble Science of Politics*, 23–62.

[134] Stewart's role as a biographer and reader of Smith is an ongoing theme in Istvan Hont, *Jealousy of Trade: International Competition and the Nation-State in Historical Perspective* (Cambridge, MA: 2005). See as well Murray Milgate and Shannon Stimson, "The Figure of Smith: Dugald Stewart and the Propagation of Smithian Economics," *European Journal of the History of Economic Thought*, vol. 3, no. 2 (1996), 225–253.

[135] See Dugald Stewart, *Lectures on Political Economy*, vol. 2, in *Collected Works*, vol. 9, ed. William Hamilton (London: 1856), 441.

become prevalent on the eve of the French Revolution.[136] Individuals who "derived their whole knowledge of our government from *The Spirit of Laws*" came to be under the impression that the English government was "composed of three branches, which form constitutional and irresistible checks on each other."[137] Stewart argued that in reality, neither the king nor the House of Lords was in a position to regularly block measures that were approved by the House of Commons. "With respect to . . . the King," he declared, "it now seems to be an acknowledged fact, that he never *can* exercise his negative without endangering the public tranquility. The last time it was exerted was in the year 1692."[138] And although the monarch could dissolve Parliament, that power was effective only when the people were "at variance with the measures of their constitutional representatives."[139] According to Stewart, "neither the King nor the House of Lords possess now that independence and co-ordinate importance which our popular language and popular theories ascribe to them."[140] "Consequently . . . the whole practical efficiency of our Government is either centered within the walls of the House of Commons, or operates by the intermediation of that assembly."[141]

Like so many of the authors we have examined, Stewart argued that what actually moderated the House of Commons was not an external check against its decisions coming from the king and lords but rather the influence that both branches had acquired within the House of Commons' deliberations – their "very great indirect influence on its proceedings" is how he termed it.[142] He claimed that "the perfection of our government" was for this arrangement to moderate the House of Commons without undermining its capacity to control the Crown.[143] It should give "the sovereign a sufficient degree of parliamentary weight to produce a *general* support to public measures without an implicit confidence in ministers."[144]

I noted that Stewart trained many of the great British intellectuals of the early nineteenth century. One of them was Francis Jeffrey, who would use the pages of the *Edinburgh Review* to defend this same account of the English constitution. Today, Francis Jeffrey is nearly a forgotten figure in the history of political thought.[145] But as M. J. C. Vile recognized, he was one of the premier theorists of parliamentarism.[146] Until Walter Bagehot

---

[136] Ibid., 440.   [137] Ibid., 441, 440.

[138] Ibid., 443. In reality, the veto was last used in 1708, by Queen Anne.   [139] Ibid.

[140] Ibid., 444.   [141] Ibid.   [142] Ibid., 449.   [143] Ibid.   [144] Ibid.

[145] Jeffrey is still read for his literary criticism. One of the few monographic studies of Jeffrey is Phillip Flynn *Francis Jeffrey* (Camden: 1978).

[146] Vile, *Constitutionalism and the Separation of Powers*, 237–239.

and the third Earl Grey a half century later, no British writer would lay out its principles with comparable sophistication.

Jeffrey's foremost political commitment was to a powerful representative assembly that deliberated over the common interest, held executive officials responsible, and represented public opinion. Like Necker and de Staël, he was convinced that the absence of such a body in France was what led to the Revolution. Before 1789, France had "no contrivance for ascertaining the sentiments of the actual strength of the nation, – and for conveying those sentiments, with the full evidence of their authenticity, to the actual administrators of their affairs."[147] This was because there was no "parliament . . . which really and truly represents the sense and opinions – we mean the general and mature sense, not the occasional prejudices and fleeting passions – of the efficient body of the people and which watches over and controls every important act of the executive magistrate."[148]

Jeffrey believed that the key to instituting such an assembly was to integrate the other constitutional powers into the regular process of parliamentary debate. "It is impossible to deny," he wrote, "that, according to the present constitution of the House of Commons, the Crown, the Executive government, or the Ministry, has a great influence in its deliberations."[149] When a bill was still in the process of being formulated, ministers could advance it or oppose it within Parliament. Jeffrey argued that the genius of the English constitution was to "employ the different tendencies of the royal, aristocratical, and popular influences, rather to modify the measures of government in their concoction than to counteract and oppose each other afterwards."[150] The result was that "the collision and shock of . . . rival principles, is either prevented or prodigiously softened by this early mixture of their elements."[151] Jeffrey wrote about the advantage of this arrangement at length:

> If a measure to which the Lords were adverse was proposed in the Commons, it would be desirable that the reasons and the influence which produced their hostility should be directed against it *in that House*; and if a measure, from which the Sovereign was resolved to withhold his acquiescence was proposed in either House, it would, in like manner, be desirable that this repugnance should be disclosed *in the course of their deliberations*, and matters prevented,

---

[147] Francis Jeffrey, "Leckie on the British Government," *Edinburgh Review*, vol. 20, no. 40 (1812), 331.

[148] Ibid., 333–334.

[149] Francis Jeffrey, "Cobbett's Political Register," *Edinburgh Review*, vol. 10, no. 20 (1807), 413.

[150] Ibid., 412.   [151] Ibid.

if possible, from coming to extremities by the interposition of the royal veto on a measure zealously patronized by the Parliament.[152]

As this passage makes clear, the true "collision" that Jeffrey feared was one in which the Crown tried to veto legislation. He was convinced that the House of Commons had come to possess "a degree of weight and authority, against which it would no longer have been safe for any other power to have risked an opposition."[153] "No ministry, for a hundred years back," he wrote, "has had courage to interpose the royal negative to any measure which has passed through the House of Parliament, even by narrow majorities; and there is no thinking man, who can contemplate, without dismay, the probable consequences of such a resistance."[154] "The whole frame and machinery of the constitution, in short, is contrived for the express purpose of preventing the kingly power from dashing itself to pieces against the more radical power of the people."[155] This was accomplished by making the government an active participant within the House of Commons.

It is hard to imagine that when Jeffrey crafted his image of "the kingly power ... dashing itself to pieces against the more radical power of the people," he was not thinking about the collapse of the French Constitution of 1791 – an event he later wrote about in the *Edinburgh Review*.[156] But what he was immediately responding to were developments in England. Influenced by the French and American revolutions, the late eighteenth and early nineteenth centuries saw prominent English radicals such as Thomas Paine, William Cobbett, Francis Burdett, and even to some degree Jeremy Bentham all question the dominance of the House of Commons over the executive.[157] Jeffrey was appalled that "Mr. Cobbett talks repeatedly of the irregularity of Parliament interfering with the King's choice of ministers, with which, he says, they have no more to do than with the choice of his running footmen."[158] He claimed that Cobbett as well as Francis Burdett "regard the revival or active development of the King's prerogative, as an important part of that beneficial reform, which

---

[152] Ibid., 412.   [153] Ibid., 414.   [154] Ibid.
[155] Jeffrey, "Leckie on the British Government," 339.
[156] For Jeffrey's harrowing description of the collapse of the French monarchy in 1792, see Jeffrey, "Mad. de Staël sur la Revolution Françoise," 300–301.
[157] For a discussion of the turn against parliamentary institutions by British radicals during the era of the French Revolution, see Vile, *Constitutionalism and the Separation of Powers*, 110–118.
[158] Francis Jeffrey, "Parliamentary Reform," *Edinburgh Review*, vol. 14, no. 28 (1809), 302.

they think would be effected by purging the Common's House of all admixture of Royal or aristocratical influence."[159]

Jeffrey warned that if ministers were removed from the House of Commons and the monarch enabled to independently exercise his prerogatives, the result would be "by far the greatest calamity that could be inflicted upon us by our own hands."[160] The English constitution would meet the same fate as the Constitution of 1791:

> To set the sovereign of this country again to stand upon his prerogative, and to meet the encroachments of a democratical House of Commons with no other aid than a set of ministers appointed without any connection with that House, would be to expose the monarchy and the constitution to a fate infinitely more certain and terrible than that which fell upon them in the time of King Charles.[161]

Jeffrey and Stewart both thought Hume was the great eighteenth-century theorist who had recognized that the power of the House of Commons required it to be contained differently – by the influence of the other parts of the constitution rather than by their prerogatives.[162] Another author cited by Stewart on multiple occasions was "Rousseau's ingenious fellow citizen," Jean Louis de Lolme.[163] While Stewart acknowledged that his sharp critique of Montesquieu and Blackstone "may be extended" to de Lolme as well, he insisted that his criticisms were "by no means equally applicable" to the latter author.[164] Stewart argued that it was de Lolme who offered the defining account of how the House of Commons served as the control on the Crown, protecting "the rights and liberties of the subject."[165] De Lolme's great achievement was to demonstrate that only an elected legislative assembly could adequately perform this function and that it was in this respect that England surpassed the republics of antiquity.[166] "It is from the *executive power* that the principal dangers to liberty are always to be apprehended," Stewart declared, and he claimed that the control of the House of Commons was the most effective practice ever invented for preventing those dangers.[167]

Following de Lolme, Stewart argued that the executive power should be unitary, so that its actions could be more easily supervised, and that it should be given to a hereditary monarch so as to limit usurpation by "ministers" or "popular leaders":

---

[159] Ibid.   [160] Ibid.   [161] Ibid.
[162] See Jeffrey, "Cobbet's Political Register," 415; Stewart, *Lectures on Political Economy*, 444.
[163] Stewart, *Lectures on Political Economy*, 438.   [164] Ibid., 441.   [165] Ibid., 426.   [166] Ibid.
[167] Ibid., 425.

The minister, however aspiring; the popular leader, however turbulent . . . sees every channel obstructed by which he might hope to raise himself to dominion over his fellow-citizens. In Rome and other ancient republics, the want of a common superior encouraged popular and military leaders successively to aim at the sovereign authority, till the people at length sought a refuge from the miseries brought on them by the dissensions of the contending parties, in submission to absolute despotism. In this view, the monarchical part of our Constitution (restrained and limited as it is . . .) is one of the strongest bulwarks of British liberty.[168]

Jeffrey agreed that hereditary monarchy alone could "disarm the ambition of dangerous and turbulent individuals, by removing the great prize of supreme authority, at all times, and entirely, from competition."[169] This argument would also be made by John Millar, who was a professor at the University of Glasgow rather than at Edinburgh, but whose writings on law and history were influential for the Edinburgh Whigs.[170] In his *Historical View of the English Government*, Millar argued that the combination of parliamentary control over ministers and constitutional monarchy had enabled "the English government . . . to possess the advantages both of a monarchy and a republic."[171] "The dignity and authority of a hereditary monarch" prevented usurpation, while the House of Commons' control over ministers prevented them from infringing upon liberty.[172] Although ministers were "nominated or displaced at the discretion of the Crown," Millar noted that "their continuance in office was . . . brought under the control of the two houses of parliament, and more especially under that of the Commons."[173]

A powerful assembly that represented the people and controlled the executive; a constitutional monarch who maintained his position in the state through *dignity* rather than *prerogatives*; ministers who served in Parliament, defended the government's interests, and prevented constitutional disunity – this political order was being defended by major British thinkers at the turn of the nineteenth century, just as it was being advocated in France by Necker and de Staël. The only salient difference between the theories of parliamentarism put forward in Edinburgh and Coppet concerned the issue of representation. The Edinburgh Whigs

---

[168] Ibid., 427.   [169] Jeffrey, "Leckie on the British Government," 323.
[170] The influence of Millar upon the authors of the *Edinburgh Review* is noted in Fontana, *Rethinking the Politics of Commercial Society*, 4–6.
[171] John Millar, *An Historical View of the English Government*, ed. Mark Phillips and Dale Smith (Indianapolis: 2006), 702.
[172] Ibid.   [173] Ibid., 701.

continued to envision the House of Commons as representing not the nation but rather the people in contradistinction to the aristocracy. It was far from the *représentation nationale* that Sieyès had envisioned and that the overthrow of the privileged orders in France had made inescapable. The Edinburgh Whigs also tended to defend the traditional English electoral system in all its complexity. They argued that by giving different constituencies different electoral qualifications, England achieved the best possible representation of the interests and opinions prevalent in society.[174] While Simonde de Sismondi and Germaine de Staël's son Auguste agreed with the Edinburgh Whigs that a variegated suffrage was better, the other major figures in the Coppet Circle thought that the English system was prone to corruption: they argued for uniform property requirements.[175]

Parliamentary corruption did become a major issue in Edinburgh as well as Coppet, however. Jeffrey and Stewart viewed the Crown's electoral spending and legislative patronage as essential supports of parliamentary government.[176] But there were other authors who wrote for the *Edinburgh Review*, including several of Stewart's former students, who took the opposite position. Henry Brougham, one of the most important liberal thinkers in nineteenth-century Britain and a founding member of the *Review*, was a staunch opponent of patronage. He argued that the House of Commons' most important role was to hold ministers accountable, ensuring that the "inviolable" and "irresponsible" authority of the Crown was always exercised according to the public interest.[177] How could it accomplish this, he asked, if a plurality of its members were financially dependent upon that very administration, so that Parliament "identified, as it is too apt to ... with the executive, rather than with its constituents?"[178] Brougham was the Edinburgh Whigs' most important theorist of

---

[174] The most important defense of this system was articulated by James Mackintosh, "Universal Suffrage," *Edinburgh Review*, vol. 31, no. 61 (1818), 174–177, 181–192; see as well Henry Brougham, "Speech on Parliamentary Reform," *Works of Henry Lord Brougham*, vol. 10 (Edinburgh: 1873), 319–386; and Jeffrey, "Parliamentary Reform," 303.

[175] See Simonde de Sismondi, *Études sur les constitutions des peuples libres* (Paris: 1836), 81–87, 110–111, 136–146; Auguste de Staël, *Lettres sur Angleterre* (Paris: 1825), 294–296. However, these views were strongly at odds with the elder statesmen/women of Coppet. See Germaine de Staël, *Des circonstances actuelles qui peuvent terminer la Révolution*, 299–300; and Benjamin Constant, "Pensées diverses sur les élections," *Oeuvres complètes*, t. 11, ed. Etienne Hofmann (Berlin: 2011), 420–421.

[176] Jeffrey, "Parliamentary Reform," 304; Stewart, *Lectures on Political Economy*, 446–451.

[177] This theme redounds through his writings. See Henry Brougham, "Mr. Canning – Parliamentary Reform," in *Contributions to the Edinburgh Review by Henry Lord Brougham*, vol. 2 (London: 1856), 498; Henry Brougham, "Dangers of the Constitution," *Contributions*, 438; and finally Henry Brougham, "Queen Consort," *Contributions*, 408.

[178] Brougham, "Dangers of the Constitution," 437–438.

political parties.[179] But in a period when the Whig party had been out of office for decades, he did not share Burke and de Staël's confidence that party connections would keep representatives from being bribed to support the government.

Because of his opposition to corruption, Brougham was an early supporter of electoral reform in England. Though he wished to maintain England's diversity of electoral qualifications, he argued that the elimination of corrupt boroughs and the enfranchisement of unrepresented communities, leading to "the freest representation of all classes," would reduce the number of parliamentary representatives who owed their seats to the Crown.[180] Brougham's argument was reiterated by James Mackintosh, who likewise saw the necessity of "counteracting the growing influence of the Crown in the House of Commons."[181] Mackintosh warned that absent major reform, this influence would threaten "the right of the House of Commons to interpose, with decisive weight, in the choice of ministers, as well as the adoption of measures."[182]

Another important Whig author during this period who opposed patronage was John Russell, destined to be among the most important British statesmen of the nineteenth century. In *An Essay on the History of the English Government and Constitution*, published in 1821, Russell emphasized that the presence of ministers in the House of Commons was essential to English politics. It led to "harmony ... between the different and hitherto jarring parts of the constitution," by allowing "an individual member of Parliament" to also be "the adviser of his sovereign."[183] But even as Russell recognized that it was important for ministers to have the support of Parliament, else "their measures will be thwarted, their promises will be distrusted," he claimed that it was of still greater importance for the House of Commons to function as a control on the executive.[184] He therefore lamented that "the influence of the Crown is so greatly and so dangerously increased" and that, since Walpole, so many ministers selected

---

[179] See Henry Brougham, "The State of the Parties," *Edinburgh Review*, vol. 46, no. 92 (1827), 431–432.

[180] Brougham, "Mr. Canning – Parliamentary Reform," 493. For more of the specifics of Brougham's opposition to corruption emanating from the Crown, see Henry Brougham, "Parliamentary Reform," *Contributions*, vol. 2, 364–371.

[181] James Mackintosh, "Parliamentary Reform," *Edinburgh Review*, vol. 34, no. 68 (1820), 483. For further critiques of corruption by Mackintosh, see ibid., 486–487, 492–494.

[182] Ibid., 498.

[183] See Earl John Russell, *An Essay on the History of the English Government and Constitution: From the Reign of Henry VII. to the Present Time* (London: 1823), 162.

[184] Ibid., 159.

from Parliament have thought "to serve the Crown by corrupting that assembly, and poisoning the sources from which their authority was derived."[185]

In the remaining chapters of this book, I will show how authors committed to the English parliamentary model were finally able to solve the nagging dilemma of corruption. One crucial step occurred in 1832. Pushed by many of the Whigs I discussed in this chapter – including Russell, Brougham, Mackintosh, and Jeffrey – the Great Reform Act was passed that year. By eliminating many of the most corrupt electoral districts, the Reform Act had the result of dramatically reducing the Crown's parliamentary influence. In its aftermath, English writers would be forced to find new foundations for parliamentarism. But they were not the first to do so. Almost two decades before the Reform Act, a figure at the intersection of the Edinburgh Whigs and the Coppet Circle would come up with an entirely novel interpretation of the English constitutional model, one in which corruption had no essential role. That figure was Benjamin Constant – the subject of the next chapter.

---

[185] Ibid., 428, 161.

CHAPTER 4

Reinventing Parliamentarism: The Significance of Benjamin Constant

The past three decades have witnessed a revival of interest in Benjamin Constant, who is now widely regarded as a liberal theorist of the first rank.[1] However, despite the recent profusion of scholarship on Constant, his most important contribution to liberalism remains largely unappreciated.[2] In an era when parliamentarism defined liberal thought and practice, he was its greatest theorist. His account of a parliamentary constitution would become the nineteenth-century paradigm of a liberal state, to such an extent that when Max Weber argued in 1918 for Germany to adopt a parliamentary regime modeled on England, many of his formulations could have been lifted straight out of Constant's writings from a century earlier.

Constant's account of a parliamentary constitution was revolutionary in two ways. Unlike the earlier authors examined in this book, he argued for a constitutional monarch who was not involved in political decisions – "the king reigns but does not govern" became his followers' slogan.[3] He also provided a convincing demonstration that the English parliamentary model did not require widespread patronage to function, thus severing its long-standing association with political corruption. The result of these two innovations was to significantly strengthen parliament's position vis-à-vis the executive. In Constant's theory, the hereditary monarch was entirely

---

[1] For a discussion of the "Constant revival," see Helena Rosenblatt, "Why Constant? A Critical Overview of the Constant Revival," *Modern Intellectual History*, vol. 1, no. 3 (2004), 439–453.

[2] Constant's theory of parliamentarism has been treated by scholars, particularly in France, but even the best such treatments do not capture the extent of its influence on European liberalism, or how important parliament as an institution was in Constant's political thought. See Pasquino, "Sur la théorie constitutionelle de la monarchie de Juillet"; Lucien Jaume, "Le concept de 'responsabilité des ministres' chez Benjamin Constant," *Revue française de droit constitutionnel*, no. 42 (2002), 227–243; Lucien Jaume, "La théorie de l'autorité chez Benjamin Constant," *Historical Reflections / Réflexions Historiques*, vol. 28, no. 3 (2002), 455–470; Paul Bastid, *Benjamin Constant et sa doctrine* (Paris: 1966).

[3] While Constant did not use this phrase, which was popularized by Adolphe Thiers, he similarly wrote "the king reigns but does not administer." Benjamin Constant, "Un dernier mot sur le refus du budget," in *Recueil d'articles 1829–1830*, ed. Éphraïm Harpaz (Paris: 1992), 136.

separated from the executive power, while the ministers who did exercise that power were deprived of their traditional patronage in parliament.

Constant was a compulsive gambler, and in his constitutional theory, he made a daring wager. He gambled that if a state had all the crucial elements of English parliamentarism – a powerful representative assembly, responsible ministers who served in the assembly, a constitutional monarch, a system of political parties – then further strengthening the assembly's position would not lead to legislative usurpation but rather would multiply the benefits of parliamentary rule. Parliamentary deliberation would become an even greater factor in national political life, while the accountability of executive officials to parliament would be fully secured. Many of Constant's contemporaries feared that a king who reigned but did not govern and ministers who served in parliament were meager checks on the legislature. However, he contended that this framework was sufficient to restrain the legislature, and that it offered the strongest possible safeguards for political liberty.

Constant developed his constitutional theory during the 1790s and early 1800s, when he was still a republican. He published it in 1814 and 1815, as France was transitioning to a parliamentary government. And for the rest of his life, he would struggle to enact it through parliamentary politics. Like Burke, Constant was a parliamentary actor as well as a parliamentary theorist. It is therefore necessary to provide a brief overview of the history of parliamentarism in France.

Napoleon fell from power in April of 1814, and over the next 13 months, France instituted not one but two parliamentary governments modeled on England. The first was the Charter of 1814, which Louis XVIII granted in May of that year and which went into effect in June. The following March, Napoleon escaped from exile and returned to France. In April of 1815, he proposed his own parliamentary constitution, which was adopted in a national referendum, though never implemented. The author of that constitution was Benjamin Constant.[4] This explosive series of events foreshadowed the many difficulties that would afflict French parliamentarism. France had two different monarchies during the first half of the nineteenth century, the Bourbon Restoration (1814–1830) and the July Monarchy (1830–1848). In neither was the relationship between the king

---

[4] For scholarly treatments of the Charter of 1814 and the history of its implementation, see Alain Laquièze, *Les origines du régime parlementaire en France: 1814–1848* (Paris: 2002), 37–76; Rosanvallon, *La monarchie impossible*, 15–55. For the constitutional framework of 1815 and Constant's role, see Alain Laquièze, "Benjamin Constant et l'Acte Additionnel aux Constitutions de l'Empire du 22 Avril 1815," *Historia Constitucional*, no. 4 (2003), 197–234. These constitutional frameworks are printed in Duguit and Monnier, *Les constitutions et les principales lois politiques de la France*, 180–198.

and the Chamber of Deputies ever properly settled, nor the freedom of the press durably established. Corruption and cabinet instability emerged as serious dilemmas – as did the limited suffrage. While French political culture became invested in the ideal of a deliberative assembly, there was widespread scorn for France's actual parliaments.[5]

Yet despite these challenges, parliamentarism was more successful at achieving political stability with constitutional liberty than any political framework of the French Revolution. For that reason, it proved remarkably durable, outlasting all the revolutionary upheavals of the nineteenth century. The 1830 Revolution was followed by another parliamentary monarchy modeled on England (i.e., the July Monarchy). While the July Monarchy did not survive the 1848 Revolution, the French commitment to parliamentarism did. The Second and Third Republics would both have parliamentary governments.

Benjamin Constant was elected to the Chamber of Deputies in 1817, and he remained involved in parliamentary politics until his death in 1830. I will argue that during this period, his overriding political aim was to rescue French parliamentarism from its pathologies. He defended the freedom of the press, fought to strictly circumscribe the role of the monarch, and argued for an expansion of the suffrage – though one that would have left France still far short of democracy.[6] He also struggled to combat parliamentary corruption. While he failed to salvage France's first parliamentary regime and died shortly after its collapse in 1830, his efforts are indispensable for understanding his political theory.

I will begin the chapter by analyzing Constant's theory of parliamentarism. I will consider his conceptions of representation, deliberation, and responsibility; his defense of constitutional monarchy and responsible cabinet government; and his response to the threat of legislative usurpation. I will also argue, against most scholars, that the principles of Constant's thought were directly at odds with Montesquieu's account of the English constitution. The chapter will then explore Constant's involvement in French parliamentary politics.

---

[5] In part this was because the bar for rhetoric that was set by the assemblies of the French Revolution seemed so high. For the contested culture of parliamentary deliberation in France, see Jean Starobinski, "The Pulpit, The Rostrum, and the Bar," in *Realms of Memory: The Construction of the French Past*, vol. 2: *Traditions*, ed. Pierre Nora and Lawrence Kritzman, tr. Arthur Goldhammer (New York: 1997), 418–440; Thomas Bouchet, "French Parliamentary Discourse, 1789–1914," in *Parliament and Parliamentarism*, ed. Pasi Ihaleinen et al. (New York: 2016), 162–175.

[6] While Constant wished to see "a greater number of Frenchmen called to exercise their political rights," he did not wish to enfranchise the lower classes. "Electors too poor would not have been, despite their great number, anything but the instruments of the rich ... In the intermediate class lies enlightenment, industry, and an equal interest in liberty and order: the law which gives power to this class is a law which is wise and principled." See Benjamin Constant, "Des Chambres, depuis leur convocation jusqu'au décembre 1816," in *Oeuvres complètes*, t. 10, vol. 1, ed. Kurt Kloocke (Berlin: 2010), 376.

Here I will especially focus on Constant's opposition to parliamentary corruption and his understanding of political parties.

Representation and Deliberation: The Promise of Parliament

Constant was born in Lausanne, Switzerland, in 1767. Like de Staël, he was a champion of the English parliamentary model who also sympathized with two of the most radical doctrines of the French Revolution. The first was republicanism: although Constant would eventually come to favor constitutional monarchy, he preferred a republic well into the early 1800s, as he labored over his never-published work *De la possibilité d'une constitution républicaine dans un grand pays.*[7] The second was social equality. Constant cheered the French Revolution's attack on aristocratic privilege. From "an impenetrable cloud which covers its birth," he declared, "we see the human species advance toward equality."[8] Even after his conversion to constitutional monarchy, he continued to defend the more equal society created by the Revolution.[9]

Constant's most important *institutional* commitment – both during his republican phase and after – was to a powerful representative assembly. "In a large nation," he wrote, "liberty cannot exist ... without strong, large, and independent assemblies."[10] "It is representative assemblies alone that can infuse life into the political body."[11] In *De la possibilité d'une constitution républicaine dans un grand pays*, Constant explicitly argued for "the supremacy of the legislative power over the executive power."[12] "The legislative power and the assemblies charged with it are the premier power," he wrote; they are "the first of all powers in rank and dignity."[13]

Constant based his argument for the supremacy of the legislature on the principle that it alone could represent the people. "In order to represent

---

[7] For Constant's rejection of monarchy in this text, see Benjamin Constant, "De la possibilité d'une constitution républicaine dans un grand pays," in *Oeuvres complètes*, t. 4, ed. Maria Luisa Sanchéz Mejía and Kurt Kloocke (Tübingen: 2005), 401–426. Many of Constant's earliest political writings were in defense of the republican constitution of 1795. See Benjamin Constant, "De la force du gouvernement actuel de la France et de la nécessité de s'y rallier," in *Oeuvres complètes*, t. 1, ed. Jean-Daniel Candaux and Lucia Omacini (Tübingen: 1998), 366–375.

[8] Constant, "De la force du gouvenement actuel de la France et de la nécessité de s'y rallier," 374.

[9] Despite his admiration for English political institutions, Constant was always critical of the power of the aristocracy in England. See, for instance, Benjamin Constant, *Commentary on Filangieri*, ed. Alan Kahan (Indianapolis: 2015), 54–67.

[10] Benjamin Constant, *Principes de politique applicables à tous les gouvernements représentatifs et particulièrement à la constitution actuelle de la France* (Paris: 1815), 59.

[11] Ibid., 65.

[12] Constant, "De la possibilité d'une constitution républicaine dans un grand pays," 431.

[13] Ibid., 431, 521.

the people, one must be one with it," he declared. "This principle is the basis of the representative system: as soon as it is consecrated, the representative system is secure."[14] No other political power but the legislature could possibly "be one" with the people, for that required "a certain number of individuals proportionate to the area of the nation," who together could "know and predict the people's needs."[15] On the crucial issue of political representation, Constant was the heir to Henry Parker. Only a legislative assembly was large and diverse enough to serve as the image of the nation. Therefore, only the legislature could represent the nation in political decisions.

Constant was among the great nineteenth-century theorists of parliamentary deliberation, and his conception of the legislature as a deliberative body emerged straightforwardly from his belief in its representative character. What made the legislature representative was that its members came from "every part" of the nation and stood for a variety of interests and opinions.[16] The only way such a large and diverse group could possibly arrive at collective decisions was through a long process of debate and discussion.

Constant believed strongly in the educative value of deliberation. "One hundred deputies, nominated by a hundred sections of the state, bring into the assembly the particular interests of their electors," he wrote.[17] But when "forced to *deliberate* together, they soon become aware of the respective sacrifices which are indispensable."[18] He argued that this process was the only way to arrive at the common good, or general interest. "What is the general interest," he asked, "if not the negotiation worked out between all the particular interests? What is the general representation, if not the representation of all the particular interests which must compromise over the objects which are common to them?"[19] As Bryan Garsten has emphasized, this conception of the general interest led Constant to reject all electoral systems designed to filter out partial interests.[20] What he wanted was open parliamentary debate *between* partial interests. As each representative is "partial for his constituents," Constant wrote, "the partiality of each, brought together, will have all the advantages of the impartiality of all."[21]

While Constant presumed that each representative would be "partial for his constituents," he was convinced that parliamentary deliberation made representatives more *enlightened* in their partiality. It forced them to "see

[14] Ibid., 619.   [15] Ibid., 435.   [16] Ibid., 562.   [17] Ibid., 564.   [18] Ibid.
[19] Ibid., 563.
[20] See Garsten, "From Popular Sovereignty to Civil Society in Post-Revolutionary France," 254.
[21] Constant, "De la possibilité d'une constitution républicaine dans un grand pays," 564.

every side of each question that was presented, and every opinion attacked and defended."[22] The result was a more nuanced understanding of political issues. Parliament's character as a representative assembly – composed of "men different with respect to their habits, their relationships, and their social positions" – contributed to the range of potential viewpoints.[23] So did the rules of parliamentary procedure, and Constant was particularly fond of the English rule that prohibited representatives from reading prewritten speeches. He wrote

> it is only when orators are obliged to speak without preparation that a true discussion is engaged in. Everyone, struck by the arguments he has just heard, is naturally led to examine them ... The views he has encountered combine with and modify those he already holds, suggesting to him answers which present the same issue from different points of view.[24]

Following de Lolme, Constant argued that the clash of viewpoints in parliament involved not only representatives but also the public.[25] This occurred through the medium of the press. "Pamphlets accompany each political question into the heart of parliament," he wrote.[26] "The whole thinking part of the nation intervenes, in this way, in the questions which interest it."[27] Constant was one of the great nineteenth-century defenders of the freedom of the press. While this was largely because of his commitment to individual liberty, it was also due to the reciprocal relationship he identified between the press and parliamentary deliberation.

Political Responsibility and Constitutional Monarchy

Although Constant argued that only the legislature could represent the people when he was a republican, there is no indication that he changed his view on this when he came to favor monarchy.[28] Like de Staël, he recognized that endorsing constitutional monarchy meant accepting an unelected hereditary assembly that represented the aristocracy. But he

---

[22] Benjamin Constant, *De la liberté des brochures, des pamphlets et des journaux* (Paris: 1814), 8.
[23] Benjamin Constant, *Réflexions sur les constitutions, la distribution des pouvoirs, et les garanties, dans une monarchie constitutionnelle* (Paris: 1814), 50.
[24] Benjamin Constant, *Principles of Politics Applicable to All Representative Governments, Political Writings*, ed. Biancamaria Fontana (Cambridge: 1988), 222.
[25] For his debt to de Lolme on the benefits of freedom of expression, see Constant, *De la liberté des brochures, des pamphlets et des journaux*, 26.
[26] Ibid., 8.   [27] Ibid.
[28] For indications of this, see Constant, *Réflexions sur les constitutions*, 27, 68, 118, 154; Benjamin Constant, "Questions sur la législation actuelle de la presse en France-IV," in *Oeuvres complètes*, t. 10, vol. 2, ed. Kurt Kloocke (Berlin: 2010), 698.

made clear that this body (i.e., the Chamber of Peers) did not represent the people or express public opinion. It represented what he called "the long duration" of the state, and as we will see, he presumed that in any sustained confrontation with the Chamber of Deputies, it would be forced to back down.[29] He treated elections to the Chamber of Deputies as the definitive expression of the public will.[30]

No less important than the legislature's function as a *deliberative* body was its role in securing the *responsibility* of executive officials. Even if the executive power was subordinate to the legislature, Constant recognized that executive officials would necessarily possess significant discretion. Unexpected situations would invariably arise in which ministers would be forced to exercise their own judgment.[31] Because of the potential for this discretion to be abused, it was essential that parliament regularly evaluate the conduct of the executive. "We thus arrive at the matter of responsibility," Constant wrote, "without which all constitutions would be nothing but empty forms."[32] He declared this "the most important . . . of all constitutional questions."[33]

Constant argued that parliament was ideally equipped to hold high-ranking executive officials responsible. It could subject them to "scrupulous investigation," and it could also engage in "a public conversation, over each fact, over each complaint, over each measure that seems illegal."[34] As a deliberative body, rather than a judicial body, parliament could consider not only whether ministers had broken the law but also whether they were governing in a manner conducive to the common good.[35] Constant recognized that ministers would rarely be impeached and prosecuted, for "in questions of this nature crime and innocence are seldom entirely evident," but he emphasized that parliament's inquiries into executive decisions were still of great value.[36] They might lead to a minister's resignation – even if not to his prosecution – and they reminded ministers that their first duty was to the nation. In turn, the nation was reminded of its fundamental right to control those who governed:

> Responsibility must, above all, secure two aims: that of depriving guilty ministers of their power, and that of keeping alive in the nation – through

---

[29] Constant, *Principles of Politics*, 185. For a discussion of Constant's trepidation about the Chamber of Peers, see Levy, *Rationalism, Pluralism and Freedom*, 194–198.
[30] See especially Constant, "Questions sur la législation actuelle de la presse en France-IV," 698.
[31] Constant, "De la possibilité d'une constitution républicaine dans un grand pays," 575.
[32] Ibid., 590.   [33] Ibid.
[34] Benjamin Constant, "Annales de la session de 1817 à 1818," in *Oeuvres complètes*, t. 11, 188.
[35] Constant, *Principles of Politics*, 230.   [36] Ibid., 239.

the watchfulness of her representatives, the openness of their debates, and
the exercise of freedom of the press applied to the analysis of all ministerial
actions – a spirit of inquiry, a habitual interest in the maintenance of the
constitution of the state, a constant participation in public affairs, in a word
a vivid sense of political life.[37]

To keep ministers continually responsible to the nation, Constant agreed
with Burke that parliament should have the right to remove any ministry
from power. "In England," he wrote admiringly, "the ministry loses its
position if it finds itself in the minority."[38]

Constant made only one revision to the traditional English account of
political responsibility. However, it was extraordinarily radical. He argued
that "the indispensable condition for the exercise of political responsibility"
was that the monarch play no part in governing.[39] Constant did not want to
change anything about the way ministers were appointed. He recognized
that in England, ministers were selected by the monarch – and then either
acquiesced to or rejected by the House of Commons over the course of
parliamentary debates.[40] It was this practice that he hoped to institute in
France as well. What he insisted was that the king should never use these
appointments to favor a particular political agenda or direct his ministers
regarding how to act. "The king wishes that the people are happy, well-
governed, and enjoy their rights. He chooses ministers in order that they
administer in this direction," Constant wrote.[41] But when it came to
determining which decisions would best lead there, "the ministers choose
them."[42] Constant claimed that the "great aim" of "constitutional monarchy" was to "separate the executive power" from the king.[43] This was
nothing less than "the key to all political organization."[44]

Constant argued that unless the executive power was independent of the
king, it was impossible to combine hereditary monarchy with political
responsibility. If representatives challenged a minister's decision, and that
minister was acting as the king had directed, then one of two situations
would occur. Either the king would be dragged into the political arena and
forfeit his higher legitimacy, or representatives would hesitate to confront
the minister, so as not to challenge the monarch. In the former case,
"discussion or resistance" would inevitably "compromise the head of
state," while in the latter, all political responsibility would be lost.[45] The

[37] Ibid.   [38] Ibid., 225.   [39] Ibid., 191.
[40] Benjamin Constant, "Du droit de dissolution," in *Recueil d'articles 1829–1830*, 523–524.
[41] Benjamin Constant, "Second lettre sur la prérogative royale," in *Recueil d'articles 1829–1830*, 177.
[42] Ibid.   [43] Constant, *Principles of Politics*, 191.   [44] Constant, *Réflexions sur les constitutions*, 1.
[45] Constant, *Principles of Politics*, 191.

king's inviolability would become an "attribution of ministerial authority;" and "the king himself, descending from the height where he was placed . . . becomes a sort of minister, before which all liberty disappears, because he associates, with the inviolability he possesses, attributions incompatible with that inviolability."[46] Political responsibility had long required that representatives criticize ministers *as if* they were acting independently of the monarch. Constant's argument was that unless political institutions conformed to this logic, the responsibility of ministers could never be secure, for it was always possible that a monarch involved in governing would decide to put his entire political weight behind a particular minister, and parliament would hesitate to challenge the minister, so as to avoid an explosive confrontation with the king.

Constant noted that for the sake of political responsibility, ministers had to explain and justify all their decisions to parliament. They could lose their positions or even face criminal prosecution. How was that fair if they were merely doing the monarch's will? And how could the monarch serve as an able chief executive if his deputies could be changed at will by the assembly? Unless ministers were independent of the monarch, "their responsibility would be absurd and unjust."[47] In making these arguments, Constant drew on ideas that were circulating in France, where, as I showed in Chapter 3, Sieyès was increasingly open about his desire for a distinction between executive and monarchical power, as well as England, where a similar position was staked out by Charles James Fox and his Whiggish allies against George III. In his *Historical View of the English Government*, which was published in 1804 and dedicated to Fox, John Millar fore-shadowed one of Constant's crucial arguments. He claimed that as it was ministers, rather than the king, who were "alone responsible for ordinary acts of mal-administration . . . these ministers must be allowed exclusively to direct and govern the state machine; for it would be the height of injustice to load them with the crimes of another, nor could it be expected that any man of spirit would submit to be a minister upon such terms."[48] Political responsibility was therefore incompatible with the active consti-tutional monarch that Burke and de Lolme had both defended. It required

---

[46] Benjamin Constant, "Des chambres (VII article) projet de loi sur les journaux," in *Oeuvres complètes*, t. 10, vol. 1, 468.

[47] Constant, *Principles of Politics*, 184.

[48] Millar, *Historical View of the English Government*, 701. For a discussion of Millar, his relationship to Fox, and the emergence of a more radical Whiggism in historiography as well as politics, see Hugh Trevor-Roper, "Lord Macaulay: The History of England," in *History and the Enlightenment*, ed. John Robertson (New Haven: 2010), 196–200.

the king depicted in *Cato's Letters*, who delegated the powers of governing to his ministers and could "float above" the strife and "dissensions" of politics like a god.[49]

Constant versus Montesquieu: Parliament and Public Opinion

Because Constant's mature political theory was based on the English constitution, scholars have often presumed that he was a disciple of Montesquieu.[50] They argue that he shared Montesquieu's appreciation for a system of equal checks and balances and amended Montesquieu's account only by introducing the idea of a neutral power.[51] This is a tempting hypothesis, but it overlooks a decisive difference. Constant favored a far more powerful legislature and a far more constrained executive than Montesquieu. While this was evident across Constant's entire career, it became particularly apparent once he turned away from republicanism.

During his republican period, Constant endorsed largely the same constitutional framework as de Staël. He envisioned a bicameral legislature (in which one branch played the role of a more elite senate), while the executive power was to be held by a committee that the legislature appointed.[52] Unlike the Directory, this committee would be able to veto legislation, and its ministers would sit in the legislature.[53] Finally, an additional committee would serve as the *neutral power*. This last idea was Constant's key addition to de Staël's account of a parliamentary republic. Like Sieyès and a number of other figures writing during the 1790s, Constant thought that every constitution needed one power that played

---

[49] Constant, *Principles of Politics*, 187.

[50] For arguments to the effect that Constant follows Montesquieu, see Holmes, *Benjamin Constant and the Making of Modern Liberalism*, 4–5, 134; Biancamaria Fontana, *Benjamin Constant and the Post-Revolutionary Mind* (New Haven: 1991), 48–50; K. Steven Vincent, *Benjamin Constant and the Birth of French Liberalism* (New York: 2011), 107, 174–176; Markus Prutsch, *Making Sense of Constitutional Monarchism in Post-Napoleonic France and Germany* (New York: 2013), 1, 4, 37; Craiutu, *A Virtue for Courageous Minds*, 227, 289; Jeremy Jennings, "Constant's Idea of Modern Liberty," in *The Cambridge Companion to Benjamin Constant*, ed. Helena Rosenblatt (Cambridge: 2009), 87.

[51] A claim of this kind is found in Fontana, *Benjamin Constant and the Post-Revolutionary Mind*, 50; Vincent, *Benjamin Constant and the Birth of French Liberalism*, 189; Craiutu, *A Virtue for Courageous Minds*, 227–234.

[52] Though Constant never exactly defined the two branches, he most likely was intending to follow de Staël on this point. See, in particular, his conception of how the executive would be nominated in Constant, "De la possibilité d'une constitution républicaine dans un grand pays," 513 as well as his account of the executive on 534–535.

[53] Ibid., 542–543.

no active role in the state – its function was to prevent the powers that *did* play an active role from either collapsing into gridlock or combining to threaten liberty.[54] Its purpose was "to defend the government from the divisions of the governors, and to defend those who are governed from the oppression of the government."[55]

More specifically, Constant argued that the neutral power would possess "the means to break the coalition of executive and legislative power when it forms, as well as the means to calm the divisions that arise between the two powers."[56] The "means" that enabled it to accomplish these two tasks were its powers of "dismissal and dissolution."[57] When a conflict arose between the executive and legislature, the neutral power could dismiss the executive – allowing the legislature to appoint a new one. Or it could dissolve the legislature itself and call new elections.

In 1814, Constant broke definitively with republicanism. That year he wrote *Réflexions sur les constitutions, la distribution des pouvoirs, et les garanties, dans une monarchie constitutionnelle*, which made the case for France to adopt a constitutional monarchy based on England. The following year, he would reiterate this argument in *Principes de politique applicables à tous les gouvernements représentatifs*, his defense of the parliamentary constitution he had written for Napoleon.[58] In both texts, Constant envisioned a bicameral legislature with one elected branch and one hereditary branch. The executive power was to be held by the king's ministers, who were to serve in the legislature just like they did in England. As I emphasized earlier, the king himself would play no executive role.

Constant argued that because the king held neither executive nor legislative responsibilities, he was perfectly positioned to serve as the neutral power. Indeed, Constant maintained that in England, this was already largely the case. An English monarch did not directly participate in political decisions; his function was instead to mediate conflicts that arose between the other powers of government. "The English constitution employs the royal power to end any dangerous conflict, and re-establish harmony among the other powers," Constant wrote.[59] Should a conflict arise between the House of Commons and the House of Lords, the king

---

[54] For a classic discussion of this dimension of French revolutionary thought, see Gauchet, *La révolution des pouvoirs*.
[55] Constant, "De la possibilité d'une constitution républicaine dans un grand pays," 627.   [56] Ibid.
[57] Ibid.
[58] That year Constant also published a treatise on political responsibility. See Benjamin Constant, *De la responsabilité des ministres* (Paris: 1815).
[59] Constant, *Principles of Politics*, 185.

could add new peers, bringing the Lords into alignment with the lower house. Or he could dissolve the House of Commons and call new elections. This was George III's course of action when the Lords rejected Fox's East India Reform Bill in 1783 – an event Constant prominently references.[60] Should a conflict arise between the House of Commons and the ministry, the king faced a similar choice. He could either dismiss the existing ministry and appoint one that a majority of the House of Commons favored, or he could dissolve the House of Commons, allowing all sides to make an appeal to public opinion.[61]

During Constant's republican period, there exist some grounds for thinking that, like Montesquieu, he wanted the legislature checked by an independent executive armed with a veto. In *De la possibilité d'une constitution républicaine dans un grand pays*, he specifically argued for an "independent" executive that (unlike the Directory) could veto legislation. Yet even then, he was quite critical of this prerogative.[62] "The veto is a means of such extremity … it is hardly ever used," he wrote, and "there are very few examples of the exercise of the veto in England."[63] He found it especially telling that George III did not veto Fox's East India Reform bill. "In 1783 … the King preferred the arguably irregular means of his personal credit over the members of the high chamber, to the legal employment of his constitutional prerogative, for rejecting Fox's India Bill."[64] Every indication suggests that Constant's parliamentary republic was intended to function like the one de Staël envisioned. The exercise of the veto against an important bill would trigger the dissolution of the legislature – making it less a means to block legislative decisions and more a means to test whether the legislature truly represented public opinion. If the executive committee was still at odds with the legislature following the subsequent election, its members *lost their positions*. Indeed, Constant introduced the neutral power specifically to facilitate this process. With its capacity to dismiss the executive and dissolve the legislature, the neutral power ensured that a clash between the legislature and executive was followed by a general election, and it forced the executive committee from office whenever it was at odds with a legislature that represented public opinion.[65]

---

[60] Ibid., 200.   [61] Ibid., 194–198, 225, 243–244.

[62] Constant, "De la possibilité d'une constitution républicaine dans un grand pays," 575.

[63] Ibid., 610.   [64] Ibid.

[65] Constant frequently emphasized the need for a power in republics that could ensure executive responsibility by forcing the highest executive officials to resign. That power was the neutral power: absent it, Constant worried, the assembly would have no choice but to criminally prosecute those officials, leading to massive political conflicts and disruptions. See *Principles of Politics*, 190.

When Constant embraced constitutional monarchy, he eliminated the executive's independence and further reduced the importance of the veto. Along with placing the neutral power in the hands of a king, rather than a committee, Constant's other crucial move was to shift where the executive power was located. In *De la possibilité d'une constitution républicaine dans un grand pays*, it was held by a committee of officials who were distinct from the legislature – though whose ministers served in the legislature. In 1814, Constant eliminated the executive committee and never replaced it. In his mature constitutional theory, the highest executive officials were ministers who sat in the legislature, and who were entirely dependent upon the legislature for their positions. They had no capacity to block legislation. Although the neutral constitutional monarch was given a veto, Constant was again quite critical of it, as it "irritates" the assembly "without disarming" it (almost certainly a reference to the experience of Louis XVI).[66] Constant argued that "dissolution is the only remedy whose effectiveness is assured."[67]

The purpose of dissolution was to test whether the legislature was acting in accord with public opinion.[68] If the ministry was at odds with a majority of the legislature, the king's natural response would be to appoint new ministers who were acceptable to the majority. But he also had one other option, which was to test whether that majority was the true majority by dissolving the legislature and calling an election. If there was a conflict between the legislature and the Chamber of Peers, the monarch faced a similar decision. Either he could add new peers and bring the upper chamber into alignment with the elected assembly, or he could call an election to test whether that assembly actually represented public opinion.[69] If the electorate endorsed the assembly's actions, Constant believed it would be extraordinarily dangerous for either the ministry or the aristocratic chamber to continue in opposition.[70] They would at that point be putting themselves manifestly at odds with public opinion, and the legislature would be entitled to begin making use of its budgetary powers to force them into submission. This is exactly what Constant would recommend in 1830, when Charles X's ministry refused to resign after it

---

[66] Ibid., 195.   [67] Ibid.

[68] For an important argument about contested claims to represent the people in Constant's thought, though different from mine, see Garsten, "Representative Government and Popular Sovereignty."

[69] Constant, *Principles of Politics*, 200.

[70] With respect to the Peers needing to give way, see ibid. For the necessity that ministers give way, which is essential to Constant's constitutional theory and parliamentary practice, see ibid., 225.

lost support in the Chamber of Deputies and was defeated in a general election.[71] So long as the legislature could lay claim to genuinely represent public opinion, there was no legitimate constitutional means by which another power could block it.

As I showed in Chapter 1, Montesquieu's account of the English constitution required checks and balances that were broadly equal. Should stalemate result, each power would be equally able to compel the other two.[72] In Constant's constitutional theory, this was simply not the case. It was the king's role to arbitrate a stalemate, and there was a major disjuncture between how he could act upon the ministry or Chamber of Peers and how he could act upon the elected assembly. By dismissing the ministry or adding new Peers, he immediately changed the agenda of either power, so that it was in line with the elected assembly. But he had no comparable way to change the assembly's agenda. All he could do was call a new election, and if the electorate ended up being in support of the assembly, nothing could be done to force its position. An elected assembly supported by public opinion rightfully found itself in a position of greater strength than any other constitutional actor. Like in de Staël's political theory, the only way another constitutional actor could really change parliament's will was through gambling that it was not supported by public opinion and that the current majority would be defeated in an election. Dissolving parliament tested that gamble and revealed whether the current assembly represented the public mind. If it did, then its actions could no longer be opposed by the other constitutional powers.

Moderating the Legislature

Constant declared that "there is nothing more salutary for . . . liberty" than a powerful legislative assembly, and he envisioned a constitutional structure in which a legislature supported by public opinion encountered no real check.[73] But he knew that the legislature could also become a threat to liberty. This was one of the defining lessons of the French Revolution.

---

[71] See Constant, "Un dernier mot sur le refus du budget," 135–144; Benjamin Constant, "Rejet partiel ou total du budget," in *Recueil d'articles 1829–1830*, 130–134, and "Pas de budget possible avec le ministère actuel," in *Recueil d'articles 1829–1830*, 205–208.

[72] Such a system requires a deeply rooted commitment to political compromise and moderation; otherwise, no (constitutionally legitimate) decision is possible when the different constitutional powers are in disagreement. See Eric Nelson, "Are We on the Verge of the Death Spiral that Produced the English Revolution of 1642–1649?" *History News Network* (December 12, 2014).

[73] Benjamin Constant, "Des désordres actuels de la France et des moyens d'y remédier par M. le comte de Montlosier," in *Oeuvres complètes*, t. 10, vol. 1, 176.

"None of our free constitutions has assigned a limit to legislative power," he wrote. "Representative assemblies ... have exercised the most unheard of arbitrary power over the whole of individual existence."[74]

Unlike Tocqueville and Mill, Constant's chief concern was not that legislative assemblies enabled the tyranny of the majority. It was rather that they enabled the tyranny of *a minority*. He agreed with de Lolme that history was replete with individuals and factions who first came to dominate the legislature and then made use of its extraordinary powers to usurp the state.[75] Constant's emphasis on usurpation rather than majority tyranny is partly attributable to his never accepting universal suffrage – whereas Tocqueville and Mill both would.[76] But that is not the whole story. Even when it came to the assemblies of the French Revolution, which were elected by a wide suffrage, what Constant emphasized was their tendency to be overpowered by organized minorities.

The Legislative Assembly of 1791–1792 was a sterling example of this. Constant wrote that "there never existed, in the Legislative Assembly, a hundred men who wished to bring down the constitutional monarchy: from the beginning to the end of its short career, that assembly was always driven in a direction opposed to its wills and desires."[77] He later reiterated this point: "the Constituent Assembly did not want to shake and weaken the monarchy and yet it shook and weakened it. The Legislative Assembly did not want to bring down the throne, and yet it did."[78] Practically every tyrannical legislature had been dominated by an ambitious faction:

> Three quarters of the Convention held in horror the assassinations of which Paris became the theatre. Nevertheless it did not delay in being subjugated by the authors of those crimes, even as they were a very small number at its heart. Whoever has pored through the authentic acts of the Parliament of England ... before the death of Charles I, must be convinced that two-thirds of the parliamentarians ardently desired the peace that their votes ceaselessly repressed, and that they regarded as horrible and blamable, the war which each day they proclaimed unanimously the justice and necessity of.[79]

---

[74] Constant, "De la possibilité d'une constitution républicaine dans un grand pays," 550.

[75] Bryan Garsten has perceptively discussed the importance of legislative usurpation in Constant's political thinking, and differentiated this from the danger of majority tyranny (Garsten, "Representative Government and Popular Sovereignty").

[76] For Constant's discussions of the suffrage, see Constant, *Principles of Politics*, 213–221; Constant, "Pensées diverses sur les élections," 420–421.

[77] Constant, "De la possibilité d'une constitution républicaine dans un grand pays," 519.

[78] Benjamin Constant, "Prospectus du journal des arts," in *Oeuvres complètes*, t. 10, vol. 1, 134.

[79] Constant, "De la possibilité d'une constitution républicaine dans un grand pays," 519.

Constant was convinced that the very same features of the legislature that made it representative and deliberative also made it susceptible to usurpation. The legislature contained a plethora of different interests and factions competing to enact their agenda. While this forced representatives to engage in deliberation and made possible all the benefits of deliberation, it was always possible that one faction – whether through ruthlessness, or eloquence, or superior organization – would simply dominate the others. Indeed, Constant viewed this as quite probable. Because of the legislature's size and pluralism, it was unlikely to have a basis of agreement or common will in advance of deliberation – only a wide variety of different wills. Yet on many questions, it would have to arrive quickly at a decision. In that situation, a faction could easily hold the entire assembly hostage. Despite his praise for parliamentary deliberation, Constant recognized it was a fragile and imperfect method. "A well unified minority, which has the advantage of attack, which frightens and seduces, reasons and menaces in turn," Constant wrote, will "dominate sooner or later the majority."[80]

Because legislative usurpation was often instigated by factions that did not represent a majority of the nation, the power of dissolution was an especially effective safeguard. Dissolving the legislature could not block an agenda that had wide public approval, for in that case, the electorate would simply send back the same representatives. But it could bring down a faction that had seized control of the assembly while not actually representing national opinion – it could reveal how far this faction really was from speaking for the whole nation. Constant lamented that the Constitutions of 1791 and 1795 had failed to include a power of dissolution. He declared that the "germ of death" in the Constitution of 1791 was that it made it an "impossibility" for "the king to dissolve the legislative assembly."[81] "Without that precaution," he wrote, "a monarchy and a constitution are chimeras."[82] While the monarch's other powers – the appointment of peers, the selection and dismissal of ministers – enabled him to shift around office holders, only through the power of dissolution could he restart the entire political process from scratch. It was a true power of last resort and one that

---

[80] Ibid., 519.

[81] Constant, "Des désordres actuels de la France et des moyens d'y remédier par M. le comte de Montlosier," 176. For Constant, the great example of the power of dissolution disarming a faction in this manner was when Louis XVIII dissolved a chamber dominated by the extreme right in 1816 (the *chambre introuvable*) and new elections led to a more moderate assembly. See Constant "Des Chambres (VII Article) Projet de loi sur les journaux," 467; Constant, "Annales de la session de 1817 à 1818," 923.

[82] Constant, "Des désordres actuels de la France et des moyens d'y remédier par M. le comte de Montlosier," 176.

maintained the king's neutrality. When dissolving parliament, the monarch did not need to take a concrete political stand and could claim simply to be canvassing public opinion, while the power to settle the crisis was given to the electorate rather than him.

In addition to dissolving the legislature when it was at odds with public opinion, the monarch's other crucial role was to prevent usurpation from arising within the legislature. Constant's argument on this point largely followed de Lolme. He argued that the presence of a constitutional monarch created a powerful limit to political ambition – "a fixed unassailable point which passions cannot reach."[83] "The things that make up the veneration by which the monarch is surrounded prevent any comparison" with other political actors, he noted.[84] Even the most popular and ambitious representative would think twice before challenging such a figure. Constant believed that the king's neutrality would only render him more insuperable. Because he was responsible for no political decision and embroiled in no political controversy, allegiances to him would transcend partisan divisions. He would come to be beloved by the entire nation – and would symbolize the values of justice, impartiality, and national unity.[85]

Constant warned that in a republic, if there occurred an unexpected or dramatic change in leadership, the recently departed ministers might be motivated to take drastic action to regain power. "In a hereditary monarchy," by contrast, "this would present no difficulty."[86] The monarch's "dignity" and popularity would serve as an imposing obstacle to usurpation: "the permanent character of his dignity" would redirect "all the efforts of their [i.e., the old ministry's] partisans against the new ministry," Constant wrote, instead of against the political structure itself.[87] After 1814, this would become Constant's key argument for the superiority of constitutional monarchy over republicanism: by establishing a highest figure in the state whom legislative representatives could not realistically hope to challenge, constitutional monarchy conditioned them to seek power legitimately.[88]

---

[83] Constant, "Principles of Politics," 190. [84] Ibid. [85] Ibid., 187. [86] Ibid., 189.
[87] Ibid.
[88] Constant's argument for the value of a hereditary monarch is so close to de Lolme's that it is difficult to believe he was not following de Lolme directly. There is, in fact, evidence that Constant was thinking about de Lolme in 1814–1815, when he came out in favor of constitutional monarchy. While de Lolme is not mentioned in either *Réflexions sur les constitutions* or *Principes de politique*, he is mentioned in another pamphlet published during that same political moment. *De la liberté des brochures, des pamphlets et des journaux*, Constant's most systematic defense of freedom of expression, came out a mere two months after *Réflexions sur les constitutions*. In it, Constant declares specifically that he will "invoke" the "authority of Delolme" in order to demonstrate that freedom of speech and expression were compatible with political authority in England. See Constant, *De la liberté des brochures, des pamphlets et des journaux*, 26. My chronology is drawn

A similar benefit was derived from the presence of ministers in parliament. As we saw in earlier chapters, this practice was usually defended because it enabled the government to influence the legislature. Because of his preoccupation with usurpation, Constant reversed that argument: the importance of having ministers in the legislature was not that it allowed the executive to influence the legislature but rather that it allowed legislative representatives to become the executive. Constant argued that where representatives could directly attain the highest government positions, they were less likely to use the legislature to attack the government. Instead of usurpation, they sought the power and honor that came with ministerial office:

> When the representatives of the people are excluded from participation in power, we have reason to fear that they will regard it as their natural enemy. If on the contrary, the ministers could be received in the bosom of the assemblies, the ambitious will direct their efforts only against men and would respect the institutions. Because their attacks will be aimed at individuals, they will be less dangerous for the assembly as a whole. No-one will want to break an instrument the use of which he could hope to win ... We see an example of this in England. The enemies of the ministry see in its power their own future authority and strength.[89]

For these reasons, Constant wrote that "the greatest advantages result from letting representatives have the ability to arrive at ministerial places."[90] It was this arrangement that had "perhaps preserved the English constitution."[91]

Constant favored a parliamentary government even when he was a republican. Like de Staël, he envisioned a republic where ministers served in parliament and held their positions only if they maintained the support of a parliamentary majority. Constant castigated the Constitutions of 1791 and 1795 for not imitating England in this respect.[92] While "legislative functions are first in genuine dignity, and the most appropriate to independent characters," he wrote, "the places of the ministry are, in a great empire, the surer route to power and to riches. They are always more desired by vulgar ambitions. If the members of the representative assemblies cannot ever participate in the executive power as ministers, it is to be feared that they will regard that power itself ... as their natural enemy."[93]

from Cecil Patrick Courtney, *A Bibliography of Editions of the Writings of Benjamin Constant to 1833*, vol. 1 (Hudson: 1981), 34–37.
[89] Constant, *Principles of Politics*, 224.
[90] Constant, "De la possibilité d'une constitution républicaine dans un grand pays," 542.
[91] Ibid., 542–543.   [92] Ibid., 544.   [93] Ibid., 543.

The presence of ministers in the legislature brought other benefits as well. Constant argued that ministers possessed greater knowledge and experience than the average representative, elevating the character of parliamentary deliberation. "Ministers will discuss the decrees necessary for administration" in parliament, he wrote, and "they will offer that knowledge of the facts which the exercise of government alone can give."[94] Parliament in turn could contest ministers' proposals, and "the government," after "yielding to reasonable objections, will amend sanctioned proposals and explain obscure formulations."[95] "Authority will be able to render a just homage to reason without compromising itself, and to defend itself with the weapons of reasoning."[96] But Constant's most extended argument for the involvement of ministers in the legislature was that it prevented usurpation. Even though he first asserted this as a republican, it was an argument that ultimately made this practice deeply consonant with constitutional monarchy. While constitutional monarchy created a limit to political ambition, a parliamentary government channeled political ambition toward legitimate ends. Together these two practices reduced the greatest threat posed by the legislature – its tendency to become a site for usurpation.

Constant and the Dilemmas of French Parliamentarism

At this point, we can summarize the essentials of Benjamin Constant's constitutional theory. He envisioned a powerful legislative assembly that held executive officials responsible, represented the predominant interests and opinions in the nation, and deliberated over the common good. Ministers would be controlled through their responsibility to the legislature, and Constant ingeniously recognized that this practice would also restrain the other representatives. Because they could enact their agenda by forcing the current ministers from office and acquiring their positions, they would eschew more radical forms of action. Competition in parliament over ministerial office restrained the legislature no less than the executive.

The presence of a constitutional monarch further conditioned representatives not to engage in usurpation. And by virtue of having neither legislative nor executive responsibilities, the monarch was perfectly positioned to serve as a neutral arbiter when the ministry was at odds with a majority of the assembly, or when the assembly clashed with the Chamber of Peers. He could facilitate the assembly's course of action by dismissing

[94] Constant, *Principles of Politics*, 224.   [95] Ibid.   [96] Ibid.

the ministry or appointing new peers, or he could dissolve the assembly and call new elections, to test whether the current parliamentary majority represented public opinion. The king could also dissolve the assembly if there was no clear majority and cabinet instability arose, or, as a last resort, if the assembly was becoming a threat to liberty.

Constant believed that this political framework ensured the exercise of power would always be debated and contested, but without any risk to political stability. "Since the parties are agitating below the sphere in which royalty truly resides," Constant wrote, "political order is no longer in peril. All is full of life in the middle, where there is intense struggle; all is tranquil at the summit."[97] His constitutional theory achieved the values long associated with English parliamentarism; however, it also solved the two enduring dilemmas of parliamentarism. It ended any risk that a hereditary monarch armed with executive powers might scheme to break free of parliamentary control, as Burke had feared of George III. And it overcame the challenge of parliamentary corruption. Since Walpole, writers had argued that without corruption, ministers would be unable to influence parliament on behalf of the Crown or maintain cabinet stability. But in parliamentarism as Constant reconceived it, this argument no longer carried the same weight. On the one hand, the mechanism through which a parliamentary regime contained the assembly was not *ministerial influence* but rather *the struggle over ministerial office*. On the other hand, should cabinet instability arise, the monarch would simply dissolve parliament and call an election, allowing the public to choose between the competing parties. As we will see later in this chapter, Constant viewed *public opinion* as a far better source of stable parliamentary majorities than patronage.

It is difficult to express how influential Constant's theory was. During the Restoration, it was taken up and reiterated by a range of authors, including Simonde de Sismondi, Baron de Vitrolles, Chateaubriand, and Lanjuinais.[98] Under the July Monarchy, as I will show in Chapter 5, it was defended by Duvergier de Hauranne, Odillon Barrot, and Adolphe Thiers.

---

[97] Constant, "Des chambres (VII article) projet de loi sur les journaux," 467.

[98] François-René de Chateaubriand, *La Monarchie selon la Charte* (Paris: 1816); Simonde de Sismondi, *Examen de la constitution Française* (Paris: 1815); Baron de Vitrolles, *Du ministère dans le gouvernement représentatif* (Paris: 1815). As for Lanjuinais, who had given up his earlier opposition to the English parliamentary model, see Jean-Denis Lanjuinais, *Constitutions de la nation française*, in *Oeuvres de J. D. Lanjuinais*, t. 2 (Paris: 1832), 200–289; for a useful account of Constant's theory and its line of influence, see Eulau, "Early Theories of Parliamentarism," 35–44.

The last of these figures, who was also among the founders of the Third Republic, would popularize the phrase that best captured Constant's vision: *le roi règne mais ne gouverne pas* ["The king reigns but does not govern."]. However, Constant's influence extended far beyond France. In Prussia, his conception of constitutional monarchy was adopted by Hegel.[99] In Spain, Belgium, Portugal, Italy, and South America, his ideas found adherents, while in Britain, as I will show in a later chapter, many of the most important liberals of the nineteenth century argued that their nation's constitutional stability and liberty rested on Victoria's role as a neutral monarch.[100] When the Victorian historian and MP Thomas Macaulay wrote that "according to the pure idea of constitutional royalty, the prince reigns, and does not govern; and constitutional royalty, as it now exists in England, comes nearer than in any other country to the pure idea," he was merely echoing Constant.[101]

But other nineteenth-century liberals remained committed to the older version of parliamentarism. They wanted a monarch who was involved in governing and could influence parliament through his ministers. Especially before Victoria, whom "everyone can see" as "the accomplished image of a constitutional sovereign entirely removed from the struggle of parties," to quote Prévost-Paradol, it was inconceivable to many liberals that Constant's neutral monarchy would actually work.[102] That a monarch who did no more than "call to power the leaders of the triumphant majority," and dissolve parliament when "there was reason to believe [the majority] had ceased to represent the general opinion" wouldn't simply be overrun – this was hard to fathom.[103]

The confrontation between these two conceptions of parliamentarism was especially heated in France. While I noted the many liberal authors who adopted Constant's theory, it was rejected by every French monarch. Nor did liberal intellectuals always side with Constant, for many were still drawn to the ideas of Burke and Necker. Foremost among them were the

---

[99] See G. W. F. Hegel, *Elements of the Philosophy of Right*, tr. H. B. Nisbet, ed. Allen Wood (Cambridge: 1991), 323. The connection between Constant's conception of monarchy and Hegel's is noted in Bernard Yack, "The Rationality of Hegel's Concept of Monarchy," *American Political Science Review*, vol. 74, no. 3 (1980), 715.

[100] Constant's wide influence was characteristically noted by Carl Schmitt, *Guardian of the Constitution*, 152. For his influence in Latin America in particular, see O. Carlos Stoetzer, "Benjamin Constant and the Doctrinaire Influence in Hispanic America," *Verfassung und Recht in Übersee/Law and Politics in Africa, Asia and Latin America*, vol. 11, no. 2 (1978), 145–165.

[101] Thomas Macaulay, *The History of England from the Accession of James II to the Present*, vol. 4 (London: 1856), 8.

[102] Lucien Anatole Prévost-Paradol, *La France nouvelle* (Paris: 1868), 123.   [103] Ibid.

Doctrinaires, a political and intellectual circle that emerged in the Restoration and included such figures as François Guizot, Hercule de Serre, Pierre-Paul Royer-Collard, Charles Rémusat, and Joseph Lainé. The Doctrinaires were a powerful force in French politics during the early Restoration, and they would remain influential into the July Monarchy. François Guizot – the Doctrinaires' most brilliant theorist – became the leading French political figure in the 1840s, when he served as foreign minister (1840–1847) and then prime minister (1847–1848).

The Doctrinaires' aim was to defend the more equal society created by the French Revolution, while combatting the radicalism to which it had also given rise.[104] Constant was of course sympathetic to this aim, and he was willing to ally with the Doctrinaires on certain occasions. But his vision of parliamentarism was at odds with theirs. Because they subscribed to the theory of parliamentarism that had been pioneered by Robert Walpole's defenders and developed by Burke and Necker, the Doctrinaires were convinced that the monarch's involvement in parliament was essential. According to Hercule de Serre, "the only means for reconciling the existence of public liberty with the force of government consists in the avowed and regular influence that the monarchical power exercises upon the Chambers."[105] This led the Doctrinaires to support the presence of ministers in parliament. However, it also led them to strongly defend the government's patronage in parliament. When a bill to diminish patronage was placed before the French Chamber of Deputies in 1817, Serre called it an "attack on the royal authority."[106] He declared that blocking administrative employees from the Chamber would make it "impossible for the government to possess the necessary action."[107] Royer-Collard warned that restrictions on functionaries in parliament would sabotage "the cooperation of the Chambers with the government."[108]

The Doctrinaires strongly opposed a neutral constitutional monarch. Royer-Collard wrote that it was "a fundamental and sacred principle that it

[104] This is the theme of most of the scholarship on the Doctrinaires, including Pierre Rosanvallon, *Le moment Guizot* (Paris: 1986); Aurelian Craiutu, *Liberalism under Siege* (Lanham: 2003); Michael Drolet, "Carrying the Banner of the Bourgeoisie," *History of Political Thought*, vol. 32, no. 4 (2011), 645–690.

[105] Hercule de Serre, "Discussion de project de loi sur les élections," in *Archives parlementaires*, ser. 2, t. 16 (Paris: 1869), 239.

[106] Hercule de Serre, "Suite de la discussion du projet de loi relatif à l'organisation des colléges électoraux," in *Archives parlementaires*, ser. 2, t. 18 (Paris: 1870), 90.

[107] Ibid.

[108] Pierre-Paul Royer-Collard, "Suite de la discussion du projet de loi relatif à l'organisation des colléges électoraux," in *Archives parlementaires*, ser. 2, t. 18, 92.

is the king who governs."[109] Guizot was equally appalled by Constant's theory. He argued the idea of a king for whom "the danger and responsibility of affairs were unsuited to his imperturbable dignity" was reminiscent of (so-called) Asiatic despotism.[110] Guizot also denied that this state of affairs obtained in England, or that it was "the inevitable consequence" that "must necessarily result" from the responsibility of ministers to parliament.[111] Guizot contended that Constant had conflated the king's "inviolability" with "infallibility."[112] All inviolability meant was the permanence of the king's position. It did not require that he never be opposed or that ministers be independent of him.

While the Doctrinaires favored the responsibility of ministers to parliament, they did so less categorically than Constant, who insisted that "the minister ... loses his post, if he finds himself in the minority."[113] The Doctrinaires recognized the need for parliamentary control over the government, but they also thought that ministers were in the assembly to influence it on behalf of the king, who needed some latitude to select the right individuals for this task. If "the government will be at the discretion of the majority of the Chamber," then how was France not a republic, Royer-Collard asked?[114] The Doctrinaires thus ended up with no stable position on the responsibility of ministers to parliament, and Guizot became particularly infamous for his flip-flops on this issue (for he seemed to want strict parliamentary control over ministers only when he was out of office). In 1821, he argued that "to contest whether the chambers should have a decisive influence over the formation of the ministry" or to "demand that the ministers be strong without the support of the chambers, is to refuse representative government."[115] Yet a mere five years earlier, he had explicitly written that "it is not the Chambers which make and unmake ministers."[116]

Despite the Doctrinaires' equivocations, their ideal was a ministry that possessed the support of parliament. Like Burke and Necker, they viewed this as a crucial source of constitutional harmony. "A homogenous cabinet, composed of men who were permeated with the same ideas concerning internal and external politics, and capable ... of rallying in the Chambers a

---

[109] Pierre-Paul Royer-Collard, *La vie politique de M. Royer-Collard: ses discours et ses écrits*, ed. Prosper de Barante, vol. 1 (Paris: 1861), 293.

[110] François Guizot, *Du gouvernement représentatif et de l'état actuel de la France* (Paris: 1816), 34.

[111] Ibid., 35.   [112] Ibid.   [113] Constant, *Principles of Politics,* 225.

[114] Royer-Collard, *La vie politique de M. Royer-Collard*, vol. 1, 217.

[115] François Guizot, *Du gouvernement de la France depuis la restauration, et du ministère actuel* (Paris: 1820), 284.

[116] Guizot, *Du gouvernement représentatif,* 30.

majority devoted to these ideas, and of establishing a true and lasting accord between the king and that majority": Guizot called this "the premier end" of representative government and claimed it had always been his lifelong political goal.[117] Such a cabinet would possess the unified authority to steer France through the hazards of postrevolutionary politics. However, its authority would be entirely compatible with liberty, as it would be challenged in parliament by an organized opposition and subject to the test of "public discussion."[118]

Constant was elected to the Chamber of Deputies in 1817, when the Doctrinaires were at the height of their influence, and he remained active in French parliamentary politics until his death in 1830.[119] Against the Doctrinaires, he maintained steadfastly that a neutral constitutional monarchy was "the only basis, the indispensable basis" for constitutional government.[120] Rejecting this, he warned, would "bring down the whole constitutional edifice."[121] Just as he had argued that an English monarch's separation from the executive power was inherently required by the responsibility of ministers to Parliament, he contended this was no less true of the French constitutional charter of 1814, which made "the King inviolable and the ministers responsible."[122] A strict distinction "between royal authority and ministerial authority" necessarily followed.[123]

The most important context in which Constant defended his constitutional theory was the debate over the freedom of the press – the most extensive political battle he was involved in during the Restoration. In the aftermath of Napoleon's stunning return from Elba, restrictions on the press were put in place to shore up the fragile regime – along with a number of other "laws of exception."[124] These laws were defended by the Doctrinaires as necessary for stability. However, Constant categorically opposed them.[125]

[117] François Guizot, *Mémoires pour servir à l'histoire de mon temps*, t. 8 (Paris: 1867), 9–10.

[118] François Guizot, "Présentation et discussion du projet de loi relatif à la réélection des Députés promus à des fonctions publiques salariées," in *Histoire parlementaire de France, recueil complet des discours prononcés dans les Chambres de 1819 à 1848*, t. 1 (Paris: 1863), 46.

[119] For discussions of Constant in parliament, see Vincent, *Benjamin Constant and the Birth of French Liberalism*, 197–201; especially Robert Alexander, "Benjamin Constant as a Second Restoration Politician," in *The Cambridge Companion to Constant*, ed. Helena Rosenblatt (Cambridge: 2009), 146–170.

[120] Constant, "Questions sur la législation actuelle de la presse en France-IV," 694.   [121] Ibid.

[122] Ibid., 693.   [123] Ibid.

[124] For a discussion of this debate and Constant's involvement, see Lucien Jaume, *L'Individu effacé ou le paradoxe du libéralisme français* (Paris: 1997), 407–444.

[125] Ibid., 413–418. For another broad survey of the debate over the freedom of the press during the early Restoration, see Jeremy Jennings, "A Note on Freedom of the Press in Restoration France," *Journal of Modern Italian Studies*, vol. 17, no. 5 (2012), 568–573.

Denying that there was a trade-off between individual liberty and stability, he called a free press the "flame of popular government."[126] He also posited a direct connection between the freedom of the press and a neutral constitutional monarch.

The reason for this connection was as follows. If the king was involved in governing, then to attack the government was to criticize the king, who was inviolable and beyond reproach. "Criticism of laws" would "be forbidden, as showing a lack of respect for ... the King," Constant warned, and "the criticism of proposals for laws, the opposition to these proposals in the Chamber, their discussion in journals or in pamphlets must be equally forbidden ... if one perceives the Monarch where one should only see ministers."[127] Without a neutral monarch, all liberty of political expression was threatened. While Guizot had insisted that "inviolability" was not the same as "infallibility," Constant predicted that in practice the two would be conflated. Only when "laws, proposals for laws, acts of government, measures of administration" were perceived to "appertain to the ministry" alone, could they freely "be criticized" by the ministry's opponents.[128]

The other important issue on which Constant opposed the Doctrinaires was patronage. The bureaucracy that France inherited in 1814 from Napoleon contained 250,000 positions, nearly all appointed by ministers in parliament, while at no point during the Restoration or July Monarchy were more than 250,000 individuals eligible to vote in parliamentary elections.[129] This created extraordinary potential for corruption. Conceivably, every French voter could be an employee of the ministry in power, and many were given jobs or promised government favors in exchange for their votes.[130] Ministers made use of patronage to win over representatives as well as voters. Constant calculated in 1818 that one-third of the

---

[126] Constant, "Questions sur la législation actuelle de la presse en France-IV," 695.   [127] Ibid.
[128] Ibid., 696.
[129] This figure is taken from H. A. C. Collingham, *The July Monarchy: A Political History of France, 1830–1848*, ed. R. S. Alexander (New York: 1988), 71.
[130] One of the most detailed contemporary analyses of the way ministers in French parliamentary politics used the administrative powers at their disposal to influence elections was made by Gustave Beaumont – Tocqueville's friend and close intellectual collaborator. See Gustave Beaumont, *De l'Intervention du pouvoir dans les élections* (Paris: 1843). For more recent scholarly analyses of electoral and legislative patronage during this period, see Bernard Silberman, *Cages of Reason: The Rise of the Rational State in France, Japan, the United States and Great Britain* (Chicago: 1993), 120–129; Louis Girard, "La réélection des députés promus à des fonctions publiques, 1828–1831," in *La France au XIX siècle: Mélanges offerts à Charles Hippolyte Pouthas* (Paris: 1973), 227–244; Francois Julien-Laferrière, *Députés fonctionnaires sous la monarchie de Juillet* (Paris: 1970); Paul Bastid, *Les institutions politiques de la monarchie parlementaire française (1814–1848)* (Paris: 1954), 232–236, 265–267.

Chamber of Deputies was employed in a government position.[131] By 1848, it would be two-thirds of the Chamber.[132]

In Constant's writings, there is a fascinating parallel between censorship and patronage, as both were means through which a government could avoid having its power openly contested. Through censorship, ministers could prohibit written opposition, whereas through patronage, they could use the force of personal interest to prevent representatives from challenging them in parliament. If a ministry "purports to place, by fear or ruse, on the benches of the national assembly, its own men, named by it, paid by it, revocable by it; if it wishes that the employees of the government are at the same time the authorized representatives of the people," Constant warned that there would no longer be real debate.[133] Parliament would become "the theatre of a long monologue, divided between demands and responses, but recited in a choir of the same voices."[134] Whereas censorship struck at debate and discourse in the broader public, patronage prevented a "public conversation" from emerging in parliament.[135]

Constant believed that because parliamentary representatives were "the surveillors, the controllers of ministers," those "ministers . . . are of all individuals those who should be left the least influence over the nomination of the men who are to surveil and control them."[136] He feared that as a result of the growing numbers of functionaries in parliament, the "assembly . . . would not be a representative body, it would be a council of state" and incapable of holding the government responsible.[137] But at other moments, Constant made the opposite argument. He warned that patronage led not to an assembly dominated by ministers but rather to no stable ministry at all. This was a major dilemma in France, where five different prime ministers held power between 1815 and 1821.[138] Whereas Walpole had argued that

---

[131] Constant, "Annales de la session de 1817 à 1818," 190.

[132] The figure is taken from Silberman, *Cages of Reason*, 123.

[133] Benjamin Constant, "Seconde lettre de M. Benjamin Constant à M. Charles Durand," in *Oeuvres complètes*, t. 11, 378.

[134] Ibid.   [135] Constant, "Annales de la session de 1817 à 1818," 188.

[136] Benjamin Constant, "Pressions électorales exercées en province," in *Recueil d'articles 1820–1824*, ed. Éphraïm Harpaz (Geneva: 1981), 197.

[137] Benjamin Constant, "Des élections de 1818," in *Oeuvres complètes*, t. 11, 816.

[138] Richelieu's first ministry lasted the longest of these five, approximately three years, but it underwent substantial internal revolutions the entire time. In the first year alone, over half the men holding positions changed. See Léon Muel, *Gouvernements, ministères et constitutions de la France depuis cent ans: Précis historique des révolutions, des crises ministérielles et gouvernementales, et des changements de constitutions de la France depuis 1789 jusqu'en 1890* (Paris: 1891), 128–129. For an account of the parliamentary politics of this period, see Robert Alexander, *Re-writing the French Revolutionary Tradition* (Cambridge: 2003), 81–94.

patronage was essential for preventing cabinet instability, Constant argued the opposite: patronage was the most important source *of* cabinet instability. In a nation with as many competing factions and ambitious individuals as France, it was impossible to create a stable parliamentary majority through distributing offices. "In making yourself agreeable to parties which want places, you turn away all the others who also want places," he wrote, "sacrificing the majority which murmurs for places, to the minority which demands them."[139]

Most importantly, ministers would only "half-satisfy" representatives with the jobs they were giving them.[140] As soon as those representatives began demanding better jobs, ministers were forced into an impossible dance, "jumping from one minority to the other . . . dividing, subdividing, and exciting the parties . . . using vengeance to push exasperated factions to vote in its direction."[141] Through this strategy, Constant argued, "a ministry can create a majority that will last for a few months."[142] Put simply, negotiations over patronage were a poor substitute for real parliamentary deliberation. Whereas deliberation revealed a common interest shared by different factions, patronage was a zero-sum game in which winning over one faction alienated the others.

To combat patronage, Constant called for a prohibition on functionaries serving in the Chamber of Deputies. "It is said that in the Chamber of Deputies there are one hundred twenty or one hundred thirty public functionaries dependent on the ministry for their salaries, their fears, their hopes," he wrote, and he demanded that this number be reduced twentyfold.[143] With the exception of cabinet ministers, he argued that government employees should not sit in parliament.[144]

Constant was also one of the leaders of a growing liberal opposition party, the Indépendants, which he believed capable of governing without patronage. The Indépendants program was simply the principles of Constant's political thought. They defended "constitutional monarchy, because it is constitutional," he wrote, and "respect the hereditary transmission of the throne because this transmission protects the calm of the people from the struggle of factions."[145] They were committed to "the

---

[139] Benjamin Constant, "D'une assertion de M. Bailleul dans sa brochure contre M. de Chateaubriand," in *Oeuvres complètes*, t. 11, 244.

[140] Ibid.   [141] Ibid.   [142] Constant, "Annales de la session," 189.

[143] Ibid., 190. Constant maintained that the proportion of executive officers sitting in the legislature should never exceed 1 in 100 representatives. In practice, this meant that none but the ministers should be allowed to serve. See Constant, "Des élections de 1818," 814.

[144] Constant, "Des élections de 1818," 814.

[145] Benjamin Constant, "Des élections prochaines," in *Oeuvres complètes*, t. 10, vol. 2, 777.

responsibility of ministers," and to "the liberty of the press and news-papers, so that each individual can argue without seeing his arguments mutilated by the censure."[146] Finally, they were opposed to the "meetings" and "negotiations" and "transactions" over patronage that dominated French parliamentary life.[147] They refused to use patronage as a means of acquiring power.[148]

Constant supported the Indépendants out of disgust with the centrist ministries that governed between 1815 and 1821, and which, frequently supported by the Doctrinaires, had instituted censorship and governed through corruption. But he also believed that by achieving power, the Indépendants would transform the very character of French politics. They would demonstrate that "no party, no association, no gathering of men, in power or out of power, which does not rally around national principles, will attract any popular assent," and that the way for a minority party to become the majority was to win the nation over to its principles.[149] A struggle between competing parties of principle would unfold in the Chamber and before the nation, and while the party that had public opinion on its side would govern, the opposition would immediately make a new appeal to "the mass of the nation," as "popular favor" was its only path out of "minority status"[150] Through this principled struggle, ministries would attain sufficient political support to stay in office for an extended period, even as their actions were perpetually challenged by an opposition. As political parties came to base their strength in principle and public opinion, patronage would fade in importance. If the governing party did turn to patronage, that merely signified it was losing popular support – and would soon be unseated by its opponents.

While Burke and de Staël had argued that the function of a political party system was to minimize the corrupting effect of patronage, Constant was considerably more ambitious. He believed that once public opinion became the ultimate arbiter between parties, it was possible to do without patronage entirely. This was essential, not because patronage led directly to the

---

[146] Constant, "Pensées diverses sur les élections," 422. For an account of the liberal opposition that Constant was a part of during the early Restoration, see Alexander, *Re-writing the French Revolutionary Tradition*, 105–134. For a treatment more focused on intellectual currents, see Andrew Jainchill, *Reimagining Politics after the Terror: The Republican Origins of French Liberalism* (Ithaca: 2008), 287–294.

[147] Constant, "D'une assertion de M. Bailleul dans sa brochure contre M. de Chateaubriand," 244.

[148] Ibid.

[149] Benjamin Constant, "De la doctrine politique qui peut réunir les partis en France," in *Oeuvres complètes*, t. 10, vol. 1, 328.

[150] Ibid.

destruction of virtue and liberty – Constant was usually not susceptible to such eighteenth-century Whiggish fears – but rather because it undermined the struggle for power in the legislature that Constant saw as characteristic of parliamentarism. It reduced that struggle to a scramble for places, or, if representatives became reluctant to oppose the ministers who employed them, sapped it of energy. "The representative system is a system of struggle," Constant wrote. "If there is no struggle, the representative system would be the worst of all systems."[151] He opposed patronage so categorically because he believed so strongly in parliamentary politics.

Coda

When Constant died in 1830, his vision of parliamentarism and his ideal of a monarch who reigned but did not govern remained unaccomplished. This was obviously the case in France, where the entire political system had just been toppled following Charles X's refusal to acquiesce to the Chamber of Deputies. But it was also true of Britain. While Constant claimed that his constitutional theory was based on the "facts" of the "English constitution," George IV, who died only months before Constant, was an avowed opponent of Catholic emancipation – hardly recognizable in the role of "neutral power."[152] What Constant had grasped, however, was the historical tendency of English politics. The powers that an English monarch could still easily exercise – above all the powers of dissolution and dismissal – were not suited for governing a nation. To use them toward that end would be an extraordinary gamble. However, these powers *were* suited for making the monarch into an umpire who mediated between the other constitutional actors and facilitated the rule of public opinion. After Victoria came to the throne in 1837, this conception of monarchy would become increasingly widespread in Britain. In the decades following Constant's death, few prominent British liberals would disagree with his account of a parliamentary regime. In France, by contrast, liberal theorists would remain divided over Constant's program. They would also continue to struggle over parliamentary corruption. It was in this context that Alexis de Tocqueville, the most original French liberal author to write in the wake of Constant, worked out his theory of parliamentarism.

[151] Constant, "Annales de la session," 952.
[152] Constant, *Principles of Politics*, 185. Constant in fact notes George IV's refusal to acquiesce on rights for Catholics and somewhat unconvincingly denies that this was at odds with the king's neutrality (ibid., 191–192).

CHAPTER 5

Democracy in America, Parliamentarism in France: Tocqueville's Unconventional Parliamentary Liberalism

Chapters 3 and 4 have shown how European liberals turned to parliamentarism following the French Revolution. But France was not the only nation that rejected parliamentarism in the late eighteenth century. The United States did so as well, and unlike the French Constitutions of 1791 and 1795, the American Constitution proved remarkably durable. By giving the executive power to an elected president, who could claim the same popular legitimation as Congress, America had shown how a system of checks and balances might potentially succeed.

If Montesquieu's *Spirit of the Laws* and the French constitutions of the 1790s were the great alternatives against which classical parliamentarism initially developed, the American Constitution would become its defining antagonist in the middle decades of the nineteenth century. The argument that proponents of parliamentarism would make against the American Constitution would be very different from what we have seen in previous chapters. Their claim was not that the American Constitution provided no effective way to restrain the legislature, as Burke and Constant had argued about the Constitution of 1791, but rather that it failed to secure the supremacy of the legislature over the executive in the first place.

In the following two chapters, I will examine a series of nineteenth-century authors who asked about the relative merits of American constitutionalism and liberal parliamentarism. Chapter 6 will take up John Stuart Mill and his Victorian contemporaries, while this chapter considers Alexis de Tocqueville, a figure who had practically no choice but to compare parliamentarism with the American Constitution. Tocqueville first made his name by traveling to the United States and writing a book called *Democracy in America*. However, he then went on to spend nearly 15 years in French parliamentary politics. Despite his admiration for American political life, the contention of this chapter is that he preferred parliamentarism for European states, and I will show that he developed a highly original theory of parliamentarism, which cannot be reduced either to Constant's influential account or to that of the Doctrinaires.

This chapter will begin with an examination of *Democracy in America*. I will consider Tocqueville's attraction to American institutions as well as his reasons for thinking they could not be exported to a European nation like France. The rest of the chapter will consider Tocqueville's parliamentary career, a dimension of his life that has been neglected by scholars. Tocqueville first ran for the French Chamber of Deputies, unsuccessfully, in 1837. However, he was triumphant two years later and served in the Chamber until the fall of the July Monarchy in 1848. Following the 1848 Revolution, he was again elected to the legislature of the Second Republic. He served briefly as minister of foreign affairs and was on the commission that drafted the Second Republic's constitution. He also wrote a brilliant memoir (*Souvenirs*) that recounted his political activities and castigated the corruption of his fellow representatives. Examining Tocqueville's political career is essential if we wish to understand how he characterized parliamentarism and why he preferred it for France.

Taming the American Legislature

In *Democracy in America*, Tocqueville analyzed a political regime very different from parliamentarism. He noted that not only a constitutional monarchy but also a parliamentary government was missing in the United States. "The President has no entry into Congress," he wrote, "his ministers are excluded as he is, and it is only by indirect pathways that he makes his influence and his opinion penetrate this great body."[1] However, Tocqueville's analysis of the American political system shared a common preoccupation with the earlier French advocates of parliamentarism. Like them, he viewed the legislature as the indispensable institution for representing the people in modern states, even as he also feared it was prone to despotism. Tocqueville viewed the American state legislatures as particularly dangerous. "In America, the legislature of each state is faced by no power capable of resisting it," he lamented.[2] "Nothing can stop it in its tracks, neither privileges, nor local immunity, nor personal influence, not even the authority of reason, for it represents the majority that claims to be the only instrument of reason."[3] An American state legislature "has no limit to its action other than its own will."[4]

---

[1] Alexis de Tocqueville, *Democracy in America*, vol. 1, ed. Eduardo Nolla, tr. James Schleifer (Indianapolis: 2012), 206.
[2] Ibid., 149.   [3] Ibid., 149–150.   [4] Ibid., 150.

What gave legislative assemblies such power was their claim to directly represent the popular majority. "The legislature is, of all political powers, the one which most willingly obeys the majority," Tocqueville wrote.[5] His most well-known passages about the tyranny of the majority depict it as a form of social coercion. However, throughout the first volume of *Democracy in America*, majority tyranny is constantly associated with an overreaching legislature. In "the United States," Tocqueville argued, "the omnipotence of the majority ... favors the legal despotism of the legislator."[6] Perhaps the most telling instance of this comes in the conclusion to his famous chapter, "Of the Omnipotence of the Majority in the United States and Its Effects," which uses passages from Jefferson and Madison to illustrate the tyranny of the majority. Remarkably, the passage that Tocqueville takes from Jefferson does not appear to have anything to do with the majority at all and is simply about the danger of an unchecked legislature. It reads, "the executive power, in our government, is not the only, and perhaps not the principal object of my concern, the tyranny of legislators is now and will be for many years to come the most formidable danger."[7] Tocqueville associated the tyranny of the majority with "the tyranny of legislators" to such a degree that he could literally refer to them interchangeably.

Unlike Constant, Tocqueville feared the despotism of an electoral majority rather than usurpation by a legislative minority, but he agreed with Constant that the legislature's tendency to become omnipotent derived from its claim to represent the people. In the United States, he wrote, "sovereign power is handed over to the authority that makes the laws. That authority can rapidly and irresistibly abandon itself to each of its desires."[8] Tocqueville saw a profound parallel in this regard between the American state legislatures and the legislative assemblies of the French Revolution.[9] But he contended that the American federal Constitution was different. While the American founders could not "destroy the inclination that leads legislative assemblies to take hold of government," Tocqueville wrote, "they have made this inclination less irresistible."[10] They had managed to effectively contain the legislature through a system of checks and balances.

---

[5] Alexis de Tocqueville, *Democracy in America*, vol. 2, ed. Eduardo Nolla, tr. James Schleifer (Indianapolis: 2012), 403.
[6] Ibid., 416.   [7] Ibid., 426.   [8] Ibid., 407.   [9] Ibid., 408.
[10] Tocqueville, *Democracy in America*, vol. 1., 202.

Tocqueville viewed the American presidency as an especially crucial check on the legislature. He argued that the president "executes the constitutional desires of the legislatures with more skill and sagacity than they would be able to do themselves," and "is a barrier against the abuse of their power."[11] Put simply, the president "prevents their omnipotence from degenerating into tyranny," and Tocqueville claimed that the failure of the state constitutions to include a similarly strong executive contributed to their legislatures' despotic tendencies.[12] In contrast with authors such as Necker, Guizot, and Constant – who attributed the destruction of the Constitution of 1791 to Louis XVI's use of his veto – Tocqueville maintained that the president's most important regular check against Congress lay in his veto power.[13] "There can only be an unequal struggle," he wrote,

> between the President and the legislature, since the latter, by persevering in its intentions, always has the power to overcome the resistance that opposes it. But the qualified veto at least forces it to retrace its steps; it forces the legislature to consider the question again; and this time, it can no longer decide except with a two-thirds majority of those voting.[14]

Yet while Tocqueville viewed the American presidency as an effective check on Congress, he made clear even in *Democracy in America* that this institution came with profound drawbacks and that it was neither possible nor desirable to imitate American presidentialism in France. He would instead recommend the same framework as the other authors I have examined: a powerful representative assembly that was moderated through constitutional monarchy and the presence of responsible ministers in the assembly. Tocqueville did not argue – as John Stuart Mill and Walter Bagehot later would – that parliamentarism was intrinsically superior to the American Constitution, but he never claimed it was inferior either. Tocqueville was not interested in systematically ranking different constitutional arrangements, but when it came to the specific question of how to establish liberty in a European nation like France, he could not escape, and indeed embraced, the very same logic as all the other figures in this book.

Tocqueville's Defense of Parliamentarism

Tocqueville's lifelong political goal was to construct an enduring liberal regime in France. He believed the crucial institution for achieving this was

---

[11] Ibid., 201.   [12] Ibid., 201, 404.   [13] Ibid., 203.   [14] Ibid.

constitutional monarchy. "A Republic is an ill-balanced form of government, promising more freedom and giving less than a constitutional
monarchy," he wrote.[15] Tocqueville argued that one of the most important
advantages of constitutional monarchy was that it prevented the highest
position in the state from becoming the object of political struggle – a view
he shared with Benjamin Constant.[16] But unlike Constant, Tocqueville
never advocated a *neutral* monarch who was without executive powers. To
the contrary, he defended constitutional monarchy largely because it made
possible a stronger executive. "To want the representative of the State to be
simultaneously armed with great power and elected is, to my mind, to
express two contradictory desires," he declared.[17] "To make hereditary
royalty change to a state of elected power ... its sphere of action must be
contracted in advance; its prerogatives gradually reduced."[18] While the
United States could make do with an elected president because of its
international isolation and relative internal stability, this was not an option
in continental Europe.[19] "The more precarious and perilous the position
of a people, the more the need for consistency and stability makes itself felt
in the direction of foreign affairs," Tocqueville argued, "and the more
dangerous the system of election of the head of State becomes."[20] Because
of France's "situation ... among the peoples of Europe," monarchy was
the only option.[21]

Tocqueville believed that for monarchy not to be incompatible with
liberty, it was absolutely essential that the monarch be under the control of
an even more powerful representative assembly, which prevented him from
exercising power arbitrarily. For Tocqueville, the "subordination" of the
monarch to the legislature was one of the two essential conditions that was
required for a liberal political order to emerge in France – the other being a
greater degree of local self-government.[22]

To enable legislative control over the monarch, Tocqueville strongly
recommended a parliamentary government. He believed that where "the
head of executive power is irresponsible," as was the case in a hereditary
monarchy, there was no other option but for "ministers to be placed under
the eyes, in the heart, and under the hand even, of the legislative

---

[15] Alexis de Tocqueville, *Recollections: The French Revolution of 1848*, ed. J. P. Mayer (New Brunswick: 1987), 200–201.
[16] Tocqueville, *Democracy in America*, vol. 1, 211–217.   [17] Ibid., 212.   [18] Ibid.
[19] Ibid., 217–218.   [20] Ibid.   [21] Ibid., 218.
[22] Alexis de Tocqueville to Eugène Stoffels (October 5, 1836), in *Lettres choisies; Souvenirs: 1814–1859*, ed. Françoise Mélonio and Laurence Guellec (Gallimard: 2003), 865.

assembly."[23] The presence of ministers in parliament and their responsibility to parliament were crucial bulwarks against an arbitrary executive. However, Tocqueville recognized that these practices also enabled the executive to influence parliament, for they meant that "the King is represented, within the Chambers, by a certain number of agents who set forth his views, uphold his opinions and make his maxims of government prevail."[24] In a parliamentary government, the calibration of executive and legislative power became a process that was worked out within parliament itself: the king made use of his ministers to influence parliament's agenda, while parliament struggled to control their decisions.[25]

As Tocqueville emphasized in the first volume of *Democracy in America*, one major dilemma with this arrangement was cabinet instability. Because ministers could not govern without the support of the legislature, both powers had to be in agreement for the state to function. "It is an established axiom in Europe that a constitutional king cannot govern when the opinion of the legislative chambers is not in agreement with his."[26] The king "needs the chambers," and "the chambers need him," Tocqueville wrote; "they are two powers that cannot live without each other."[27] "The gears of government stop at the moment when there is discord between them."[28] Indeed, between 1830–1835, when Tocqueville researched and wrote the first volume of *Democracy in America*, such "discord" was at an all-time high in French politics. No less than 12 different prime ministers held office during the 1830s.[29] But despite the persistent threat of cabinet instability, Tocqueville thought that this arrangement offered the best hope for achieving liberty and stability in France. It enabled the "energetic central government" that he associated with monarchy, even as it also ensured "that this central power has a clearly delineated sphere . . . and, that it is forever subordinated,

---

[23] Alexis de Tocqueville, "Discours sur l'élection du président de la république," in *Oeuvres complètes*, t.3, vol. 3, ed. André Jardin (Paris: 1990), 213.

[24] Tocqueville, *Democracy in America*, vol. 1, 206.

[25] Tocqueville was convinced that this system worked best with a monarch who generally "took his ministers from the majority, and his policies from his ministers," like a "King of England." The only monarch who came close to practicing this in France, he believed, was Louis XVIII. See Alexis Tocqueville and Nassau William Senior, *Correspondence & Conversations of Alexis de Tocqueville with Nassau William Senior from 1834 to 1859*, vol. 1, ed. M. C. M. Simpson (London: 1872), 243.

[26] Tocqueville, *Democracy in America*, vol. 1, 210.   [27] Ibid.   [28] Ibid.

[29] For an analysis of conflicts between ministries and parliaments in nineteenth-century France, see Laquièze, *Les origines du régime parlementaire en France*, 354–359. For accounts of the parliamentary instability and intrigue during the July Monarchy in particular, see Collingham, *The July Monarchy*, 200–219; Robert Koepke, "The Failure of Parliamentary Government in France, 1840–1848," *European Studies Review*, vol. 9 (1979), 433–455.

in its tendencies, to public opinion, and to the legislative power that represents public opinion."[30]

Tocqueville viewed American presidentialism as particularly unsuitable for France. Although the American president was less powerful than a French monarch, he was also less controlled by the legislature, as he and his ministers were not strictly responsible to Congress. Were such a figure to have the extraordinary powers of the centralized French state at his disposal, Tocqueville predicted that one of two things would happen. Either the president would become a danger to liberty, or, to avoid that situation, he would be stripped of his powers and independence – leading to an executive who could neither serve as a moderating influence on the legislature nor provide the leadership that France needed in international affairs.[31] Constitutional monarchy and parliamentary government were the solution to this dilemma. By combining a king who was permanent and inviolable with ministers who were beholden to parliament, this arrangement created an executive that was completely under parliamentary supervision but could still provide the steady government France needed.

Tocqueville's reluctance to bring American presidentialism to France was especially apparent in the aftermath of the 1848 Revolution. He was on the commission that drafted the Constitution of France's Second Republic, and, despite misgivings, he defended it before the National Assembly.[32] Revealingly, he did not push for an executive modeled on the United States. He accepted a much weaker president with no veto power, while insisting that the president's ministers be drawn from and responsible to the legislature. Why did Tocqueville defend what he himself called an "unheard of" arrangement – a republic where the popularly elected president's cabinet sat in parliament?[33] The reason was the

---

[30] Tocqueville to Stoffels (October 5, 1836), 865.

[31] Like Constant and de Staël, Tocqueville viewed the Constitution of 1795 as an example of a constitution that had weakened the French executive to the point where it was no longer an immediate threat to liberty but at the price of depriving it of all strength and independence. See Alexis de Tocqueville, "France before the Consulate," in *Memoirs, Letters, and Remains of Alexis de Tocqueville*, tr. anon (London: 1861), 263–275.

[32] For one of the few analyses of Tocqueville's thinking about the executive during this period see Lucien Jaume, "Tocqueville et le problème du pouvoir exécutif en 1848," *Revue française de science politique*, vol. 41, no. 6 (1991), 739–755.

[33] Tocqueville, "Discours sur l'élection du président de la république," 213. Jaume is right to note that the constitution does not precisely specify that ministers *must* be members of the Assembly or create a *formal* process of ministerial responsibility, which Tocqueville seems to suggest (Jaume, "Tocqueville et le problème du pouvoir exécutif en 1848," 750–752). But given that the Charters of 1830 and 1814 also did not include such provisions, Tocqueville was not wrong to assume that this same form of politics would develop under the Second Republic.

overriding necessity "to monitor the executive power in its principal acts."[34] The "immense clientele" that the French president had at his disposal through his control over the bureaucracy and military made it too dangerous for his ministers not to be in the legislature and responsible to it for their every action.[35] "To have the president elected by the people, without danger to the Republic," Tocqueville declared, "the sphere of his prerogatives must be strictly curtailed."[36]

In the aftermath of the 1848 Revolution, Tocqueville was also concerned about the power of the National Assembly – a unicameral legislative body elected by universal male suffrage – and in a private note from the period he reiterated his position from *Democracy in America* that "the chronic malady of democracies" was "the mobility, capriciousness and tyranny of legislative power."[37] However, the first constitutional necessity was to ensure control over the executive, even if that meant expanding the powers of the legislature beyond what Tocqueville would have wished. This dilemma goes a long way toward explaining Tocqueville's preference for constitutional monarchy. Without that institution, there was no obvious way to institute a legislature that controlled the executive without also making the legislature itself too powerful. The American constitutional model led to an executive that was insufficiently responsible, and by introducing parliamentarism, one brought it under legislative supervision. But the risk then became that the legislature itself would become omnipotent. In that context, making the executive *permanent* and *hereditary* was a way to strengthen its position vis-à-vis the legislature without diminishing legislative control over the executive. Put simply, France was better off instituting a parliamentary republic than a republic modeled on the United States, but parliamentarism with constitutional monarchy was superior to a parliamentary republic.

Tocqueville's position in 1848 can be further elucidated through a comparison with Édouard Laboulaye. A major French intellectual, one of the founders of the Third Republic, and the man responsible for the Statue of Liberty, Laboulaye did most of his important political writing during the Second Empire.[38] He was always a great admirer of

---

[34] Alexis de Tocqueville, "Notes," in *Oeuvres complètes*, t. 3, vol. 3, 208. See also Alexis de Tocqueville, "L'élaboration de projet constitution," in *Oeuvres complètes*, t. 3, vol. 3, 106–107.

[35] Alexis de Tocqueville, "Réflexions sur les pouvoirs du président et de l'assemblée," *Oeuvres complètes*, t. 3, vol. 3, 224–225.

[36] Tocqueville, *Recollections*, 177.   [37] Tocqueville, "Notes," 208.

[38] I am indebted to the discussion of Laboulaye in Stephen Sawyer, *Demos Assembled: Democracy and the International Origins of the Modern States, 1840–1880* (Chicago: 2018), 76–98.

Tocqueville. However, in an important essay written in July 1848, he rejected the Tocquevillian argument for a parliamentary republic.[39] Laboulaye recognized that in a constitutional monarchy, parliamentary government was indispensable. But he argued that in a republic, where the head of state was an accountable elected official, it was unnecessary. The "responsibility of the president authorizes more extended prerogatives," he wrote, and a "greater liberty" for executive action.[40] Moreover, the most important task facing a republic was precisely to augment the executive, so it could be equal to the legislature. Laboulaye thus wanted France in 1848 to directly imitate the American Constitution.[41] He argued that by separating cabinet ministers from the legislature, France would remove a common source of corruption and ensure "the perfect independence of the president, who otherwise would be dominated by ministers commonly chosen by the majority of the assembly."[42] As I have shown, Tocqueville strongly rejected this line of thinking. He believed that absent the peculiar conditions of the United States – its lack of centralization, its distance from European powers – an independent executive posed a real threat to liberty. The key to a durable French republic was parliamentarism.

The only part of the American Constitution that Tocqueville saw as plausibly imitable in France was the Senate. This was an institution he doubly admired, for he was a strong defender of a bicameral legislature and a great believer in indirect election. Tocqueville argued that because they were elected indirectly, senators "represent exactly the governing majority of the nation; but they represent only the elevated thoughts that circulate in its midst, the generous instincts that animate it, and not the small passions that often trouble it and the vices that dishonor it."[43] As I noted earlier in this book, the assemblies of the French Revolutionary period were elected like the members of the American Senate: electors did not

---

[39] See Édouard Laboulaye, "Alexis de Tocqueville," in *L'état et ses limites suivi d'essais politiques* (Paris: 1886), 138–202.

[40] Édouard Laboulaye, *Considérations sur la Constitution* (Paris: 1848), 91.

[41] Laboulaye's belief that absent constitutional monarchy, it was essential to have an American-style republic, was long-lasting. See Édouard Laboulaye, *Questions constitutionnelles* (Paris: 1872), ii–viii. Ironically, however, Laboulaye would go on to deliver several historic speeches affirming the Third Republic – which deviated fundamentally from the American institutions he had earlier supported. See, for instance, Édouard Laboulaye, "Rapport fait, au nom de la commission des lois constitutionnelles (a) chargée d'examiner le projet de loi organique sur les rapports des pouvoirs publics," *Journal officiel de la République française* no. 156 (1875), 4160–4162.

[42] Laboulaye, *Considérations sur la Constitution*, 91.

[43] Tocqueville, *Democracy in America*, vol. 1, 321.

directly select the members of the national legislature but instead selected representatives to intermediate assemblies; those intermediate assemblies then decided who would serve in the national assembly. In 1817, France turned away from this model and instituted direct elections to parliament.[44] While this move was defended by Constant and Guizot, Tocqueville's experience in the United States led him to believe it was a mistake.[45] Although he was largely skeptical of imitating the American Constitution in France, he did want to reintroduce a system of indirect election.[46]

In addition to securing the responsibility of the executive, Tocqueville thought that a powerful representative assembly was indispensable for stimulating public political involvement. Like Constant, he was convinced both that debates in parliament could engage the general public and that the key to achieving this was an organized parliamentary opposition. Distinguishing the position of the ministry from that of the opposition, Tocqueville wrote, "the one supports itself by power ... the other by public opinion. Its lever is public favor; its arms in the struggle it sustains are ardent convictions and disinterested passions, which it gives birth to and sustains in the nation."[47] As that last line makes clear, Tocqueville credited a parliamentary opposition with both awakening and sustaining public political commitment. While on the "terrain" of experience and interest, "the opposition can never fail, whatever it does, to be inferior to its adversaries," Tocqueville argued that "its great power always resides in sentiments and in general ideas."[48]

By virtue of not having to defend particular decisions, the opposition could appeal more directly to first principles, elevating national politics into a contest over the general interest. Tocqueville wrote:

---

[44] The intellectual significance of the shift in 1817 is discussed in Rosanvallon, *Le Peuple introuvable*, 43–56, 121; Alan Spitzer, "Restoration Political Theory and the Debate over the Law of the Double Vote," *Journal of Modern History*, vol. 55, no. 1 (1983), 54–70.

[45] See François Guizot, *The History of the Origins of Representative Government in Europe*, tr. Andrew Scoble, ed. Aurelian Craiutu (Indianapolis: 2002), 344–352; Constant, *Principles of Politics*, 201–213. Mill also notably favored direct election of representatives. See John Stuart Mill, *Considerations on Representative Government, Collected Works*, vol. 19, ed. J. M Robson (Toronto: 1977), 482–487.

[46] See Tocqueville, *Democracy in America*, vol. 1, 320–321; Alexis de Tocqueville, "Notes pour un discours," in *Oeuvres complètes*, t. 3, vol. 2, ed. Francois Melonio (Paris: 1985), 211. Indirect election was, however, defended by the reactionary Ultras. Tocqueville's famously conservative family upbringing may have primed him to be more sympathetic to this procedure. See Rosanvallon, *Le Sacre du citoyen*, 271–300.

[47] Alexis de Tocqueville, "Lettres sur la situation intérieure de la France," *Oeuvres complètes*, t. 3, vol. 2, 117.

[48] Ibid., 116.

Although in politics as elsewhere, men appear quite bad when taken one by one, as a group they admire and love political faith, fidelity to party, disinterestedness, righteousness and loyalty. The public brings to the great theatre of the world the passions of the *parterre*. It only applauds what seems to it generous and honourable.[49]

Like his broader case for parliamentarism, this argument was grounded in uniquely European circumstances. France had no developed institutions of local self-government. That extraordinary site of political involvement, public discussion, and civic education simply did not exist as it did in New England. Parliament was France's only hope for constituting a public political realm. Yet Tocqueville did not think that parliamentary politics would lose its value if local self-government were introduced. Local self-government was incapable of creating a meaningful public discussion about problems of *national* significance – which France's revolutionary struggles and situation in Europe rendered unavoidable. Without a vibrant political struggle at the national level, Tocqueville feared that local politics would be reduced to a selfish contest between regional notables, entrenching the narrow materialism that he saw as endemic to France's *petite bourgeoisie*.[50] Only parliamentary politics was capable of inspiring great convictions and sustaining a national culture of political engagement.

Tocqueville in Parliament

While Tocqueville favored parliamentarism for many of the same reasons as other French liberals, the way he conceived of it was highly distinctive. The best way to elucidate his unique understanding of a parliamentary regime is to examine his political career. As I noted at the beginning of the chapter, Tocqueville was elected to the French Chamber of Deputies in 1839, and he remained involved in French politics until the end of the Second Republic. For much of that period, the two dominant factions in French political life

---

[49] Ibid., 117.
[50] This concern about French local politics redounds through Tocqueville's letters and notes from the 1830s and 1840s. See, for instance, Tocqueville's letter to Pierre-Paul Royer-Collard (15 August 1840), *Oeuvres complètes*, t. 11, ed. André Jardin (Paris: 1970), 90; Alexis de Tocqueville, "Discussion de l'adresse," *Oeuvres complètes*, t. 3, vol. 2, 205. Tocqueville's suspicion of French local interests was a major reason he favored a system of indirect elections, as he believed France's current system "divides the realm into an infinite multitude of small pieces," preventing parliament from serving as a space of debate over issues of general significance (ibid.). Jennifer Pitts has also shown that a major reason why Tocqueville was desperate for France to compete with England as a colonial power was because he thought that the resulting nationalist sentiments would awaken the French from their materialist and individualist slumber. See Pitts, *A Turn to Empire*, 189–230.

represented approaches to parliamentarism that this book has already explored. By situating Tocqueville between them, it is possible to understand his distinctive conception of a parliamentary regime.

Between 1840 and 1848, the leading figure in French parliamentary politics was François Guizot, who held the position of foreign minister before becoming prime minister. Guizot was a key member of the Doctrinaires, the intellectual group I explored in the last chapter. While the Doctrinaires defended the more equal society created by the French Revolution, I argued that their conception of parliamentarism was similar to that of Walpole, Burke, and Necker, and that they were inclined to favor patronage. By contrast, the liberal opposition to Guizot was led by disciples of Benjamin Constant. The most important opposition leader, Adolphe Thiers, was also France's most influential advocate of a neutral constitutional monarch. It was Thiers who popularized the phrase "the king reigns but does not govern" (*le roi règne mais ne gouverne pas*). He called for a regime in which "the king reigns, the ministry governs, the chambers judge."[51]

Thiers argued that this constitutional framework was the only option for a European nation seeking to be free, and he predicted that it would be adopted "in Spain, in Italy, in Germany, in Russia."[52] Like Constant, Thiers believed that it was already coming into being in France and England.[53] While he recognized that the United States offered an alternative constitutional model, he made many of the same arguments against it as Tocqueville did. He contended that "France's geographic and military situation," along with "the disturbances attached to the election of a president" and "the need for a degree of stability within the continual movement of a representative regime," all cried out for monarchy. But for monarchy to be compatible with "liberty" and "the necessity for the nation to govern itself," it was necessary not only that the king's ministers be responsible to a powerful legislative body – as Tocqueville argued – but also that those ministers be wholly autonomous of the monarch. "The king does not administer or govern; he reigns," Thiers wrote: *le roi n'administre pas, ne gouverne pas: il règne.*[54] He led one of the two liberal parliamentary

---

[51] See Adolphe Thiers, "Le roi règne mais ne gouverne pas," included as an appendix in de Hauranne, *De la réforme parlementaire et de la réforme électorale*, 277. For one of the few discussions of Thiers as a political thinker, see Alain Laquièze, "Adolphe Thiers, théoricien du régime parlementaire. Ses articles dans *Le National* en 1830," *Revue française d'histoire des idées politiques*, vol. 5 (1997), 59–88.

[52] Thiers, "Le roi règne mais ne gouverne pas," 272.   [53] Ibid., 278.

[54] Ibid., 274. Stephen Sawyner notes that in the aftermath of the 1848 revolution, Thiers would question his support for monarchy – and wonder whether the American republic might be an apt model for France (*Demos Assembled*, 102).

factions opposed to Guizot; however, the leader of the other, Odillon Barrot, was also a long-standing proponent of this configuration.[55] So was Duvergier de Haurrane – the most prominent intellectual in the liberal parliamentary opposition other than Tocqueville. According to de Haurranne, it was Constant "more than anyone else" who "had contributed to our constitutional education."[56]

These figures were not *merely* disciples of Constant. In certain respects, they were more radical than he was, such as in their desire to expand the limited French suffrage to include the working class.[57] They also had a more English orientation than Constant. The 1830 Revolution was frequently taken to be parallel to 1688, which meant that the history of England in the eighteenth century offered a powerful model for nineteenth-century France.[58] One example of this renewed attention to English history was Thiers' preoccupation with parliamentary control over the budget. While Constant did not devote significant attention to this power until the end of his life, for Thiers, there was never any doubt that the legislature's financial powers were what enabled it to supervise the government.[59] The legislature's right to "refus[e] ... the budget," he argued, was "indispensable for completing the prerogatives of the [legislative] majority."[60] Without this crucial power, the legislature could do no more than "disapprove" of the executive's actions.[61] It was the legislature's control over finances that enabled it to comprehensively supervise and control the executive.

The liberal opposition's intense focus on parliamentary corruption was equally telling. Its adherents were convinced that patronage had corrupted

---

[55] See Odillon Barrot, *Mémoires posthumes de Odilon Barrot*, vol. 1 (Paris: 1875), 325.

[56] De Hauranne, *De la réforme parlementaire et de la réforme électorale*, 34–35.

[57] To be clear, however, they did not favor *universal suffrage*. For the debate over the suffrage during this period and the liberal opposition's position in it, see Rosanvallon, *Le sacre du citoyen*, 350–387.

[58] For the debate over these parallels and how far the English model should be followed, see Theodore Zeldin, "English Ideals in French Politics during the Nineteenth Century," *Historical Journal*, vol. 2, no. 1 (1959), 40–58. See as well, Jeremy Jennings, "Conceptions of England and Its Constitution in Nineteenth-Century French Political Thought," *Historical Journal*, vol. 29, no. 1 (1986), 65–85.

[59] In Chapter 4, I noted Constant's affirmation of legislative control over the budget and its importance for controlling the executive in the lead-up to the 1830 Revolution. However, earlier in his life, he had been skeptical of this as a control on the executive. See "De la possibilité d'une constitution républicaine dans un grand pays," 581–582. This difference between Constant and Thiers is emphasized in Laquièze, "Adolphe Thiers, théoricien du régime parlementaire," 64–65.

[60] Adolphe Thiers, "Du refus absolu du budget," in *Études historiques sur la vie privée: politique et littéraire de M. A. Thiers*, ed. Alexandre Laya (Paris: 1846), 49.

[61] Ibid.

the Chamber of Deputies and the nation. Unless the assembly took dramatic action, Guizot and Louis-Philippe would use the power of corruption to escape parliamentary accountability and govern arbitrarily.[62] According to de Hauranne, this was exactly the danger that "the two greatest political writers of England, Bolingbroke and Burke, have perfectly explained."[63] Just as in England "after 1688," so in nineteenth-century France, "prerogative has been succeeded by influence, and violence by corruption."[64]

Although Tocqueville was aligned with the liberal opposition to Guizot, he famously never fit in with them. Partly this was for reasons of temperament. Tocqueville was personally disgusted by Thiers, whom he found simultaneously opportunistic and dogmatic.[65] But there was also a crucial ideological difference. Unlike Thiers and de Hauranne, Tocqueville was not beholden to Constant's ideal of a "king who reigns but does not govern." While he wanted a monarch whose ministers were responsible to the legislature, he never suggested that the king delegate all active political powers to ministers and be neutral with respect to political decisions. Whenever such a proposal was on the table, Tocqueville kept his distance.[66] As I have shown, he favored the "consistency and stability" that a hereditary monarch brought to executive action. Indeed, in a note from the period, he acknowledged that he would have perhaps preferred "a stronger royal power."[67] Nor was he convinced that *only* a neutral king was compatible with political responsibility. While he felt no fondness for Louis-Philippe and was deeply concerned about parliamentary corruption, he did not think that the king and his ministers were in a position to deprive the nation of liberty.

---

[62] For these themes, see, for instance, Charles Rémusat, "Députés fonctionnaires publics," in *Annales du Parlement français*, vol. 9 (Paris: 1848), 364–372; Adolphe Thiers, "Discours sur les députés fonctionnaires, prononcé le 17 mars 1846, à la Chambre des Députés," in *Discours parlementaires de M. Thiers*, vol. 7 (Paris: 1880), 108; de Hauranne, *De la réforme parlementaire et de la réforme électorale*, 113–138.

[63] De Hauranne, *De la réforme parlementaire et de la réforme électorale*, 301.   [64] Ibid.

[65] See Tocqueville's letters to Gustave Beaumont on October 21, 1841; September 19, 1842; December 14, 1846, *Oeuvres complètes*, t. 7, vol. 1, ed. André Jardin (Paris: 1967), 292, 451, 473, 601–606. See also Tocqueville, *Recollections*, 19.

[66] See Alexis de Tocqueville to Francisque de Corcelle (December 20, 1838/January 2, 1839), *Oeuvres complètes*, t. 15, vol. 1, ed. Pierre Gibert (Paris: 1983), 105–109, where Tocqueville declares his lack of support for "the coalition's" campaign on behalf of this position in 1838. Nor did Tocqueville have any sympathy for the banquet campaign of 1847 (*Recollections*, 18–28). As his letters to Corcelle make clear, he was extraordinarily reticent to discuss the whole issue of the monarch's prerogatives.

[67] Tocqueville, "Notes pour un Discours," 208.

Unlike the leaders of the opposition, Tocqueville accepted an active constitutional monarch.[68] Why, then, did he not side with Guizot? It is worth noting that Guizot was himself quite troubled by this, declaring in a letter to Tocqueville, "I have never understood why you were not one of us."[69] Tocqueville differed with Guizot on several issues. He wanted France to adopt a more aggressive posture in foreign affairs, and by the late 1840s, he had come to accept the idea of expanding the suffrage.[70] For our purposes, however, the most important disagreement between Tocqueville and Guizot concerned corruption. Whereas Tocqueville believed that legislative and electoral patronage was corroding political life in France, Guizot was among the greatest defenders of this practice. He saw patronage as a crucial tool for building stable ministries and fostering unity between the legislature and executive.[71] He used patronage relentlessly during the 1840s to achieve these ends.[72] Like Burke and de Staël, he claimed that so long as patronage was distributed through political parties that were united by larger principles, it would not corrupt parliament.[73] Tocqueville emphatically disagreed.[74] It was in large part because of this issue that he ended up sitting with the liberal opposition.[75]

Throughout the 1840s, Tocqueville fought for severe restrictions on patronage. Like Constant, he sought to prohibit lower-level functionaries from serving in parliament. He also demanded the modernization of the French administrative state. Although usually thought of as an

---

[68] On this point, see Tocqueville, *Recollections*, 64; Tocqueville to Francisque de Corcelle (January 2, 1839), 109.

[69] Quoted in André Jardin, *Tocqueville: A Biography*, tr. Lydia Davis and Robert Hemenway (Baltimore: 1988), 314.

[70] For an account of Tocqueville's broader opposition to Guizot, see ibid., 343–404. Tocqueville was surprisingly slow in coming to advocate the expansion of the suffrage; see Robert Gannett, "Tocqueville and the Politics of Suffrage," *Tocqueville Review*, vol. 27, no. 2 (2006), 209–226.

[71] The similarity between Guizot and Walpole is noted in Zeldin, "English Ideals in French Politics during the Nineteenth Century," 44–45.

[72] Cabinet stability was particularly important to him. See in particular François Guizot to Lord Aberdeen" (April 26 1852), collected by Douglas Johnson, in "Guizot et Lord Aberdeen en 1852. Échange de vues sur la réforme électorale et la corruption," *Revue d'histoire moderne et contemporaine*, vol. 5, no. 1 (1958), 66–67.

[73] See Francois Guizot, *Des moyens de gouvernment et d'opposition dans l'état actuel de la France*, ed. Claude Lefort (Paris: 1987), 131–139, 213–232.

[74] Unlike Guizot, Tocqueville thought that the permanent nature of the monarch's position, along with the vast hold of the centralized state in the French political imagination, would more than maintain a French king's position vis-à-vis parliament without patronage. On this point, see Alexis de Tocqueville, "Préparation au discours que je voulais prononcer le 11 février 1842 et que la clôture m'a empêché de prononcer," in *Oeuvres complètes*, t. 3, vol. 2, 248; Alexis de Tocqueville, "Incompatibilités parlementaires," in *Oeuvres complètes*, t. 3, vol. 2, 250–251.

[75] Alexis de Tocqueville, "Notes de Tocqueville, 1847?" in *Oeuvres complètes*, t. 3, vol. 2, ed. Francois Melonio (Paris: 1985), 727.

uncompromising opponent of bureaucracy, Tocqueville's career in French politics was devoted not to fighting bureaucracy but rather to reforming it.[76] He sought to make bureaucratic office contingent upon competitive examination and to create a standardized process of career advancement such as existed in Prussia, so politicians would no longer be able to distribute jobs and promotions in exchange for political support.[77] His justification for these reforms was similar to that offered by Constant three decades earlier. Tocqueville argued that patronage was a dangerous substitute for parliamentary deliberation and the rule of public opinion. It motivated political parties to secure power by appealing to personal financial interests rather than principles.

Tocqueville's experience in parliament led him to believe that patronage profoundly undermined deliberation. Because all that mattered were the negotiations going on behind the scenes to determine who would get what job, "debates in parliament" had become "exercises of wit rather than serious discussions."[78] They were bereft of "all originality, all reality, and ... all true passion."[79] "What was most lacking" in the Chamber of Deputies, Tocqueville wrote, "was political life itself."[80] As it became apparent that parliamentary debates were mere spectacle, citizens lost all interest. "The whole nation" had become "bored" with national politics, he argued; profoundly dispirited by the high levels of corruption, "the nation does not desert certain political opinions, it deserts politics itself."[81]

Nor was the use of patronage confined to parliament. While the ministry was distributing offices among representatives, those same representatives were passing many of the offices down to the electorate. "The corruption of the deputy by the minister," Tocqueville wrote, led to the corruption "of the elector by the deputy."[82] "Each elector sees more and more in politics the means of making a fortune."[83] But if many French citizens took to politics as a way to "make a fortune," an even greater

---

[76] This argument is made at greater length in William Selinger, "*Le grand mal de l'époque*: Tocqueville on French Political Corruption," *History of European Ideas*, vol. 42, no. 1 (2016), 73–94.

[77] For Tocqueville's argument on behalf of these reforms, see Tocqueville, "Discussion de l'adresse," 204–205; Alexis de Tocqueville, "La proposition Gauguier sur les incompatibilités parlementaires," in *Oeuvres complètes*, t. 3, vol. 2, 240–242. To be clear, the class of functionaries Tocqueville wished to exclude from the assembly was not as large as that which Constant sought to exclude. As I noted in Chapter 4, Constant wanted to prohibit all administrative officers except the ministry from serving in the Chamber, while Tocqueville was willing to include some functionaries beneath the ministry (ibid., 241).

[78] Tocqueville, *Recollections*, 10.   [79] Ibid.   [80] Ibid.

[81] Alexis de Tocqueville, "Notes politiques," in *Oeuvres complètes*, t. 3, vol. 2, 217.

[82] Alexis de Tocqueville, "Fonctions publiques," in *Oeuvres complètes*, t. 3, vol. 3, 215.

[83] Tocqueville, "Notes pour un discours," 209–210.

number stopped paying attention entirely and found themselves "estranged from political life."[84] Political corruption contributed to the retreat from public life that Tocqueville had warned about in the second volume of *Democracy in America* and famously titled *individualism*.

Where Tocqueville broke with Constant was regarding how this process of corruption would end. Constant had argued that patronage would lead to no clear parliamentary majority and continual cabinet instability. However, Tocqueville was forced to be more pessimistic. Over the course of the 1840s, Guizot succeeded in bringing a remarkable degree of stability to the French Chamber of Deputies, even as he also made unprecedented use of patronage. Like Burke during the administration of Lord North, Tocqueville drifted closer to the pessimism of Bolingbroke and the eighteenth-century "country party." He feared that patronage would corrupt public spirit entirely.[85] "In nations with free institutions," he warned, "public spirit is the soul of government."[86] "Absolute monarchies can live without political life and the action of public opinion. Free governments cannot, because it is necessary for the daily movement of the whole political machinery."[87]

But unlike Burke and Bolingbroke (or, for that matter, his fellow members of the liberal opposition), Tocqueville was unconvinced that corruption would lead to traditional tyranny. The prospect of Guizot and Louis-Philippe governing despotically never struck him as plausible.[88] While many French citizens were in the pocket of the government, far more had become apathetic, because they were *discouraged* by the widespread corruption (this emphasis on apathy and discouragement is the major difference between Tocqueville's account of corruption and Bolingbroke's or Burke's). Should the government really try to rule despotically,

[84] Tocqueville, "Discussion de l'adresse," 198.
[85] For Tocqueville's broad argument that cynicism and narrow self-interest had prevented an effective opposition from forming, see Tocqueville, "Lettres sur la situation intérieure de la France", 95–121; Alexis de Tocqueville, "Discours prononcé à la Chambre de députés," in *Oeuvres complètes*, t. 3, vol. 2, 745–758.
[86] Tocqueville, "Notes de Tocqueville," 724.   [87] Ibid.
[88] In part, this was because he found these two figures so contemptible. They were far too caught up in meaningless spectacle of parliamentary politics to think of usurping it. Tocqueville was not *completely* unconcerned about the abuse of executive power. During the July Monarchy, he waged an unsuccessful battle in the Chamber of Deputies to force administrators to be tried before regular courts instead of special administrative courts, a practice that he thought encouraged abuse. But this concern was never at the heart of his campaign against corruption. See Alexis de Tocqueville, "De la responsabilité des agents du pouvoir," and "Compétence des tribunaux administratifs en matière de délits de voirie," in *Oeuvres complètes*, t. 3, vol. 2, 155–178.

there would be a return to great politics, and many of those apathetic citizens would be inspired to take action. This was an eventuality that Tocqueville was of course ambivalent about, but the crucial point is that for much of the 1840s, he thought it very unlikely. The effect of patronage was to "corrupt the people without defying them" and "twist the spirit of the Constitution without changing the letter."[89] Parliamentary corruption contributed to the worst tendencies of modern politics – materialism, individualism, selfishness, narrowness. It deprived France of a vibrant public realm. But it was unlikely to reawaken the spirit of despotism.

In addition to promoting administrative reform, Tocqueville's other response to corruption was to strive to create a better parliamentary opposition. His fear was not only that the liberal opposition was too divided to defeat Guizot but also that upon gaining power, the opposition would be forced to turn to the same strategy as Guizot – having attained no durable basis of support in public opinion. To escape this fate, Tocqueville argued that it was essential for the opposition to express clear principles, which could attract the nation to its side.[90]

Tocqueville's efforts to develop a new liberal opposition party are reminiscent of Constant. Indeed, during the early 1840s, he envisioned a party with a program very similar to the Indépendants. It would be devoted to preserving basic individual liberties – especially freedom of the press and freedom of association.[91] By 1847, Tocqueville had moved farther to the left.[92] He no longer believed that appealing to basic individual liberties would be sufficient to unseat Guizot and awaken the French public. Working with Jules Armand Dufaure, the parliamentary figure he most admired at the time, Tocqueville envisioned a liberal opposition party centered on the political rights and well-being of the working class.[93] But although his ideological position had shifted, the way Tocqueville conceived

---

[89] Tocqueville, *Recollections*, 64.
[90] See Tocqueville, "Lettres sur la situation intérieure de la France", 117–118; Alexis de Tocqueville, "Mefiance à l'égard du ministere et de son éventuel successeur," in *Oeuvres complètes*, t. 3, vol. 2, 91–92.
[91] Tocqueville, "Lettres sur la situation intérieure de la France," 119.
[92] Alexis de Tocqueville, "Manifest pour la nouvelle équipe *Du Commerce*," in *Oeuvres complètes,* t. 3, vol. 2, 124–125. For discussions of Tocqueville's move to the left, see Hugh Brogan, *Alexis de Tocqueville: A Life* (New Haven: 2006), 415–420; Roger Boesche, "Tocqueville and Le Commerce: A Newspaper Expressing His Unusual Liberalism," *Journal of the History of Ideas* vol. 44, no. 2 (1983), 277–292.
[93] See Alexis de Tocqueville, "Question financiére," in *Oeuvres complètes*, t. 3, vol. 2, 734–737; Alexis de Tocqueville, "Fragments pour une politique sociale," in *Oeuvres complètes*, t. 3, vol. 2, 742–744; Tocqueville, "Note."

of an opposition party remained constant.[94] Its role was to reinvigorate national politics, so that public opinion rather than patronage could became the basis of a parliamentary majority. While Tocqueville shared Burke and Necker's conception of parliamentary regime, he subscribed to Constant's vision of a party system. He believed that a principled partisan struggle over power was essential – not because it limited the scope of patronage, but because by making public opinion the ultimate arbiter of which party was in power, it rendered patronage unnecessary.

Appraising Tocqueville's Liberalism

Over the past generation, scholars have frequently inquired into the intellectual relationship between Guizot and Tocqueville.[95] They have also puzzled over what Tocqueville might have thought about Constant, who is almost never mentioned in Tocqueville's writings.[96] My discussion of Tocqueville has sought to clarify these questions. I have shown that Tocqueville agreed with Constant and the Doctrinaires that the survival of liberty in France required parliamentarism, yet he differed with both regarding how a parliamentary regime should be instituted. What he sought was a middle ground between Constant and the Doctrinaires in which the monarch did not give up an active role in the state but did give up his corrupt "influence" in parliament. Such a compromise had no chance of success in the politically charged context of the 1840s. Guizot's intransigence regarding corruption and the suffrage (combined with the opposition's fervent belief that liberty itself was threatened) sparked the 1848 Revolution. It was then that Tocqueville began his tragic quest for a parliamentary republic.

---

[94] During the months leading up to the 1848 revolution, Tocqueville perceived for the first time in his political career a possible return to "great parties" as the working class confronted the bourgeois regime of the July Monarchy. So more than truly giving birth to general principles and sentiments, he began to describe the role of a parliamentary opposition party to be that of channeling and drawing on sentiments already somewhat in existence. See Alexis de Tocqueville, "De la classe moyenne et du peuple," in *Oeuvres complètes*, t. 3, vol. 2, 738–741.

[95] See, for instance, François Furet, "The Intellectual Origins of Tocqueville's Thought," in *Tocqueville et l'espirit de la Démocratie*," ed. Laurence Guellec (Paris: 2005), 121–140; Melvin Richter, "Tocqueville and Guizot on Democracy: From a Type of Society to a Political Regime," in *History of European Ideas*, vol. 30, no. 1 (2004), 61–82; Aurelian Craiutu, "Tocqueville and the Political Thought of the Doctrinaires," *History of Political Thought*, vol. 20, no. 3 (1999), 456–493.

[96] A classic treatment of this question is George Armstrong Kelly, *The Humane Comedy: Constant, Tocqueville, and French Liberalism* (Cambridge: 1992). For a compelling account of Tocqueville's relationship to a whole variety of French political theorists during the early nineteenth century see Welch, *De Tocqueville*, 7–48.

Tocqueville was no more successful than Constant at salvaging French parliamentarism; however, he never gave up on parliamentarism as an institutional framework. Several months after the demise of the Second Republic, he wrote a letter to the Comte de Chambord, the Bourbon heir to the throne, signaling his support – but only on the condition that Chambord accept a parliamentary assembly. "A parliament in which discussion occurs freely and in full publicity seems to me to be the *sine qua non* of constitutional monarchy," Tocqueville wrote.[97] While he called for this parliament to be "a sincere representation of the nation" and for "a genuine liberty of the press," he manifestly did not expect the monarch to be neutral regarding political decisions.[98] Tocqueville sought to achieve the same liberal ends as Constant but always via subtly different constitutional means.

Given how magnificent Tocqueville's account of American politics is, it is tempting to think that the parliamentary order he envisioned for France was merely second best, and it is true that he favored this regime in part because its foundation had already been laid. "My conviction," he wrote during the July Monarchy, is that "our current institutions are sufficient for reaching the end I have in view."[99] However, Tocqueville was convinced that his constitutional vision for France was also admirable in itself, and that it would lead to extensive popular political participation as well as individual liberty. He viewed American constitutional democracy and European parliamentarism as different but valid paths that a state might follow, depending upon its circumstance. Chapter 6 will take up a group of nineteenth-century liberal authors who were not content with that answer and set themselves the task of weighing and evaluating these two alternatives.

---

[97] Alexis de Tocqueville, "Note pour le Comte de Chambord," in *Oeuvres complètes*, t. 3, vol. 3, 469.
[98] Note Tocqueville's indication in the letter that a strong monarch is a prerequisite for constitutional government in France (ibid.).
[99] See Tocqueville to Stoffels (October 5, 1836), 366.

CHAPTER 6

John Stuart Mill and the Victorian Theory of Parliament

During the middle decades of the nineteenth century, three visions of parliamentarism struggled for supremacy in France. While Constant and his followers argued for parliamentarism with a neutral monarch, I showed in Chapter 5 how Tocqueville and Guizot each defended parliamentarism with an active monarch only to split over the issue of patronage. Similar positions were also articulated in nineteenth-century Britain. But there, unlike in France, it was Constant's vision that triumphed decisively. Under Victoria, there came to be widespread agreement that the monarch should reign but not govern, and that ministers should exercise leadership in Parliament without using patronage.

This chapter has two aims: first, to explore the rich reflections on parliamentarism that were expressed by Victorian thinkers and second, to use that examination of Victorian political thought to offer a new interpretation of John Stuart Mill. In recent decades, there have been few accounts of Mill's thought that do justice to the other liberal authors of his moment – such as Walter Bagehot, Thomas Macaulay, George Cornewall Lewis, and the third Earl Grey.[1] I will argue that Mill subscribed to the same constitutional principles as these other Victorian liberals and staunchly defended a parliamentary regime. His great aim in *Considerations on Representative Government* was to show how the institutions and values of Victorian parliamentarism could be made to accommodate the rise of mass democracy.

With the exception of Mill, Victorian liberalism barely figures in the historical consciousness of contemporary political theory.[2] This chapter

---

[1] For several classic studies of these authors together with Mill, however, on quite different topics than are explored in this chapter, see John Burrow, *Whigs and Liberals: Continuity and Change in English Political Thought* (Oxford: 1988); Collini et al., *That Noble Science of Politics*.

[2] By saying this, I by no means intend to deny the excellent scholarship that has been done on this period and to which I am indebted. My point here is simply an intuitive conjecture about the historical imagination of contemporary political theory and how Florentine republicanism, Athenian

seeks to remedy that. Because Britain was the dominant political power of the nineteenth century, its government became an object of study across the globe. The writings on parliamentarism explored in this chapter had a profound influence, shaping the subsequent history of political thought in ways we now barely recognize.[3] While there is much we rightly bemoan about the Victorian period, it is also the case that Victorian authors expressed an extraordinarily rich set of arguments about the value of being governed by a representative assembly. In the process, they offered an important alternative to the model of liberal constitutionalism associated with the United States. If Tocqueville believed that a nation might equally adopt the American constitutional model or parliamentarism, depending upon its circumstances, the Victorian theorists I will be examining viewed the American model as decisively inferior. Their critique of the American Constitution is among the most powerful ever articulated.[4]

This chapter will begin with a general survey of constitutional theory in Britain during the mid-nineteenth century. My aim here is not to be exhaustive or delve into all of the details and complications of Victorian politics. I hope merely to capture some of the most widely shared ideas of the period and to demonstrate their affinity with the thought of Benjamin Constant. I will then home in on Walter Bagehot, the most famous, and, I will argue, the most idiosyncratic, Victorian theorist of parliamentarism. The chapter will then turn to John Stuart Mill. It will close with an examination of parliamentary corruption, a crucial theme in Mill's writings as well as in Victorian thought more broadly.

The Triumph of Parliament

Nineteenth-century British theories of parliamentarism were profoundly shaped by two events. The first was the Great Reform Act of 1832, which eliminated a number of corrupt or "rotten" boroughs and increased the

---

democracy, and the thinking of the American Founders all somehow seem more relevant to contemporary concerns than classical British parliamentarism.

[3] Several of the most important strands of influence will be traced in the conclusion. The impact of British parliamentarism is witnessed by its widespread adoption in postcolonial states. It was, for example, chosen over both the presidential model and other alternatives during the founding of the Indian Constitution. See Granville Austin, *The Indian Constitution: Cornerstone of a Nation* (New Delhi: 1966).

[4] Although not discussed in this chapter, the Victorian critique of the American Constitution was heavily influenced by discussions of the American Civil War – which authors such as Mill and Bagehot commented on extensively. For an excellent introduction to this topic, see Georgios Varouxakis, "'Negrophilist' Crusader: John Stuart Mill on the American Civil War and Reconstruction," *History of European Ideas*, vol. 39, no. 5 (2013), 729–754.

size of the electorate, so that it encompassed more of the middle class. Just as opponents had predicted, one of the most important consequences of the Reform Act was to reduce the Crown's influence in the House of Commons.[5] Because Britain did not have an administrative state comparable to that in France, electoral spending was a crucial part of the Crown's strategy for influencing Parliament.[6] By eliminating many of the boroughs where the Crown had traditionally exercised electoral patronage, the Reform Act deprived the government of a key source of parliamentary support.[7]

The second crucial event occurred in 1837, when Victoria became queen. She would reign until her death in 1901 and was the exemplary constitutional monarch of the nineteenth century. Thanks to the posthumous publication of her correspondence, we know she was quite involved in political affairs behind the scenes. However, her public image was one of scrupulous neutrality.[8] British theorists viewed Victoria as an almost magical instantiation of the monarch that Constant and Thiers had envisioned: a queen who truly "reigns but does not govern." The constitutional theorist Alpheus Todd wrote that Victoria "has scrupulously and unreservedly bestowed her entire confidence upon every ministry in turn with which public policy, or the preference of Parliament, has surrounded the throne."[9] William Hearn, the leading scholar of English constitutional law prior to A. V. Dicey, likewise argued that since Victoria, the cabinet had become the "real organ of executive government."[10] When it came to political decisions, Victoria claimed only, in Bagehot's words, "the right to be consulted, the right to encourage, the right to warn."[11]

While the ascendancy of the House of Commons has been a theme throughout this book, by the middle of the nineteenth century, it had

---

[5] See especially J. J. Park, *The Dogmas of the Constitution* (London: 1832); Peter Aiken, *A Comparative View of the Constitutions of Great Britain and the United States of America* (London: 1842), 110–117. The decrease in the monarch's influence in Parliament following the Reform Act is a major theme in Angus Hawkins's recent history of Victorian political ideas: *Victorian Political Culture: "Habits of Heart and Mind"* (Oxford: 2015), 66–98.

[6] This influence is discussed in Namier, *The Structure of Politics at the Accession of George III*, 139–142, 194–211.

[7] Older forms of corruption did not disappear after 1832, however. See Norman Gash, *Politics in the Age of Peel: A Study in the Technique of Parliamentary Representation, 1830–1850* (New York: 1971), 203–238, 323–392.

[8] For an early critique of the nineteenth-century conception of the Crown in light of Victoria's correspondence, see Laski, *Parliamentary Government in England*, 335–336.

[9] Alpheus Todd, *On Parliamentary Government in England*, vol. 1 (London: 1867), 187.

[10] William Hearn, *The Government of England: Its Structure and Its Development* (London: 1867), 8.

[11] Walter Bagehot, *The English Constitution, Collected Works*, vol. 5, ed. Norman St John-Stevas (Cambridge MA: 1974), 253.

reached unprecedented heights. The Crown had stopped using its veto long before this period, but it was now also forced to give up much of its electoral influence. On certain occasions, the House of Commons was still checked by the House of Lords, and a prodigious number of cabinet officials during the Victorian period came from the Lords rather than the Commons.[12] But the Lords had also lost much of its influence after 1832. According to Dicey, the most influential legal theorist of the second half of the nineteenth century, "the general rule that the House of Lords must in matters of legislation ultimately give way to the House of Commons is one of the best-established maxims of modern constitutional ethics."[13]

Walter Bagehot argued that British politics was defined by "the daily practical supremacy" of the "popularly elected branch of the legislature," making the House of Commons "the true sovereign."[14] Mill was equally clear on this point. "The House of Commons," he wrote, was "the real sovereign of the state."[15] There were prominent figures in British political life – notably Robert Peel and Victoria's husband Prince Albert – who wanted to strengthen the monarch.[16] But this position was never ascendant after the 1830s. Victorian liberals were especially convinced that Britain's limited constitutional monarchy, when combined with parliamentary government, was more than sufficient for moderating the House of Commons.[17] They believed that Britain had achieved the ideal of a free state: it was, without any threat of usurpation, substantially governed by a representative and deliberative assembly.

Although there is little evidence that Victorian theorists were directly influenced by Benjamin Constant, their constitutional theories were remarkably similar to his. Like Constant, they argued that the most important benefit of constitutional monarchy was the barrier it posed to

---

[12] See Jenkins, *Parliament, Party, and Politics*, 12.
[13] See Dicey, *Introduction to the Study of the Law of the Constitution*, 458.
[14] Walter Bagehot, "Presidential and Ministerial Governments Compared," in *Collected Works*, vol. 6, 166.
[15] John Stuart Mill, *Considerations on Representative Government, Collected Works*, 423.
[16] For an account of Peel's vision and its defeat, see Angus Hawkins, "'Parliamentary Government' and Victorian Political Parties, c. 1830–c. 1880," *English Historical Review*, vol. 140, no. 412 (1989), 638–669. It is for this reason that Guizot was an admirer of Peel, even writing a biography of him. See François Guizot, *Sir Robert Peel: étude d'histoire contemporaine* (Paris: 1858).
[17] Most but not all of the authors examined in this chapter belonged to the Liberal party, and a commitment to "the virtues of 'parliamentary government'" was among the key strands of "official liberalism" (Jenkins, *Parliament, Party, and Politics*, 17). However, as Angus Hawkins has argued, a crucial development in Victorian political life was the acquiescence to this state of affairs among conservatives, which Hawkins associates with the death of Peel and the ascent of Derby. See Angus Hawkins, "Lord Derby and Victorian Conservatism: A Reappraisal," *Parliamentary History*, vol. 6, no. 2 (1987), 280–302.

political ambition. Todd warned that "without the blessing of headship, in the person of an hereditary sovereign," it was likely that "the good government of the country would be jeopardized, if not overthrown, by the strife and cupidity of rival factions contending for the mastery."[18] Through constitutional monarchy, "the most elevated position in English society is thereby withdrawn from the arena of political competition, which is an incalculable benefit to the whole community."[19] Bagehot likewise claimed that "constitutional monarchy ... restrains ambitions which might otherwise become too fierce."[20] Victoria's neutrality was thought to have made her especially beloved, rendering it inconceivable that any politician would challenge the political order. According to the liberal author and MP William Massey, under Victoria "in no instance has the power of the Crown been so exercised as to expose it to check, or censure, or embarrassment of any kind."[21] The result was that "it may be asserted, without qualification, that a sense of general content, of sober heartfelt loyalty, has year by year been gathering around the throne of Victoria."[22]

If political ambition was limited by a popular hereditary monarch, it was channeled through the presence of ministers in Parliament. John Russell, one of the major statesmen of the Victorian period, argued that the survival of the English political system since 1688 was due to the fact that "ambitious men, instead of attempting, according to their several views, to abolish the monarchy, or dispense with Parliaments" were instead motivated to compete legitimately for power within Parliament itself.[23] "Whatever struggles have been made ... have been made within the House of Commons," he wrote.[24] Instead of overstepping the limits of the constitution, politicians have "sought to reach the king's closet through the favor of the people's representatives."[25] William Hearn made a similar claim:

> Where in former times the only remedy for misgovernment real or supposed was a change of dynasty, the evil is now corrected at no greater cost than that of a ministerial crisis ... Where formerly ministers clung to office with the tenacity of despair, and rival statesmen persecuted each other to the death, the defeated Premier now retires with the reasonable prospect of

---

[18] Todd, *On Parliamentary Government in England*, vol. 1, 204.   [19] Ibid., 205.
[20] Walter Bagehot, "The Residence of the Queen," in *Collected Works*, vol. 5, 421.
[21] William Massey, "May's *Constitutional History of England*: 1760–1860," *Edinburgh Review*, vol. 115, no. 233 (1862), 241.
[22] Ibid.
[23] John Russell, *An Essay on the History of the English Government and Constitution: From the Reign of Henry VII. to the Present Time* (London: 1865), 95.
[24] Ibid.   [25] Ibid.

securing by care and skill a triumphant return; and both he and his successors mutually entertain no other feelings than those to which an honorable rivalry may give rise."[26]

In his classic treatise on parliamentarism, the third Earl Grey contended that a parliamentary system was exceptionally equipped to avoid the worst pathologies of political ambition. Grey argued that in most monarchies, "flattery" and a "base compliances to mistresses and favorites" were the preferred means of political advancement, while "free governments ... have often been distracted, and sometimes ultimately overthrown, by sanguinary tumults and civil wars arising from contests for power among ambitious men."[27] Under parliamentary government, by contrast, competition for power was woven into parliamentary deliberation, so that the only way to attain higher office was through persuading one's peers. The result "was to render ambitious men less unscrupulous in their conduct in this than in other countries."[28]

In addition to channeling political ambition, Grey argued that the presence of ministers in Parliament brought organization and leadership. "It is the nature of popular assemblies," he wrote, "in a still greater degree than of men acting individually, to shrink from looking unpleasant truths in the face, and to listen with the greatest favor to those who tell them what they wish to believe."[29] While this problem was not completely resolved, it was greatly reduced by "throwing on the Executive Government the duty of guiding the deliberations of the legislature."[30] The belief that elected assemblies were dangerous and irresponsible when not led by executive officials was widespread. Thomas Macaulay argued that it was "by means of ministries ... that the English government has long been conducted in general conformity with the deliberate sense of the House of Commons, and yet has been wonderfully free from the vices which are characteristic of governments which are administered by large tumultuous and divided assemblies."[31] The point was made even more emphatically by George Cornewall Lewis, one of the architects of English civil service reform. Lewis argued that "the action of a popular assembly is liable to become capricious, inconsistent, and unjust, unless it be regulated and controlled by ministerial power."[32] Without such

---

[26] Hearn, *The Government of England*, 126–127.
[27] Earl Grey, third earl, *Parliamentary Government Considered with Reference to a Reform of Parliament* (London: 1858), 23, 24.
[28] Ibid., 33.   [29] Ibid., 18.   [30] Ibid., 19.
[31] Thomas Macaulay, *The History of England*, *The Complete Writings of Thomas Babington Macaulay*, vol. 8 (Boston and New York: 1900), 178–179.
[32] George Cornewall Lewis, "Earl Grey on *Parliamentary Government*," *Edinburgh Review*, vol. 108, no. 219 (1858), 280.

leadership, "the same forces and powers which ought to be usefully employed in transacting the business of the country, are in fact wasted in debates absolutely injurious to the public interests."[33] Hearn offered an equally strong defense of ministers in Parliament, declaring that "they make the difference between an organized deliberative Assembly and a mere mob."[34]

We will see later in this chapter that, unlike Walpole and Guizot, many Victorian theorists denied that ministerial leadership required patronage. They claimed that ministers had significantly greater authority than other representatives simply by virtue of their positions. "In Parliament," Macaulay wrote, ministers "speak with the authority of men versed in great affairs and acquainted with all the secrets of the State."[35] This not only gave them a leading role in Parliament, but it also transformed that assembly's whole character, ensuring that "the representative body has something of the gravity of a Cabinet."[36] By creating a sense of leadership – and a target for the opposition – ministers made possible a degree of organization in Parliament, and "in any large number of people," Hearn wrote, "if there be no organization, the sense of personal responsibility is lost in the numbers."[37] Yet Hearn took pains to emphasize that the leadership of ministers in Parliament was sustained entirely by persuasion. "The control of Ministers, powerful though it be, does not in the least interfere with the fullest freedom of action on the part of individual members. That control is merely persuasive."[38]

Victorian authors were convinced that through parliamentary govern-ment and a limited constitutional monarchy, their nation had succeeded in moderating a representative assembly that exercised unrivaled constitu-tional supremacy. What made this achievement so important was that these figures associated a powerful representative assembly with political liberty itself. Parliament prevented the government from exercising power arbitrarily, and it served as an indispensable space for deliberation, where any political proposal could be discussed and criticized.

"It is essential to our liberties," Macaulay wrote, "that the House of Commons should exercise control over all the departments of the executive administration."[39] During the nineteenth century, this control was still frequently attributed to the House of Commons' financial powers. Thomas Erskine May, author of the Victorian era's definitive tract on

---

[33] Ibid.   [34] Hearn, The Government of England, 537.
[35] Macaulay, History of England, vol. 8, 179.   [36] Ibid.
[37] Hearn, The Government of England, 537.   [38] Ibid., 537–538.
[39] Thomas Macaulay, The History of England from the Accession of James II, vol. 1 (London: 1856), 130.

parliamentary procedure, emphasized the unprecedented control over government that came with Parliament's right to refuse to supply revenue. "In all countries the public purse is one of the main instruments of power," he noted.[40] And "in England, the power of giving or withholding the supplies at pleasure is one of absolute supremacy."[41]

In his classic account of English constitutional law, Dicey likewise emphasized this power. He noted that should the government ever seek to evade parliamentary control, "large portions of the revenue would cease to be legally due and could not be legally collected, whilst every official who acted as collector, would expose himself to actions of prosecutions."[42] The entire military likewise "must be discharged, in which case the means of maintaining law and order would come to an end."[43] Because the government could not survive without the ongoing permission of the House of Commons, "no ministry has since the Revolution of 1689 ever defied the House of Commons."[44] Like Constant and de Staël, Dicey believed that these extraordinary powers were legitimated by the House of Commons' claim to represent "the will of the nation." "The essential thing," he wrote, "is that the ministry should obey the House as representing the nation."[45]

By the middle of the nineteenth century, there was no longer any question that the cabinet had to leave office when it was opposed by a majority of the House of Commons.[46] Victorian theorists strongly defended this practice, which combined, in Dicey's words, "wide discretionary authority [conferred] upon the cabinet" with "the direct control of the representative chamber."[47] Although the House of Commons did not force ministers to follow a certain line of conduct in their executive capacity, it did force them, in Grey's words, to "bring forward, explain, and defend the measures of the Executive Government."[48] That inspired a deep sense of accountability:

> Every measure of the Ministers of the Crown is open to censure in either House; so that, when there is just or even plausible ground for objecting to

---

[40] Thomas Erskine May, *A Treatise on the Law, Privileges, Proceedings, and Usage of Parliament* (London: 1868), 53. My discussion of May is indebted to Palonen, *The Politics of Parliamentary Procedure.*

[41] May, *A Treatise on the Law, Privileges, Proceedings, and Usage of Parliament,* 53.

[42] Dicey, *Introduction to the Study of the Law of the Constitution,* 447.   [43] Ibid.   [44] Ibid., 453.

[45] Ibid.

[46] For an account of the emergence of this strict convention of parliamentary responsibility, see Baranger, *Parlementarisme des origines,* 168–184.

[47] Dicey, *Introduction to the Study of the Law of the Constitution,* 464.

[48] Hearn, *Government of England,* 236.

anything they have done or omitted to do, they cannot escape being called upon to defend their conduct. By this arrangement, those to whom power is entrusted are made to feel that they must use it in such a manner as to be prepared to meet the criticisms of opponents continually on the watch for any errors they may commit, and the whole foreign and domestic policy of the Nation is submitted to the ordeal of free discussion.[49]

Grey argued that this practice made the English political system decisively superior to the American Constitution, which had never instituted effective legislative control over the executive. While Congress could "thwart the measures of the President and of his cabinet . . . if they disagree with him as to the line of policy which ought to be pursued," Grey lamented that representatives "have no authority to enforce the adoption of that which they consider to be right, or to require him to change his ministers."[50] Because there was no convention that executive officials forfeit their office when they lose the support of Congress, all that resulted from Congress challenging the president was stalemate. Henry Brougham, another important liberal author and MP during the Victorian period, likewise charged that in the United States, "the most effectual responsibility under which the servants of the State and its executive government can be placed is destroyed."[51] Whereas in the wake of the French Revolution, authors such as Necker and Constant had emphasized the failure of nonparliamentary constitutions to preserve the executive against the legislature, these Victorian writers made the opposite argument regarding the United States: they charged that the American Constitution did not sufficiently establish legislative control over the executive in the first place.

In addition to securing the responsibility of state officials, Victorian authors argued that a powerful representative assembly made possible a genuinely deliberative politics. In "parliamentary debate," the Canadian analyst James de Mille wrote, "we see well-informed and well-trained intellects turning all their powers to the discussion of a subject from many points of view, in which two opposite forces struggle for victory. In such a struggle, all the highest intellectual forces are put forth."[52] This ideal of parliamentary deliberation has come to be an important theme in recent scholarship, as historians of political thought have glimpsed in the Victorian era an understanding of "government by discussion" very different from the one currently pervasive in democratic theory. Kari Palonen has

---

[49] Grey, *Parliamentary Government*, 20–21.   [50] Ibid., 22.
[51] Henry Brougham, *The British Constitution, Works of Henry Lord Brougham*, vol. 11 (Edinburgh: 1873), 412.
[52] Cited in Palonen, *From Oratory to Debate*, 16–17.

emphasized the importance of parliamentary procedure – what de Mille called "the form of parliamentary debate" – to Victorian accounts of parliamentary deliberation.[53] Greg Conti has shown how the Victorian conception of Parliament as a "deliberative assembly" was tied to a specific account of representation, according to which the House of Commons was "the mirror of the nation" and contained representatives of all the relevant interests and opinions in society.[54]

Whether the House of Commons lived up to the ideal of a representative and deliberative assembly was subject to much dispute. Even though the Reform Act had increased the representation of the middle class, the vast majority of MPs were still wealthy landholders, just as in the eighteenth century, and the working class was largely excluded from formal political participation.[55] The question of how to further expand the suffrage thus became omnipresent in British politics during the second half of the nineteenth century.[56] But despite its limitations as a representative body, Parliament was responsive to popular opinion like never before in its history. A range of interest groups and ideological coalitions sought to influence its deliberations, and they were frequently successful, as the Second Reform Act and repeal of the Corn Laws both attest.[57] Public opinion was widely felt to be the determining factor in parliamentary politics.[58] As Macaulay wrote:

> The House of Commons is now supreme in the state, but is accountable to the nation. Even those members who are not chosen by large constituent bodies are kept in awe by public opinion. Everything is printed: everything is discussed: every material word uttered in debate is read by a million of people on the morrow. Within a few hours after an important division, the lists of the majority and the minority are scanned and analyzed in every town ... At present, therefore, the best way in which a government can secure the support of a majority of the representative body is by gaining the confidence of the nation.[59]

The struggle for "the confidence of the nation" was carried on by political parties, which showed an increasing degree of organization in Parliament

[53] Ibid., 16, 63–153.   [54] For these arguments, see Conti, *Parliament the Mirror of the Nation*.
[55] Jenkins, *Parliament, Party and Politics*, 102–103.
[56] For a powerful recent account of the debate over expanding the suffrage prior to the Second Reform Act of 1867, see Saunders, *Democracy and the Vote in British Politics*.
[57] Jenkins, *Parliament, Party and Politics*, 70–75.
[58] The rise, power, and diversity of public opinion and its influence upon the political sphere is explored throughout K. Theodore Hoppen, *The Mid-Victorian Generation, 1846–1886* (Oxford: 1998).
[59] Thomas Macaulay, *The History of England, Complete Writings*, vol. 6, (Boston and New York: 1899), 293.

as well as in local constituencies.[60] According to Bagehot, a system of parties was the very "essence" of a parliamentary government.[61] But while parties organized the struggle for parliamentary leadership, they did not dominate the House of Commons in the way they would by the turn of the twentieth century. Because most representatives did not depend upon the party for their seat, it was possible for them to vote against their party on a range of issues. Divisions in the House of Commons frequently did not follow party lines, making Parliament a setting in which minds could potentially be changed through persuasion.[62]

Just as Victorian liberals believed that the American Congress was found wanting when it came to the responsibility of executive officials, they also thought it failed as a deliberative body. Because legislative deliberation was divorced from competition over the highest executive offices, representatives put no energy into Congressional debate. Nor did the public have any reason to pay attention. Grey expounded at length upon Parliament's superiority over Congress in this regard:

> If men's passions and feelings were not so much excited by political struggles, it is not likely they would read, as they do, the debates in Parliament in which these subjects are discussed, and in which, amidst all the trash and sophistry that disfigure them, the keen encounter of intellects seldom fails in the end to lead to the discovery of truth ... The former function our Parliament discharges much more perfectly than the Congress of the United States, – probably, in part, because the debates in Congress are not read with the same interest, from their having no immediate effect on the tenure of power by those to whom the Executive Government is entrusted.[63]

Grey argued that, unlike in the United States, "the mode in which our Parliamentary contests have been carried on, has had the further and great advantage of contributing much to instruct the Nation at large on all the subjects most deeply concerning its interests, and to form and guide public opinion."[64]

---

[60] See John Phillips, *The Great Reform Bill in the Boroughs: English Electoral Behaviour, 1818–1841* (Oxford: 1992).

[61] Quoted in Angus Hawkins, *Parliament, Party and the Art of Politics in Britain, 1855–59* (London: 1987), 3.

[62] For a discussion of parties' role in Parliament prior to the late nineteenth century, see Jenkins, *Parliament, Party and Politics*, 28–55. In addition to structural factors, the especially fluid party system of the mid-nineteenth century was due to the splits between Peelites and the Conservative party, as well as between Radicals and Liberals, creating the more dynamic parliamentary context that is explored in Hawkins, *Parliament, Party, and the Art of Politics*.

[63] Grey, *Parliamentary Government*, 34–35.   [64] Ibid., 34.

Walter Bagehot and the Critique of American "Presidentialism"

Today, Walter Bagehot is the most famous nineteenth-century theorist of parliamentarism. It is his account of legislative supremacy, constitutional monarchy, and a responsible cabinet government that is still read and quoted.[65] Yet Bagehot's relationship to the broader tradition of parliamentarism examined in this book can be difficult to pin down. Born in 1826, he was already a notable essayist by his early twenties, when he wrote a series of articles on the 1848 Revolution. He would become one of the most important journalists of the Victorian era, serving as chief editor of *The Economist.* His works of political and social theory were no less influential, and in *The English Constitution,* which emerged out of a series of essays that he wrote during the early 1860s, he claimed to offer the first realistic account of the English political system. He maintained that nobody before him had properly examined parliamentary government and distinguished it from the eighteenth-century theory of checks and balances.

As this book has hopefully made clear, Bagehot greatly overstated his originality. Indeed, M. J. C. Vile went so far as to argue that *The English Constitution* was not original at all – he claimed that *everything* Bagehot said about English institutions was already well known.[66] In many respects, Vile was correct. Bagehot saw *The English Constitution* as consisting of a House of Commons that exercised "daily practical supremacy" over the state; ministers accountable to and drawn from that assembly who held the highest executive positions; and a monarchy and House of Lords that were more important for their "dignified" role than as active powers. I have shown that these were staple ideas of French and British political thought since the eighteenth century.

But if Bagehot's account of the structure of parliamentarism was not novel, his account of its principles was exceedingly unconventional. Unlike the other authors I have examined, he did not believe the "supremacy" of the House of Commons was necessary to ensure the responsible exercise of

---

[65] For relatively recent discussions of Bagehot's account of the English Constitution, see Kari Palonen, "Parliamentarism as a European Type of Polity: Constructing the Parliamentarism versus Presidentialism Divide in Walter Bagehot's *English Constitution,*" in *The Meanings of Europe: Changes and Exchanges of a Contested Concept,* ed. Claudia Wiesner and Mieke Schmidt-Gleim (New York: 2014), 74–90; Paul Smith, "Introduction," in Walter Bagehot, *The English Constitution,* ed. Paul Smith (Cambridge, 2001), vii–xxvii; Hugh Brogan, "America and Walter Bagehot," *Journal of American Studies,* vol. 11, no. 3 (1977), 335–356.

[66] Vile, *Constitutionalism and the Separation of Powers,* 235–238.

executive power or the liberty of individuals. Macaulay had proclaimed, "it is essential to our liberties that the House of Commons should exercise control over all the departments of the executive administration," a conviction that went back to Burke and Bolingbroke. Bagehot never articulated such a view. Writing with his oft-noted sarcasm, he mocked "historical twaddle about the rise of British liberty" and "responsible government," and professed himself stunned that "the fiction of the responsibility of ministers" was so "universally believed."[67] Minsters lost office when their party lost a majority in Parliament. Almost never did their character and conduct have anything to do with it. "Under the established system of governing cliques," Bagehot claimed that "the House of Commons is incapable of enforcing the responsibility of any member of the administration."[68] Indeed, he went so far as to declare, in a line that would have seemed like sacrilege to many of the authors I have examined, that a minister in Parliament "may wield his authority ... with as little chance of being called to account as an Eastern despot or French emperor."[69]

Bagehot did acknowledge, though in a quite early essay, that one role of the House of Commons was "the old but still important function of watching and checking the ministers of the Crown."[70] And he believed that the supervision of ministers by Parliament had a salutary effect. "The constant proximity of Parliament is the real force which makes ministers what they are," he wrote, "which prevents their being arbitrary – which prevents their being eccentric – which ensures their attending to public opinion – which enforces a substantial probity throughout the administration."[71] But if "the constant proximity of Parliament" conditioned ministers to act appropriately, it was unrealistic to expect Parliament to intervene if they acted otherwise.

Political responsibility was unimportant to Bagehot because, unlike the other authors in this book, he was skeptical that Parliament's control over government was what secured individual liberty. This skepticism was derived in large part from his observation of the French Second Empire – the Caesarist regime *par excellence* of his day. While the press was highly censored in France and legislative assemblies could not (until the very end

---

[67] Walter Bagehot, "Responsible Government," in *Collected Works*, vol. 6, 99, 101. The realism and irony in Bagehot's political thinking is emphasized in John Burrow, "Sense and Circumstances: Bagehot and the Nature of Political Understanding," in *That Noble Science of Politics*, 161–81.

[68] Bagehot, "Responsible Government," 102.   [69] Ibid.

[70] Walter Bagehot, "The Non-Legislative Functions of Parliament," in *Collected Works*, vol. 6, 42.

[71] Walter Bagehot, "The Unseen Work of Parliament," in *Collected Works*, vol. 6, 46.

of Napoleon III's rule) exercise control over government, Bagehot felt that the vast majority of French individuals lived their lives free of arbitrary state coercion. What France had lost under Caesarism was not individual liberty but a culture of political deliberation.[72] That would become the sole normative value Bagehot associated with parliamentarism.[73]

Along with so many other Victorian authors, Bagehot believed that the American Constitution offered the only real alternative to parliamentarism, and he made the comparison between these two regimes the linchpin of *The English Constitution*. "The practical choice of first-rate nations is between the Presidential government and the Parliamentary," he declared; "it is between them that a nation which has to choose its government must choose."[74] Like Henry Brougham and the third Earl Grey, he argued that the fundamental disadvantage of the American Constitution was that it failed to secure the supremacy of the legislature. In America, he wrote, "the popular branch of the legislature cannot obtain a daily practical supremacy such as the House of Commons has in England."[75] Congress had many of the same powers as the House of Commons – it could impeach the president and deprive the government of funding.[76] But these powers never culminated, as they did in England, in the strict dependence of executive officials on the legislature. Even if the president lost the support of Congress, he "must be retained till the next stated day of presidential election, however unfit, incompetent, and ignorant he may be."[77] All Congress could do was block the president's agenda, just as the president could do no more than block the agenda of Congress.

For this reason, Bagehot believed that the American Constitution made stalemate inevitable. The administration of Andrew Johnson, in which "a hostile legislature and a hostile executive were so tied together, that the legislature tried ... to rid itself of the executive by accusing it of illegal

---

[72] Among Bagehot's many essays on France under Napoleon III, see, in particular, "France or England," "The Emperor of the French," "Caeasareanism as It Now Exists," and "The Mercantile Evils of Imperialism," in *Collected Works*, vol. 4, 89–95, 105–119. For an astute discussion of Bagehot on Caesarism and its larger context, see Georgios Varouxakis, *Victorian Political Thought on France and the French* (Basingstoke: 2002), 57–103, 165–170.

[73] Alternatively, one might say that Bagehot was the rare figure who defended parliamentarism as a system of "positive liberty," as it made possible individual and collective initiative. See especially Walter Bagehot, *Physics and Politics, Collected Works*, vol. 7 (London: 1974), ed. Norman St. John-Stevas, 13–144.

[74] Bagehot, *The English Constitution*, 202.

[75] Bagehot, "Presidential and Ministerial Governments Compared," 166.   [76] Ibid., 166–167.

[77] Walter Bagehot, "The Defect of America: Presidential and Ministerial Government Compared," in *Collected Works*, vol. 6, 164.

practices," exemplified the American system's great defect.[78] Bagehot claimed that "the quarrel in most countries would have gone beyond the law and come to blows."[79] While this is reminiscent of Necker or Constant's reaction to the Constitution of 1791, it is worth noting again that Bagehot's analysis was the reverse of theirs. They believed that an independent executive armed only with a veto would be destroyed by a legislature claiming to represent the popular majority. Bagehot's concern, by contrast, was that the legislature in the United States did not have sufficient means to assert its superiority over the executive in the first place. The consequence was not executive usurpation – as Tocqueville had feared would occur if this arrangement were introduced in France – but rather stalemate. Neither constitutional power was clearly superior; each could singlehandedly block the other's agenda.

Bagehot argued that unlike the American Constitution, English parliamentarism fostered unity between the executive and the legislature. "The excellence of the British Constitution is that it has achieved this unity," he wrote, and "the success is primarily due to the peculiar provision of the English Constitution, which places the choice of the executive in the 'people's House.'"[80] The result was a more effective government. "Policy is a unit and a whole," he noted; "it acts by laws – by administrators; it requires now one, now the other," and "unless it has an absolute command of both its work will be imperfect."[81]

Even worse than its propensity to stalemate was the American Constitution's failure to encourage deliberation. For Bagehot, the preeminent advantage of the British political system over the American system was that it better stimulated legislative debate and public discussion. Put simply, he believed that debates in Congress mattered less than debates in Parliament. Any law that Congress passed might be vetoed, and no government would fall from power as a result of Congressional debate. This was not the case in Britain, where a "debate may change our rulers"; "it may either change or strengthen them."[82]

Bagehot claimed that because of the insignificance of Congressional deliberation, members of Congress put little thought or energy into what they said. "To belong to a debating society adhering to an executive (and this is no inapt description of a congress under a presidential constitution) is not an object to stir a noble ambition, and is a position to encourage idleness."[83] And because legislative deliberation did not have the enormous

---

[78] Bagehot, *The English Constitution*, 194.   [79] Ibid.   [80] Ibid.   [81] Ibid., 350.
[82] Walter Bagehot, "The Federal Constitution Responsible for Federal Apathy," in *Collected Works*, vol. 6, 170.
[83] Bagehot, *The English Constitution*, 221.

stakes in the American political system that it had in Britain, the American people paid practically no attention to it. "We here listen to parliamentary debates, and have a daily, critical, eager opinion on parliamentary issues," Bagehot wrote, "because those issues are decisive."[84] They could lead to "a change in government," and "a change in government is a great result." "It has a hundred ramifications; it runs through society; it gives hope to many, and it takes away hope from many . . . debates which have this catastrophe at the end of them – or may so have it – are sure to be listened to, and sure to sink deep into the national mind."[85] There was nothing parallel to this in the United States. Congressional debates were like "prologues without a play."[86]

Bagehot argued that the intense public attention to what was said in the House of Commons made possible "national instruction by parliamentary debate," which was "the best mod[e] of training nations . . . in political thought" ever discovered.[87] What made debates in parliament so instructive to a nation was, first, that an especially diverse set of perspectives were expressed and second, that the discussion was nailed down by parliamentary procedure to a specific question: this forced speakers to go beyond the exchange of vague commonplaces and to enter into the real complications of a political decision.[88] Through paying attention to parliamentary deliberation, the public learned to see beyond political generalities and to grapple with inconvenient facts and difficult choices. Parliamentary deliberation helped foster "a public opinion . . . that hourly adapts itself more nicely to the exigencies of the hour," while individuals belonging to a particular group or party were forced to encounter viewpoints they otherwise might have avoided.[89]

This clarification of the public mind through parliamentary debate was aided by the presence of an organized opposition. To gain public attention, the opposition had to carefully select several of the government's most consequential proposals and force an especially long and arresting discussion about them. "The main duty of an opposition," Bagehot wrote, "is three or four times in a session to arrest the attention of the nation; to compel it to consider the questionable measures of the government" and "form an opinion whether those measures ought or ought not to be carried."[90]

---

[84] Ibid.   [85] Ibid., 216–217.   [86] Ibid., 217.

[87] Bagehot, "The Federal Constitution Responsible for Federal Apathy," 170; Walter Bagehot, "The Progress of Imperialism in France," in *Collected Works*, vol. 4, 174.

[88] For an especially powerful and detailed description of this advantage of parliamentary deliberation, see Bagehot, "The Non-Legislative Functions of Parliament," 42.

[89] Bagehot, "France or England," 91.

[90] Walter Bagehot, "The Leadership of the Opposition," in *Collected Works*, vol. 6, 62.

Bagehot believed that the education of public opinion through parliamentary debate was simply impossible in the United States. Members of Congress had little incentive to engage in the kind of meaningful discussion that would clarify political issues, and the public had no reason to pay attention. In the United States, "public opinion" was therefore "apathetic and indeterminate."[91] The ultimate reason for this was that the president and his cabinet were neither selected from Congress nor dependent upon Congress for their positions. Instead of being subordinate to the legislature, the executive had its own independent source of popular legitimacy, depriving legislative deliberation of the profound significance it had in Britain.

By making the executive subordinate to the legislature, the British system also led to superior executive officials being selected. Representatives were more "conscious of the exact nature of public business" than the electorate, Bagehot argued, and they were personally acquainted with the candidates competing for executive office.[92] The nation "is not so much a bad judge as no judge," when it came to picking a president, he wrote.[93] "The House of Commons sees Lord Palmerston every day; the American people never saw Mr. Lincoln at all."[94] Whereas "an election by the people is a choice by distant people who ... have no close opportunities of investigating the respective merits of competing statesmen," Bagehot maintained that "the choice of a parliament is the choice of comparatively skilled men that have the best opportunities of judging those statesmen who strive as gladiators in the arena before them."[95]

Most importantly, Parliament could at any moment make a change in leadership. "It can act, judge, and decide whenever it happens to be sitting," so if "Palmerston should be unequal to a sudden exigency" another leader would be found. But a whole country "cannot be continually choosing its rulers."[96] A president elected under the American system "must be retained till the next stated day of presidential election, however unfit, incompetent, and ignorant he may be."[97] Nor did Parliament's determination of who held executive office deprive the public of a chance to be politically involved. To the contrary, it contributed to public political engagement. While cabinet officials could be changed by the House of

[91] Bagehot, "The Federal Constitution Responsible for Federal Apathy," 170.
[92] Bagehot, "The Defect of America: Presidential and Ministerial Government Compared," 161.
[93] Ibid., 162.
[94] Ibid., 163. This may not be the best example, as few Americans would probably wish to trade Lincoln for Palmerston. But Bagehot's larger argument is not without merit.
[95] Ibid.   [96] Ibid., 164.   [97] Ibid.

Commons, it was also possible that the House of Commons itself would be dissolved – should the cabinet rejected by Parliament be able to potentially find support from the electorate. At any moment, a debate in the House of Commons might occasion an election. This possibility kept the British public perpetually attuned to political affairs.[98]

While Bagehot has long been famous for defending parliamentarism, I have shown that his argument for it was remarkably idiosyncratic. Unlike the other authors examined in this book, Bagehot did not associate parliamentarism with individual liberty, and he de-emphasized the value of political responsibility. His entire case rested on the profound benefits of spirited parliamentary deliberation, and it was on this ground that he argued for parliamentarism's superiority over the American Constitution. Bagehot is often treated as a representative of his age, while John Stuart Mill is viewed as a great free thinker. But we will see that Mill's understanding of a liberal parliamentary order was considerably more conventional than Bagehot's.

John Stuart Mill

The notion that John Stuart Mill was a proponent of constitutional monarchy and parliamentary government may come as a surprise to many readers. These themes are absent in the scholarship on Mill, and he is often thought to have been a progressive, who was well in advance of general Victorian opinion. But while Mill did advocate democracy, women's suffrage, an expert administrative state, and eventually socialism, he also defended the constitutional framework that had emerged in England during the eighteenth and nineteenth centuries. He believed this framework had made the House of Commons the dominant actor in English politics. "By constitutional law," he noted, "the Crown can refuse its assent to any Act of Parliament, and can appoint to office and maintain in it any minister, in opposition to the remonstrances of Parliament."[99] However "the constitutional morality of the country nullifies these powers, preventing them from ever being used; and by providing that the head of the administration should always be virtually appointed by the House of Commons, makes that body the real sovereign of the state."[100]

Like Constant, Mill argued that the House of Commons' control over ministers led to a monarch who was uninvolved in governing. "The

---

[98] Bagehot, *The English Constitution*, 217.
[99] Mill, *Considerations on Representative Government*, 422.   [100] Ibid., 422–423.

nation," he declared, "would be offended, and think their liberties endangered, if a king or a queen meddled any further in the government than to give a formal sanction to all acts of Parliament, and to appoint as ministry, or rather as minister, the person whom the majority in Parliament pointed out."[101] Mill thought that it was Adolphe Thiers, the disciple of Constant whom I examined in Chapter 5, who first "erected the English practice of constitutional monarchy into a theory," with his "maxim, '*le roi regne et ne gouverne pas.*'"[102] While this "maxim" had never been inscribed into English law, it captured how English politics had come to operate. "The very essence" of English political practice, Mill wrote, is "that the so-called sovereign does not govern."[103]

Although it has been little noted by commentators, Mill actually preferred constitutional monarchy to republicanism. Where "a constitutional monarch does not himself govern, does not exercise his own will in governing, but confines himself to appointing responsible ministers, and even in that, does but ascertain and give effect to the national will," Mill asked, "what more could be expected from a republic?"[104] His answer: nothing. "Where is the benefit which would be gained by opening the highest office in the State … as a prize to be scrambled for by every ambitious and turbulent spirit?"[105] Like so many of the authors examined in this book, Mill thought that the most important advantage of constitutional monarchy was that it created a limit to political ambition. It was on this "ground," he noted, "that some of the best writers and thinkers, in free countries, have recommended kingly government – have stood up for constitutional royalty as the best form of a free constitution," and he believed that their argument was "in the present state of society, unanswerable."[106]

Just as Mill favored constitutional monarchy over republicanism, he preferred parliamentary government to American presidentialism. He recognized that "there is unquestionably some advantage, in a country like America, where no apprehension needs be entertained of a coup d'état, in making the chief minister constitutionally independent of the legislative body, and rendering the two great branches of the government … an

[101] John Stuart Mill, "Vindication of the French Revolution of 1848," *Collected Works*, vol. 20, ed. J. M. Robson (Toronto: 1985), 362 331.

[102] Ibid. Whether Mill was aware of it, Thiers drew his theory from Benjamin Constant, though it is true that Thiers expressed it in a catchier formula. However, Constant did similarly declare, "the king reigns but he does not administer." See Constant, "Un dernier mot sur le refus du budget," in *Recueil d'articles*, 136.

[103] Mill, "Vindication of the French Revolution of 1848," 331.

[104] John Stuart Mill, "Armand Carrel," *Collected Works*, vol. 20, 199.   [105] Ibid.   [106] Ibid.

effective check on one another."[107] But he immediately went on to add that this advantage was "purchased at a price above all reasonable estimate of its value."[108] He strongly preferred to have the highest executive officials sit in the legislature and be responsible to the legislature for their positions.

Mill's arguments against American presidentialism were similar to Bagehot's. Mill was appalled by the vulgarity and empty partisanship of American presidential elections and convinced that a more competent chief executive would be selected by the legislature. "It seems . . . certain," he wrote, that a "prime minister, will be better selected by the people's representatives, than by the people themselves directly."[109] In a county where the executive posed a threat to liberty, whether due to "vast power centralized in the chief magistrate" or "insufficient attachment of the mass of the people to free institutions," Mill's recommendation of parliamentarism was even stronger.[110] "Where such peril exists," he wrote, "no first magistrate is admissible whom the parliament cannot, by a single vote, reduce to a private station."[111] In such a situation, only the complete "constitutional dependence" of the executive on the legislature could preserve liberty.[112]

Mill shared Bagehot's concern that the American constitutional model led to stalemate. Mill warned that "there ought not to be any possibility of that deadlock in politics, which would ensue on a quarrel breaking out between a president and an assembly, neither of whom, during an interval which might amount to years, would have any legal means of ridding itself of the other."[113] Because of his concern about political stalemate, Mill thought the power of *dissolution* was among the most important elements of a parliamentary regime, and, like Constant, he argued that this power was indispensable for ending stalemate within the legislature – as well as between the legislature and the executive. "When there is a real doubt which of two contending parties has the strongest following," Mill wrote, "it is important that there should exist a constitutional means of immediately testing the point, and setting it at rest. No other political topic has a chance of being properly attended to while this is undecided."[114] By quickly enabling a national election, the power of dissolution revealed which of the contending parties better represented the popular will.

---

[107] Mill, *Considerations on Representative Government*, 524.   [108] Ibid., 524–525.
[109] Mill, "Vindication of the French Revolution of 1848," 362. Mill reiterates this argument in *Considerations on Representative Government*, 525.
[110] Mill, *Considerations on Representative Government*, 526.   [111] Ibid.   [112] Ibid.   [113] Ibid.
[114] Ibid.

While Mill preferred a parliamentary regime with a constitutional monarch, he also recommended parliamentarism for republics. "It seems far better that the chief magistrate in a republic should be appointed avowedly, as the chief minister in a constitutional monarchy is virtually, by the representative body," he wrote, rather than by the people.[115] His conviction that parliamentarism was the better framework for republics would become especially evident after the 1848 Revolution. Like Tocqueville, he argued that the president of the French Second Republic should have a cabinet drawn from the legislature. However, he also insisted, far more strongly than Tocqueville, that the French president *himself* should have been appointed by the legislature.[116] He thereby reproduced, five decades later, de Staël's account of a parliamentary republic.

"It is to be feared," Mill wrote in 1848, "that the appointment of a President by the direct suffrage of the community, will prove to be the most serious mistake which the framers of the French Constitution have made."[117] He lamented that this decision would "introduce[e] . . . into the still more fermentable elements of French society, what even in America is felt to be so great an evil – the turmoil of a perpetual canvass."[118] Even the constitutional commission's rejection of a bicameral legislature, which Tocqueville viewed as its worst mistake, was less significant than its refusal to have the president be appointed by the legislature.[119] Mill argued that a president elected from within the legislature but "armed with the power of dissolving the legislature" would be "a more effectual check than any second Chamber upon the conduct of an Assembly engaged in a course of hasty or unjust legislation."[120]

In *Considerations on Representative Government*, Mill was less opposed to the constitutional model of the Second Republic than he had been in 1848. He accepted that one way of instituting a parliamentary republic was to combine a popularly elected president with ministers who sat in parliament.[121] The other approach was to have parliament itself name the highest executive official.[122] In either case, Mill argued that "the nearer it approached in practice to that which has long existed in England," where

---

[115] Ibid., 525.
[116] During the constitutional debate in 1848, Tocqueville expressly opposed this (Tocqueville, "Discours sur l'élection du président de la république," 214–222.) Later, however, he claimed to have been ambivalent about this question and acknowledged that the legislature should have selected the chief executive. See Tocqueville, *Recollections*, 178–182.
[117] Mill, "Vindication of the French Revolution of 1848," 362.   [118] Ibid.
[119] Tocqueville, *Recollections*, 173.
[120] Mill, "Vindication of the French Revolution of 1848," 362.
[121] Mill, *Considerations on Representative Government*, 428.   [122] Ibid.

"the Crown appoints the head of the administration in conformity to the general wishes and inclinations manifested by Parliament ... the more likely it would be to work well."[123]

Although Mill's intellectual debt to Tocqueville is well known, when it came to parliamentary institutions, he was far more aligned with Constant. Whereas Tocqueville accepted an active constitutional monarch, Mill favored constitutional monarchy "on one ground only, and on one condition: – that [the] constitutional monarch does not himself govern."[124] He agreed with Constant that unless the monarch did not govern, it would be impossible to secure the most important condition of political liberty: "the principle of a responsible executive."[125]

Mill argued that the recurrent crises of nineteenth-century French parliamentarism were caused by France's inability to institute a neutral constitutional monarch. Although "the condition" of a monarch who "does not govern" had been "on the whole, faithfully observed" in England, Mill claimed that "no French king ever confined himself within the limits which the best friends of constitutional monarchy allow to be indispensable to its innocuousness: it is always the king, and not his ministers, that governs."[126] Mill thought that French public opinion was also against a neutral constitutional monarch. "Those who were for a king at all" were like Tocqueville and Guizot: they favored a king "who was a substantial power in the state, and not a cipher."[127] "A constitutional monarchy, therefore, was likely in France ... to be but a brief halt on the road from a despotism to a republic."[128] This was why Mill believed a parliamentary republic was the best option for France. Even though "it was a Frenchman, not an Englishman, who erected the English practice of constitutional monarchy into a theory," Mill thought "the French had no relish" for that idea.[129]

While Mill belonged to the parliamentary tradition of Constant, he also differed with Constant on two crucial issues. The first was the suffrage. Whereas Constant had sought to prevent the working class from exercising voting rights, Mill championed an expanded suffrage. He not only agreed with Tocqueville that democracy was inevitable, he argued that Parliament could not serve as a representative and deliberative body unless the

---

[123] Ibid.   [124] Mill, "Armand Carrel," 199.   [125] Ibid.   [126] Ibid.
[127] Mill, "Vindication of the Revolution of 1848," 20.   [128] Ibid.
[129] Ibid. For a larger discussion of Mill's analysis of nineteenth-century French politics (which was extensive) and its context, see Varouxakis, *Victorian Political Thought on France and the French*, 57–102.

working class was represented.[130] Mill was concerned that poorer voters would degrade parliamentary politics, and he famously defended plural voting and proportion representation.[131] However, his ideal parliament was one with substantial working-class representation.[132]

Mill and Constant also parted ways on a more technical issue: whether ordinary members of parliament should have the right to initiate and draft legislation. Constant called this right "a necessary component of the national representation," and he lamented that under the Restoration, only the ministry could introduce laws.[133] By contrast, Mill wanted all legislation to be crafted and introduced by a select committee of experts.[134] Ordinary representatives would be able to influence legislation only indirectly by evaluating the committee's efforts or recommending bills for it to draft. Mill's position on this issue came out of his more general conviction that a representative assembly was better at judging and evaluating than it was at governing. When it came to administration, he noted that Parliament did not directly administer but rather supervised the officials who did. "Instead of the function of governing, for which it is radically unfit, the proper office of a representative assembly is to watch and control the government."[135] His contention was that a representative assembly should treat legislation in the same way it treated administration:

> When a popular body knows what it is fit for and what it is unfit for, it will more and more understand that it is not its business to administer, but that it is its business to see that the administration is done by proper persons, and to keep them to their duties ... Even in legislative business it is the chief duty – it is most consistent with the capacity of a popular assembly to see that the business is transacted by the most competent persons; confining its own direct intervention to the enforcement of real discussion and publicity of the reasons offered pro and con; the offering of suggestions to those who do the work, and the imposition of a check upon them if they are disposed to do anything wrong.[136]

---

[130] See Mill, *Considerations on Representative Government*, 466–473.

[131] Ibid., 448–466, 473–479. Mill's plan for proportional representation is drawn from Thomas Hare, *The Election of Representatives Parliamentary and Municipal, a Treatise by Thomas Hare* (London: 1865). For an analysis both of Hare's theory and the political movement for proportional representation, see Floyd Parsons, *Thomas Hare and Political Representation in Victorian Britain* (Basingstoke: 2009).

[132] Mill, *Considerations on Representative Government*, 447. In this passage, Mill famously calls for half of the House of Commons to come from the working class.

[133] Constant, *Principles of Politics*, 226.

[134] Mill, *Considerations on Representative Government*, 428–432.   [135] Ibid., 433.

[136] John Stuart Mill, "The Municipal Corporations (Metropolis) Bill [2]," *Collected Works*, vol. 28, ed. J. M. Robson and Bruce Kinzer (Toronto: 1988), 292.

Nadia Urbinati has argued it was from classical Athens that Mill got the idea of a legislature limited to judgment, criticism, and control.[137] While Mill's interest in ancient Greek democracy is undeniable, it is also the case that he was simply taking the standard Victorian conception of the House of Commons as the control on government and extending it to encompass lawmaking. When it came to administration, there was nothing novel in the idea that Parliament's preeminent task was to appoint and pass judgment. According to William Rathbone Greg, a brother-in-law of Bagehot and one of Tocqueville's best friends in England, "the House of Commons, instead of doing the work of Government, or dictating in detail how it shall be done, contents itself with naming the man or men by whom it shall be done, and removing him or them if the work is not done to their mind."[138] Bagehot agreed that this was "now the most important function of the House of Commons."[139] Nor was Mill wholly original in suggesting that this principle ought to apply to legislation as well as to administration. He noted the long-standing convention that the House of Commons' most important act, the annual budget, first be introduced by the government:

> Though the supplies can only be voted by the House of Commons, and though the sanction of the House is also required for the appropriation of the revenues to the different items of the public expenditure ... it has, no doubt, been felt, that moderation as to the amount, and care and judgment in the detail of its application, can only be expected when the executive government, through whose hands it is to pass, is made responsible for the plans and calculations on which the disbursements are grounded.[140]

Mill declared that "the principles which are involved and recognized in this constitutional doctrine, if followed as far as they will go, are a guide to the limitation and definition of the general functions of representative assemblies."[141]

The great advantage of "disjoining the office of control and criticism from the actual conduct of affairs" was that this differentiation of functions would help restrain representative assemblies, as they became more

---

[137] This is a major theme of Urbinati, *Mill on Democracy*, especially Chapters 1–3.

[138] William Rathbone Greg, "Historical Painting – Macaulay," *North British Review*, vol. 24, vol. 49 (1856), 55. While Greg agreed with this principle, he also supported eliminating the idea of cabinet unity, so that each minister would be elected head of his department separately and would stand or fall by his own competence and legislative suggestions. See William Rathbone Greg, "Cabinets and Statesmen," *North British Review*, vol. 24, no. 47 (1855), 183–196.

[139] Bagehot, *The English Constitution*, 289.

[140] Mill, *Considerations on Representative Government*, 424.   [141] Ibid.

powerful and democratic. Mill warned that "the tendency is strong in representative bodies to interfere more and more in the details of administration, by virtue of the general law, that whoever has the strongest power is more and more tempted to make an excessive use of it; this is one of the practical dangers to which the futurity of representative governments will be exposed."[142] In addition to proportional representation, plural voting, and the power of dissolution, a crucial way in which Mill hoped to moderate a future democratic Parliament was by strictly delimiting its function. This step would also secure its role as a representative and deliberative assembly. If Parliament did not directly legislate or administer, it would not have to be composed of individuals with political expertise. It could represent "a fair sample of every grade of intellect among the people which is at all entitled to a voice in public affair."[143] It might become "a place where every interest and shade of opinion in the country can have its cause even passionately pleaded, in the face of the government and of all other interests and opinions, can compel them to listen, and either comply, or state clearly why they do not."[144]

Mill was a profound believer in parliamentary deliberation. "The House of Commons is not only the most powerful branch of the legislature," he argued; "it is also the great council of the nation; the place where the opinions which divide the public on great subjects of national interest, meet in a common arena, do battle, and are victorious or vanquished."[145] Indeed, Mill claimed that "besides being an instrument of government, Parliament is a grand institution of national education, having for one of its valuable offices to create and correct that public opinion whose mandates it is required to obey."[146]

No less than Bagehot, Mill offered an account of political deliberation that was truly parliamentary in character. He viewed a culture of deliberation as unsustainable in a modern state, unless it became coextensive with the struggle to appoint and contest senior executive officials.[147] Where Mill broke with Bagehot was in claiming that Parliament was indispensable for securing political responsibility as well as deliberation. Like the

---

[142] Ibid., 428.   [143] Ibid.   [144] Ibid.

[145] See John Stuart Mill, "Recent Writers on Reform," *Collected Works*, vol. 19, 348.

[146] Ibid. For a treatment of Mill's theory of parliamentary deliberation that particularly emphasizes the legislature's role in both reflecting and educating public opinion, see Urbinati, *Mill on Democracy*, 42–122.

[147] This fact has frequently been ignored by scholars seeking to draw on Mill's views on deliberation. For instance James Fearon, "Deliberation as Discussion," in *Deliberative Democracy*, ed. Jon Elster (Cambridge: 1998), 57, 59; or Hélène Landemore, *Democratic Reason: Politics, Collective Intelligence, and the Rule of the Many* (Princeton: 2012), 75–81.

other authors examined in this study, Mill thought a fundamental obliga-
tion of Parliament was to "see that the administration is done by proper
persons, and to keep them to their duties."[148] Parliament was the only
power in the state able "to throw the light of publicity" on the government
and its actions so as "to compel a full exposition and justification of all of
them which any one considers questionable; to censure them if found
condemnable, and, if the men who compose the government abuse their
trust, or fulfil it in a manner which conflicts with the deliberate sense of
the nation, to expel them from office."[149] Like Burke and Constant, Mill
argued that the responsibility of ministers to Parliament was an indispensable "security" for "the liberty of the nation."[150]

Because scholars have not examined the full range of arguments Mill
made about political institutions (largely ignoring his statements on parliamentarism versus presidentialism, constitutional monarchy, and the
power of dissolution), his great project in *Considerations on Representative
Government* has been overlooked. It was to demonstrate how parliamentarism, as it had emerged in Britain since the eighteenth century, could
accommodate the rise of mass democracy and the creation of a
technically trained administrative state. Mill made considerable concessions to both these developments. He defended a radical expansion of the
suffrage – though on the condition that it be moderated by plural voting
and proportional representation. He also argued for an expert committee
to write all legislation and for a trained civil service to handle the execution
of laws.[151] But the larger constitutional structure that Mill envisioned was
the same one that Constant had conceived of five decades earlier. In
Considerations on Representative Government, Mill showed how it was
possible to maintain the supremacy of Parliament and preserve
Parliament's capacity to deliberate and hold executive officials responsible,
even as Parliament was elected through mass suffrage and guided by
trained experts.

Parliamentary Corruption and Victorian Liberalism

Although *Considerations on Representative Government* was about the
future of parliamentarism, Mill also wrestled with the dilemmas facing

---

[148] Mill, "The Municipal Corporations (Metropolis) Bill [2]," 292.
[149] Mill, *Considerations on Representative Government*, 432.   [150] Ibid.
[151] Mill was a staunch supporter of a professional civil service selected through competitive
examination. See John Stuart Mill, "Reform of the Civil Service," in *Collected Works*, vol. 18,
ed. J. M. Robson (Toronto: 1977), 205–212.

parliamentarism in his own time. One such dilemma was parliamentary corruption, which had been reduced though not eliminated by the Reform Act. Mill struggled against corruption across his whole life. In his youth, he vocally opposed the aristocracy's influence in English elections. As a member of Parliament during the 1860s, he fought for the strictest possible campaign finance reform. He was also a lifelong critic of parliamentary patronage, which he opposed not only in England but also in France. Put simply, Mill was among the greatest opponents of political corruption in the nineteenth century.[152]

While few Victorian thinkers matched his fervor on this issue, when it came to the specific question of *patronage*, he was within the mainstream of Victorian liberalism. As one might have expected from their general alignment with Benjamin Constant, Victorian liberals frequently saw patronage as being of no value to parliamentarism. With their commitment to a strictly limited monarchy, they did not believe the Crown needed patronage to influence Parliament. With their faith in parliamentary deliberation and the rule of public opinion, they were skeptical that cabinet stability rested on patronage either.

In his *History of England*, one of the most influential books of the Victorian era, Thomas Macaulay argued that electoral and legislative patronage had taken off in England during the eighteenth century because that was a period when the House of Commons was no longer overawed by the prerogatives of the Crown but not yet dependent on public opinion. It was "between the time when our Parliaments ceased to be controlled by royal prerogative and the time when they began to be constantly and effectually controlled by public opinion."[153] During this transitional period, ministers had no choice but to turn to patronage to win over a majority of representatives. But by the mid-nineteenth century, the expansion of the suffrage to the middle classes and the development of the press had made public opinion the ultimate arbiter of parliamentary leadership.[154] "At present," Macaulay wrote, "the best way in which a government can secure the support of a majority of the representative body is by gaining the confidence of the nation."[155]

Macaulay believed that this transformation had made parliamentary government more rather than less stable, a point on which Walter Bagehot

---

[152] For a more extended treatment on Mill and corruption, see William Selinger, "Fighting Electoral Corruption in the Victorian Era: An Overlooked Dimension of John Stuart Mill's Political Thought," *European Journal of Political Theory*, forthcoming.
[153] Macaulay, *The History of England*, vol. 6, 293.   [154] Ibid., 294.   [155] Ibid., 293.

was in agreement.[156] Bagehot argued that public opinion was a better support for parliamentary leadership than patronage and that within Parliament, shared convictions were the only reliable source of political cohesion. "A majority in parliament which is united by a sincere opinion, and is combined to carry out that opinion, is in some sense secure. As long as that opinion is unchanged, it will remain; it can only be destroyed by weakening the conviction which binds it together."[157] "A majority which is obtained by the employment of patronage," on the other hand, "is very different," Bagehot argued, for it rested on a contingent calculation.[158] As soon as the government faced a challenge, its supporters would rush to whomever seemed most likely to next have control over appointments.[159] Bagehot thus claimed that patronage was the primary source of parliamentary "instability" in English history, particularly during the eighteenth century.[160]

A key Victorian thinker who doubted that parliamentarism could function without patronage was the third Earl Grey. Despite largely supporting the 1832 Reform Act, Grey lamented that it had led to "the loss of the authority of the administration in Parliament," and he drew the lesson that the practice of patronage – which he did not hesitate to label as "akin to corruption" – was an inescapable element of parliamentarism:

> The possession and exercise, by the ministers of the Crown, of a large measure of authority in Parliament, is the foundation upon which our whole system of government rests ... this authority has from the first been maintained principally by means of the patronage of the Crown, and of the power vested in the administration, of conferring favors of various kinds on its parliamentary supporters.[161]

Grey argued that "a tendency to encourage corruption, and especially that kind of corruption which consists in the misuse of patronage must ... be regarded as inherent in the system of parliamentary government."[162]

We can glean just how controversial Grey's argument was by the forceful response against it. One critic spent nearly his entire review of *Parliamentary Government* attacking Grey's statements about patronage.[163] William Hearn wrote that "notwithstanding the respect to which Earl Grey's authority is justly entitled," his argument for patronage "may well

---

[156] See Walter Bagehot, "History of the Unreformed Parliament," in *Collected Works*, vol. 6, 284–305.
[157] Ibid., 291.   [158] Ibid.   [159] Ibid.   [160] Ibid.
[161] Grey, *Parliamentary Government*, 101–102, 39.   [162] Ibid., 45.
[163] John William Wilkins, "Parliamentary Government and Representation," *North British Review*, vol. 28 no. 54 (1858), 437–464.

be doubted."[164] Hearn argued not only that "the theory which permits the executive to tamper with the body assigned for its control by the Constitution is indefensible" but also that "the strength which is thus obtained is, as experience has amply shown, precariously unstable and unpopular."[165] George Cornewall Lewis claimed that Grey's support for patronage was "mischievous and discreditable to the cause of free government, and of British Parliamentary Government in particular."[166] He also thought Grey was simply incorrect that patronage led to stronger administrations. "Venal support is, after all, but sham support; and no party can stand which is not actuated by earnest convictions directed to a practical object."[167] This was testified to by the fact that "men contending for their principles in opposition are commonly more closely united and far better disciplined than those who enjoy the favours and emoluments of office."[168]

While Bagehot and Macaulay agreed with Constant that the corrupt use of patronage was a source of parliamentary instability, Mill expressed far deeper fears. He was convinced, like Tocqueville, that patronage undermined political life entirely, and, like Tocqueville, he came to this conclusion by observing France under the July Monarchy, where "corruption was carried to the utmost pitch that the resources at the disposal of the government admitted."[169] What Louis-Philippe's regime demonstrated, according to Mill, was that "a majority of the electors in a majority of the electoral colleges, is not too numerous a body to be bought" by the government, "and bought it is, by distributing all public employments among the electors and their protégés."[170] The result was a stunning absence of "recognized principles" in French parliamentary politics.[171] "The public mind is uninformed, and has no fixed opinion on any subject connected with government," Mill lamented.[172] "And "without clear and definite views, diffused and rooted among the public . . . there is nothing to restrain petty intrigues and cabals, or to support an honest Minister."[173] Mill declared that "the government of Louis Philippe" was "wrought almost exclusively through the meaner and more selfish impulses of mankind. Its sole instrument of government consisted in a direct appeal to men's immediate personal interests or interested fears. It never appealed to, or endeavored to put on its side, any noble, elevated, or generous

---

[164] Hearn, *The Government of England*, 380.   [165] Ibid.
[166] Lewis, "Earl Grey on *Parliamentary Government*," 293.   [167] Ibid.   [168] Ibid.
[169] Mill, "Vindication of the French Revolution of February 1848," 327.   [170] Ibid.
[171] Ibid., 302.   [172] Ibid.   [173] Ibid.

principle of action."[174] Meanwhile, French citizens who refused to take part in the web of patronage became demoralized and apathetic:

> The best spirits in France had long felt, and felt each year more and more, that the government of Louis Philippe was a demoralizing government; that under its baneful influence all public principle, or public spirit, or regard for political opinions, was giving way more and more to selfish indifference in the propertied classes generally, and, in many of the more conspicuous individuals, to the shameless pursuit of personal gain.[175]

While the July Monarchy was brought down by the 1848 Revolution, this was after years of corrupt rule. Patronage did not always produce gridlock and instability. Precisely because it led to widespread "demoralization" and "indifference," it could discourage the emergence of an effective parliamentary opposition and help a corrupt government stay in power.

The widespread Victorian confidence in parliamentarism was only strengthened by the conviction that it did not rest on patronage. As this book has shown, patronage was the source of a profound dilemma. It was a practice clearly at odds with the preeminent values of a parliamentary regime, and yet it was unclear whether a parliamentary regime could function without it. Victorian liberals believed that through a highly limited constitutional monarch and the interweaving of parliamentary debate and public opinion, Britain had solved this dilemma. Their characterization of the British constitution was similar to Constant's: it was a political system in which "the king reigns, the ministry governs, the chambers judge." Whether this political system could survive the coming pressures of mass democracy was very much an open question. It was a question, I have argued, that John Stuart Mill especially wrestled with in *Considerations on Representative Government*. But that no other political system could better ensure the responsible and deliberative exercise of power and the possibility of individual and collective freedom was something few individuals examined in this chapter would have doubted.

---

[174] Ibid., 325.
[175] Ibid., 326. While Mill was highly critical of Guizot's corrupt rule in France, it is important to note that he very much admired and drew from Guizot as a theorist. See Georgios Varouxakis, "Guizot's historical works and J. S. Mill's reception of Tocqueville," *History of Political Thought*, vol. 20, no. 2 (1999), 292–312.

Conclusion

Over the final decades of the nineteenth century, an array of European liberals would follow John Stuart Mill's lead and try to square parliamentarism with democracy. In France, authors friendly to this endeavor (notably Prévost-Paradol and Adolphe Thiers) were instrumental in the formation of the Third Republic.[1] While the Third Republic of course had no monarch, a president elected from the legislature served as a neutral mediating power – he exercised no veto and appointed a cabinet that was also drawn from the assembly.[2] This powerful experiment in parliamentary democracy was not dissimilar from the republic Mill had recommended to France in 1848. But the decades following Mill's death in 1873 would reveal a new challenge to the democratic-parliamentary regime he had sketched. This was that democracy tended to augment the position of the executive. It made the struggle for plebiscitary leadership the decisive factor in political life – not parliamentary deliberation.

The British author and statesman James Bryce was among the first to recognize this feature of democratic politics.[3] A brilliant political thinker

---

[1] While Thiers has been discussed at multiple points in this book, Prévost-Paradol has been mentioned only once. His book *La France nouvelle* was one of the crucial liberal texts in the final years of the Second Empire. *La France nouvelle* argued for a powerful legislature elected democratically through proportional representation – and which served as "the mirror of the nation" – along with a "constitutional monarch" who reigned above the parties, limited the violence of political ambition, and made use of his power of dissolution to end parliamentary gridlock or overreach. See Prévost-Paradol, *La France nouvelle*, 71, 115–155. He also favored parliamentary government and the strict responsibility of ministers to parliament, as together making possible "the strongest guarantee of political liberty" (ibid., 101).

[2] See Duguit and Monnier, *Les constitutions et les principales lois politiques de la France*, 315–321. For an account of the complex series of events that led to this result, see Robert Gildea, *Children of the Revolution: The French, 1799–1914* (Cambridge, MA: 2010), 246–260.

[3] An important precursor, however, was the nineteenth-century analysis of "Caesarism" – in particular, the French Second Empire. For recent scholarly discussions of Caesarism, see Varouxakis, *Victorian Political Thought on France and the French*; Iain McDaniel, "Constantin Frantz and the Intellectual History of Bonapartism and Caesarism: A Reassessment," *Intellectual History Review*, vol. 28, no. 2 (2018), 317–338. Unlike the analysts of Caesarism, however, Bryce

whose work is today unjustly neglected, Bryce traveled to the United States in the 1880s and ended up writing a book titled *The American Commonwealth*. While he agreed with Bagehot that there was no culture of parliamentary deliberation in the United States and that the American public was disconnected from Congress, Bryce was surprised to discover that the branch of the American government that *did* connect with public opinion was the presidency.[4] An American president, he declared, "is in some respects better fitted both to represent and to influence public opinion than Congress is."[5]

Bryce claimed that a presidential election in the United States was "a solemn periodical appeal to the nation to review its condition, the way in which its business has been carried on, the conduct of the two great parties."[6] The public was energized like in no other political contest, and the winner could legitimately claim "to be the leader of the majority and the exponent of its will."[7] An effective president was likely to maintain his hold on the popular majority: as a single individual, he could both respond to popular grievances more quickly than Congress and more easily capture public attention.[8]

In future writings, Bryce would continue to associate democracy with presidentialism.[9] Indeed, by the turn of the twentieth century, it was increasingly established that democracy led not to an omnipotent legislature (as Tocqueville and Mill had both thought) but rather to a powerful *plebiscitary executive*. This was apparent even in parliamentary nations such as Britain. A widely credited turning point was the 1879–1880 Midlothian campaign, when William Gladstone toured England and Scotland giving speeches and carried the Liberal party into power.[10] As Angus Hawkins has written, the Midlothian campaign exemplified

depicted a democratic president who represented and shaped public opinion as part of a regular constitutional order in which political opposition was unhindered.

[4] For such criticisms, which reverberate throughout the book, see Bryce, *The American Commonwealth*, vol. 1, 215, 318–321; James Bryce, *The American Commonwealth*, vol. 2 (New York: 1908), 234, 341–345, 798–799.

[5] Bryce, *The American Commonwealth*, vol. 2, 799.

[6] Bryce, *The American Commonwealth*, vol. 1, 79.

[7] Bryce, *The American Commonwealth*, vol. 2, 799.

[8] For Bryce, presidential leadership made up for certain deficiencies in the American system that Bagehot had identified. For instance, he called the party convention that chose a presidential candidate "an effort to fill the void left in America by the absence of the European parliamentary or cabinet system" (ibid., 234).

[9] See James Bryce, *Modern Democracies*, vol. 2 (New York: 1921), 466, 471–472, 552–554.

[10] See Robert Kelley, "Midlothian: A Study in Politics and Ideas," *Victorian Studies*, vol. 4, no. 2 (1960), 118–140.

a new kind of politics. Gladstone was not joining a public agitation already under way. He was shaping, with a sense of historic purpose, a militant popular mood moulded by the charismatic force of his impassioned oratory. The Midlothian campaigns were a direct challenge to the sufficiency of Parliament ... Midlothian provided him with a platform from which to speak to the nation, with a Holy wraith as a tribune of the people.[11]

Democracy led to a strengthened plebiscitary executive in part because candidates for national office like Gladstone could connect with mass opinion – inspiring Max Weber's famous reflections on charisma. But another crucial factor was the growing incapacity of representative assemblies. As Weber emphasized in *Politics as a Vocation*, an organized party system made up of individuals "living off politics" arose in tandem with democracy.[12] In the United States, this took the form of a spoils system; in England, where civil service reform was already an accomplished fact, political machines developed independently of the state.[13] Without such an apparatus, it was impossible to organize a large democratic constituency on behalf of a candidate. But as representatives became more dependent upon the party machine for their position, they could no longer afford to speak and act with the same degree of independence in parliament. The influential British writer William Lecky wrote that "since the country has committed itself to democracy, the caucus system ... has grown with portentous rapidity ... It reduces the ordinary member of Parliament to the position of a mere delegate, or puppet."[14] "The independence of Parliament has at the same time almost gone," he declared, a view echoed by Weber.[15] Because representatives were increasingly inflexible in their political allegiances, deliberation in Parliament was far less consequential, and general elections were ever more indispensable for challenging the reigning government.

The major treatments of the English constitution at the turn of the twentieth century emphasized its increasingly plebiscitary character. Sidney Low, author of *The Governance of England* (1904), argued that "for the control of Parliament, which was supposed to be regular, steady, and constant, is exchanged the control of the electorate, which is powerful,

---

[11] Angus Hawkins, *British Party Politics: 1852–1886* (London: 1998), 223–224.
[12] Max Weber, "The Profession and Vocation of Politics," in *Political Writings*, ed. Peter Lassman and Ronald Speirs (Cambridge: 1994), 318.
[13] Ibid., 334–348. Weber's discussion drew from Bryce as well as from the famous account of the party system offered in Mosei Ostrogorski, *Democracy and the Organization of Political Parties*, tr. Frederick Clarke (New York: 1902).
[14] William Edwin Lecky, *Democracy and Liberty*, vol. 1 (Indianapolis: 1981), 127.
[15] Ibid.; Weber, "The Profession and Vocation of Politics," 343.

but intermittent."[16] In *The Government of England* (1908), Abbot Lawrence Lowell made a similar argument. "The cabinet now rules the nation," he wrote, "while the nation wishes to decide what cabinet shall be that rules."[17] Ministers came into office through a personal appeal to the electorate and were able to increasingly set Parliament's legislative agenda.[18] While they were challenged by an organized opposition party that aimed to take office in the next election, Parliament no longer exercised its traditional control over government.

Weber argued that a British prime minister stands "above Parliament" like "a plebiscitary dictator," a relationship no different from "the president's superiority in relation to parliament" in the United States.[19] Indeed, influential American Progressives were convinced that a British prime minister exercised plebiscitary leadership *more* effectively than an American president and sought for that reason to bring parliamentarism to the United States. According to Herbert Croly, placing the executive in the legislature would make him "political leader of the state with full power to carry out its will."[20] "As a consequence of bestowing the leadership of the state upon one man who represents the dominant phase of public opinion," Croly argued that parliamentary democracy "develops and consolidates majority rule as it has never yet been developed and consolidated in the history of democracy."[21] If Croly was excited by this prospect, several prominent British authors were so frightened by it that they would express a new appreciation for the U.S. Constitution, precisely because it made a unified majority government difficult to achieve.[22]

Patronage, party government, and public opinion have been important themes throughout this book. Each was defended by a range of authors as essential to parliamentarism. But with the rise of mass democratic politics

---

[16] Sidney Low, *The Governance of England* (London: 1914), 81. This was a long-running theme in Low's thought. See Sidney Low, "If the House of Commons Were to Be Abolished," *Littel's Living Age*, vol. 204, no. 2636 (1895), 88–100; along with Sidney Low, "The Decline of the House of Commons," *Littel's Living Age*, vol. 205, no. 2654 (1895), 411–420.

[17] Abbott Lawrence Lowell, *The Government of England*, vol. 1 (New York: 1908), 423.

[18] Crucial to the government's agenda-setting role were changes in parliamentary procedure that by the early twentieth century "gave the government the ability to arrange practically all business in the House" (Diana Woodhouse, *Ministers in Parliament: Accountability in Theory and Practice* (Oxford: 1994), 16).

[19] Ibid.; Max Weber, "Parliament and Government in Germany," in *Political Writings*, 221.

[20] See Herbert Croly, *Progressive Democracy* (New York: 1914), 303.   [21] Ibid., 304.

[22] See Henry Maine, *Popular Government* (Indianapolis: 1976), 197–247; Lecky, *Democracy and Liberty*, vol. 1, 65–67, 116–117. For a more qualified defense of the U.S. arrangement, see Émile de Laveleye, *Le gouvernement dans la démocratie*, vol. 1 (Paris: 1891), 350–353; and vol. 2 (Paris: 1891), 140–145.

at the end of the nineteenth century, these would become the conditioning forces of political life like never before. The result was to create new resources for the plebiscitary executive that undermined its traditional dependence on parliament and made the constitutional ideals examined in this book seem increasingly unattainable.[23]

But that is only one side of the story. The other side is the *persistence* of classical parliamentarism. Despite the constraints of party government, representatives in the House of Commons frequently resisted the government's growing monopolization of Parliament's agenda and sought to maintain space for deliberation, while in France, where a modern party system was slower to develop and Bonapartism had made clear the potential dangers of plebiscitary leadership, parliament would remain dominant well into the twentieth century.[24] Parliamentary democracy was instituted across Europe in the decades before and after the First World War, frequently with the expectation that it would lead to rule by deliberative assemblies.[25]

The question of how to improve and sustain parliamentary deliberation in the age of mass politics dominated European thought during this period. One widely discussed solution was proportional representation, which exercised an extraordinary influence in the late nineteenth and early twentieth centuries.[26] Perhaps the most surprising proposal, however, was for popular referenda. We tend to associate the referendum with radical democracy and to view it as a practice at odds with parliamentary preeminence.[27] But at the turn of the twentieth century, neither of these assumptions held true. The referendum was viewed as a means of rescuing parliamentarism, and it was advocated by liberal authors who were ambivalent about democracy.

In Switzerland, it had long been established practice that a law passed by parliament would have to be submitted to popular vote if sufficient signatures were collected.[28] While radicals had long praised this practice, figures such as William Lecky, A. V. Dicey, and Émile de Laveleye – who

---

[23] For a recent study of the rise of the executive in the twentieth century that makes some similar points, see Rosanvallon, *Le bon gouvernement*, 112–183.

[24] For struggles over the cabinet's agenda-setting power in Britain, see Palonen, *The Politics of Parliamentary Procedure*, 199–244. For the continuing preeminence of parliament in French political life into the 1920s along with the slow movement to a stronger executive, see Roussellier, *Le Parlement de l'éloquence*.

[25] See Mark Mazower, *Dark Continent: Europe's Twentieth Century* (New York: 1998), 3–40.

[26] See Conti, *Parliament the Mirror of the Nation*; Rosanvallon, *Le peuple introuvable*, 179–216.

[27] Richard Tuck's interest in recovering the referendum seems premised on this notion. See Tuck, *The Sleeping Sovereign*, 245–247.

[28] This was only one of several procedures that triggered a referendum in Switzerland. For a discussion of the Swiss referendum and the wide interest it motivated during this period, see Rosanvallon, *La démocratie inachevée*, 305–329.

had no love of direct democracy and indeed came out of the tradition of thought examined in this book – likewise came to advocate it. In particular, they saw it as way to disrupt the prime minister's monopoly on parliamentary affairs. The referendum would create a regular and destabilizing challenge to the prime minister's claim to represent the popular majority, making political life more vibrant and contested during the period between general elections.[29]

Max Weber: The Last Parliamentary Liberal?

More than any other figure, Max Weber exemplifies both the crises and the persistence of liberal parliamentarism in the early twentieth century. Nobody traced the rise of the plebiscitary executive more incisively than Weber, yet despite this, he remained committed to the values and institutions of a classical parliamentary regime. In 1918, as the First World War drew to an end, he called on Germany to adopt essentially the same constitutional framework that Benjamin Constant had recommended a century earlier for France at the end of the Napoleonic Wars.

Weber is regarded by some scholars as a "decisionist" whose conception of the plebiscitary executive prefigured the authoritarianism of Carl Schmitt, while other scholars emphasize his more liberal credentials.[30] I believe the history explored in this book can clarify his position. He was *both*, not because he was confused or at odds with himself but because he believed a successful democratic regime would necessarily contain each of these elements.[31] Weber argued that the tendency of modern democracy was to elevate the executive.[32] But the defining characteristic of a free democracy, as opposed to genuine Caesarism, was the presence of a

---

[29] See A. V. Dicey, "Ought the Referendum to Be Introduced into England," *Contemporary Review*, vol. 57 (1890), 489–511; A. V. Dicey, "Democracy in Switzerland," *Edinburgh Review*, vol. 171, no. 349 (1890), 135–145; Lecky, *Democracy and Liberty*, vol. 1, 234–147; Laveleye, *Le gouvernement dans la démocratie*, vol. 2, 136–171.

[30] The classic account of Weber's continuity with Schmitt is Mommsen, *Max Weber and German Politics*. For arguments on behalf of Weber's (relative) liberalism, see Dana Villa, "The Legacy of Max Weber in Weimar Political and Social Theory," in *Weimar Thought: A Contested Legacy*, ed. Peter E. Gordon and John McCormick (Princeton: 2013), 73–100; Josh Cherniss, "An Ethos of Politics between Realism and Idealism: Max Weber's Enigmatic Political Ethics," *Journal of Politics*, vol. 78, no.3 (2016), 705–718. For a useful overview of the competing discussions of this issue, see Pedro T. Magalhães, "A Contingent Affinity: Max Weber, Carl Schmitt, and the Challenge of Modern Politics," in *Journal of the History of Ideas*, vol. 77, no. 2 (2016), 283–304.

[31] For an account of Weber that takes a somewhat similar position to mine, see Peter Baehr, "The Avatars of Caesarism in Max Weber," in *Dictatorship in History and Theory*, 155–174.

[32] Weber, "Parliament and Democracy in Germany," 221.

representative assembly that engaged in open deliberation and secured the responsibility of state officials. "Even in electoral democracies," he wrote, "parliament is indispensable as an organ for controlling officialdom and ensuring public scrutiny of the administration, as a means of excluding unsuitable officials ... and as a means of achieving compromises between the parties."[33] The "ethic of responsibility," so famously prized by Weber, was inconceivable without the regular accountability of political officials to a representative assembly. "The committees of a powerful parliament," he argued, were the only bodies able to ensure that "a nation is well informed about how its officials are conducting their affairs, so that it constantly controls and influences their work."[34] Through this continuous accountability, officials were made to justify and explain all the consequences of their actions – however unintended. They essentially had no choice but to display an ethic of responsibility if they wished to remain in power.

Following so many of the authors in this book, Weber argued that parliament's "control" over the "officialdom" was derived from its financial powers. "Today, and ever since the time when the prerogatives of the estates were first created, the right to control the budget, the power to determine the manner in which the state procures its finances, has been parliament's decisive instrument of power."[35] But like the other figures I have examined, he believed that more regular and systematic oversight was required as well and defended "a *parliamentary system* in the true sense" – that is, one in which "the leaders of administration ... require the expressly stated confidence of a majority of parliament if they are to remain in office."[36] To a greater degree than any other political system, he believed that this framework forced officials to "give an account of themselves, exhaustively and subject to verification by parliament."[37]

Weber denied that any popular power but parliament could hold executive officials responsible. "*What organ would democracy have with which to control the administration* ... if one imagines that parliamentary power did not exist? There is no answer to this."[38] While he was not opposed to the occasional use of referenda, he denied that direct democracy could ever replace a representative assembly that controlled the executive. Echoing de Lolme's argument from a century and a half earlier, Weber argued that only members of parliament had the time, experience, and motivation "to acquire the relevant facts on a subject (by cross-examining experts and witnesses under oath) and thus to control the

---

[33] Ibid., 227.   [34] Ibid., 180.   [35] Ibid., 165.   [36] Ibid.   [37] Ibid., 166.
[38] Max Weber, "Suffrage and Democracy in Germany," in *Political Writings*, 126.

actions of officials. How is this to be effected . . . by a democracy without a parliament?"[39] Nor, without a parliament, could the people exercise control over finances, which was the underlying condition for popular control over the state. "There is no country in the world where the referendum has been introduced to carry out the most important task performed by regular parliamentary work, namely the budget," Weber noted.[40] "It is plain that this would simply be impossible."[41]

Just as Weber believed that the referendum was no substitute for parliamentary control over the government, he likewise argued that it could not produce the careful, nuanced engagement with political issues that parliamentary deliberation did. "The only questions which can be resolved by referendum in a politically and technically satisfying manner are those which can be answered by a simple 'yes' and 'no,'" he argued, making the referendum unsuitable for formulating and passing "complicated laws."[42] In a parliament by contrast, "yes" and "no" were not the only options. A bill could keep being recrafted until the point of compromise was reached, allowing competing factions to "settl[e] conflicts of interest through a process of negotiation."[43] In language reminiscent of Constant, Weber argued that "*this* is the specific function performed by parliament: to make it possible to achieve the 'best' solution" to a question that was politically possible at a given moment "by a process of negotiation and compromise."[44]

As well as arguing for the strict responsibility of ministers to parliament, Weber defended the English system of parliamentary government and constitutional monarchy more broadly. He claimed that by forcing the highest-ranking executive officials to rise to power within the legislature, parliamentarism limited the effectiveness of popular demagoguery. The test of being a capable member of the House of Commons "excludes anyone who is a mere demagogue," he wrote.[45] Weber expounded upon this advantage at length:

> None of the significant English parliamentary leaders has risen to power without being trained in committee work, and without having moved through a whole series of administrative departments and being introduced to the work done there. *Only* this school of intensive work with the realities of administration which a politician goes through in the committees of a powerful *working* parliament, and in which he has to prove his worth, turns such an assembly into a place for the selection of politicians who work

[39] Ibid., 127.   [40] Ibid., 128.   [41] Ibid.   [42] Ibid.
[43] Weber, "Parliament and Government in Germany," 225.
[44] Ibid.; Weber, "Suffrage and Democracy in Germany," 128.
[45] Weber, "The Profession and Vocation of Politics," 344.

objectively (as opposed to mere demagogues). No one could honestly deny that the English parliament is the best example we have ever seen of this process.[46]

If parliamentary government limited the efficacy of demagoguery, Weber argued that constitutional monarchy served as a barrier to dangerous political ambition. "The whole strength of the British parliamentary system is connected with the fact that the highest formal position in the state has been filled, once and for all."[47] More specifically, Weber favored a *neutral* constitutional monarch who sided with no political party and was uninvolved in political decisions. Like Constant, he thought that only a neutral monarch would be able to play a mediating role when political gridlock occurred. "The hereditary monarch can neither work with elected officials nor, if he nominates the officials, can he himself take sides," Weber wrote, "without compromising his specific function in domestic politics, which is to facilitate a conflict-free solution when the political mood or distribution of power is ambiguous."[48]

While Weber was convinced that the valorization of the executive is a "tendency" in "every democracy," he believed it was "tempered" by hereditary monarchy, which kept the highest position in the state from becoming the object of plebiscitary competition.[49] Above all, however, this tendency was limited by parliament:

> In relation to the (de facto) Caesarist representation of the masses, the existence of parliament guarantees the following things: (1) the *stability* and (2) *controlled nature* of his position of power; (3) the preservation of civil *legal safeguards* against him; (4) an ordered form of *proving*, through parliamentary work, the political abilities of the politicians who seek the trust of the masses; (5) a peaceful way of *eliminating* the Caesarist dictator when he has lost the trust of the masses.[50]

Following the end of the First World War and the abdication of the kaiser, Weber was forced to give up on constitutional monarchy. Like Tocqueville in the aftermath of 1848 or de Staël during the 1790s, Weber had no choice but to seek a republic that would approximate the benefits of the English system. The popularly elected president he sought to introduce into the Weimar Republic – with all the well-known tragic consequences – was intended as a substitute for a constitutional monarch. The president was to intervene "during temporary, irresoluble crises," Weber wrote, by

---

[46] Weber, "Parliament and Government in Germany," 181–182.   [47] Ibid., 162–163.
[48] Ibid., 227.   [49] Ibid., 221.   [50] Weber, "Parliament and Government in Germany," 222.

dismissing the ministry or dissolving the legislature.[51] However, for such a figure to have the appropriate level of public legitimacy, Weber believed that he would have to be chosen by the people and exercise powers beyond those of an English monarch.[52] Unlike Tocqueville, Weber favored a neutral rather than an active constitutional monarch. But both authors sought to find a substitute for constitutional monarchy in a popularly elected president – a step that ended both times in dramatic failure.

Writing at the end of the First World War – when mass democracy and a professional administrative state were *fait accompli* – Max Weber could not conceive a better model of a free state than classical parliamentarism. In his eyes, the decisive political alternative in the twentieth century was between modern states where administration and coercion were not under parliamentary control – such as the USSR – and those in which they were.[53] Individual freedom and "the political education of the nation" could not be achieved in the former kind of state; but they were still possible in the latter kind.[54] However, such states were, in turn, faced by a profound dilemma, which was that "mass democracy ... has always had to pay for its positive successes with major concessions to the Caesarist principle of leadership selection."[55] Weber's admiration for parliamentarism never led him to turn against political equality. He recognized (like Mill) that it brought possibilities for collective action and social improvement that it would be unconscionable as well as impractical to trade away.[56] But he was equally unwilling to part with the form of freedom that was distinctively liberal and parliamentary.

The Legacy of Parliamentary Liberalism

During the 1920s, Carl Schmitt would reiterate Weber's analysis of the tension between parliamentarism and democracy. But whereas Weber had held out hope that these two systems could be productively reconciled, Schmitt was convinced of their fundamental incompatibility.[57] He

---

[51] Max Weber, "The President of the Reich," in *Political Writings*, 307.   [52] Ibid., 308.
[53] Ibid., 165; Weber, "Suffrage and Democracy in Germany," 129.
[54] Weber, "Parliament and Government in Germany," 182.   [55] Ibid., 222.
[56] See Weber, "Suffrage and Democracy in Germany."
[57] In part this is because while Weber associated democratic leadership with *charisma*, Schmitt viewed it as expressive of a deeper and more elemental political force – the sovereignty and unity of a nation – the logic of which required leadership that was beyond the legal and political controls of parliamentarism. One is tempted to say that whereas for Weber, democratic leadership was rhetorically grounded, for Schmitt it was a metaphysically grounded. See for instance, Schmitt, "On the Contradiction between Democracy and Parliamentarism," 16–17.

believed that the spread of parliamentarism in the eighteenth and nineteenth centuries was due not to its intrinsic virtues but rather to external
conditions. These included the continuing hold of an "Enlightenment"
belief in reasoned deliberation and the fact that parliamentarism was closer
than absolute monarchy to democracy – so it could attract democratic
sentiment to its side.[58] Without these contingent historical factors, which
were increasingly inoperative in the twentieth century, Schmitt thought
parliamentarism offered little in the way of attraction.

In certain ways, Schmitt's analysis was prophetic. Representative assemblies are still found throughout the world, frequently with parliamentary
governments. Yet we have lost most of our confidence that such assemblies
might be spaces for illuminating political deliberation or that high-ranking
executive officials might be decisively subordinate to them.[59] Despite the
continuing presence of constitutional monarchs and ceremonial presi-
dents, when it comes to limiting the dangerous ambition of political
leaders and preventing usurpation, we are far more likely to turn to
constitutional courts and international institutions. However, despite these
facts – and without denying that a break with classical parliamentarism
did occur – I would like to conclude by suggesting that this break is
more ambiguous than would initially appear. There are surprising continuities between classical parliamentarism and modern democracy as
well as between parliamentary liberalism and modern democratic
theory. One indication of this is just how many of the formative commentators on twentieth-century democracy expressed admiration, even
nostalgia, for classical parliamentarism. From Hans Kelsen[60] and Joseph
Schumpeter,[61] to Woodrow Wilson[62] and Walter Lippmann,[63] to

---

[58] See Schmitt, *The Crisis of Parliamentary Democracy*, 22–39; Schmitt, *Constitutional Theory*, 328–332.

[59] Jeremy Waldron notes that political and legal theorists "spend much more time discussing the appropriate limits on legislation – and the moral and philosophical basis of those limits in the idea of individual rights – than we do discussing the nature and character of the legislative power itself and its importance for a self-governing society." Such a statement could never have been made about political thought prior to 1914. See Jeremy Waldron, "The Dignity of Legislation," *Maryland Law Review*, vol. 54, no. 2 (1995), 634. For a longer statement of Waldron's argument, focusing on Kant, Aristotle, and Locke, see Jeremy Waldron, *The Dignity of Legislation* (Cambridge: 1999).

[60] See Hans Kelsen, *The Essence and Value of Democracy*, tr. Brian Graf, ed. Nadia Urbinati and Carlo Invernizzi Accetti (Lanham: 2013), 47–56, 89–90.

[61] Joseph Schumpeter, *Capitalism, Socialism, and Democracy* (New York: 1942), 269–284.

[62] Woodrow Wilson, *Congressional Government: A Study in American Politics* (Boston: 1885); Woodrow Wilson, *Cabinet Government in the United States* (Stamford: 1947).

[63] Lippmann's admiration for parliamentarism is discussed in Craufurd D. Goodwin, *Walter Lippmann: Public Economist* (Cambridge, MA: 2014), 334; Don Price, "The Parliamentary and Presidential Systems," *Public Administration Review*, vol. 3, no. 4 (1943), 318.

Hannah Arendt,[64] Jürgen Habermas,[65] and Pierre Rosanvallon,[66] the legacy of parliamentarism has informed many of the most important texts on democratic politics.

For Arendt, Rosanvallon, and Habermas, classical parliamentarism offered an ideal that we should strive to recapture under the conditions of political equality – a political order that exemplified the value of public deliberation (Habermas), or political responsibility (Rosanvallon), or honorable political rivalry (Arendt). For Americans like Wilson and Lippmann, parliamentarism constituted nothing less than a blueprint for remaking the American polity. These American progressives sought to replace the old Montesquieuian framework of checks and balances with a structure that was genuinely deliberative and engaged public opinion – like the one Bagehot had depicted in Victorian Britain.[67] For other authors, what was most important was how modern democratic institutions tended to still *empirically* resemble the parliamentary institutions of the eighteenth and nineteenth centuries. When Joseph Schumpeter sought to construct a "realistic" theory of democracy in 1942, "the classical English practice" was the example he turned to.[68] He argued that what defined democracy was not the rule of the demos but rather competition over leadership, and he was convinced that this "logic of

---

[64] Before her interest in the Athenian polis, Arendt admired classical British parliamentarism for providing a space of political action. Indeed, she was convinced that the virtues of its parliamentary system were what prevented fascism from emerging in Britain. She also lamented the decline of parliamentarism in Britain due to the growing power and prominence of the prime minister, and analyzed the far greater crisis of parliamentarism in continental Europe, where a two-party system frequently failed to develop, leading to gridlock and usurpation. See Hannah Arendt, *The Origins of Totalitarianism* (New York: 1973), 153, 251, 252–256. Even in the 1940s, however, Arendt was unconvinced that parliamentarism would be effective going forward – a more participatory framework would be required to achieve the values that existed in Britain, especially in continental Europe. On this last point, see William Selinger, "The Politics of Arendtian Historiography: European Federation and *The Origins of Totalitarianism*," *Modern Intellectual History*, vol. 13, no. 2 (2016), 417–446.

[65] In his first major work, *The Structural Transformation of the Public Sphere*, Habermas offers what can only be called a "Whig history" of the emergence of parliamentarism and the rule of public opinion in eighteenth-century Britain – and of their subsequent spread across Europe. He concludes with the crisis of parliamentarism in the twentieth century. While Habermas is critical of the limited suffrage, he is explicit that the values (though not the particular institutions) of classical parliamentarism and its public sphere must be resuscitated, so that "there [can] once again evolve a public sphere as it once existed in the form of the bourgeois public" (Jürgen Habermas, *The Structural Transformation of the Public Sphere: An Inquiry into a Category of Bourgeois Society*, tr. Thomas Burger (Cambridge, MA: 1989), 210).

[66] Rosanvallon, *Le bon gouvernement*, 253–301; Pierre Rosanvallon, *Counter-Democracy: Politics in an Age of Distrust* (Cambridge: 2008), 156–160, 169–172.

[67] For an account of the transformation in the American state eventually wrought, in no small part, by these progressive thinkers, see Karen Orren and Stephen Skowronek, *The Policy State: An American Predicament* (Cambridge, MA: 2017), 123–138; Noah Rosenblum, *The Tribe of the Eagle: Presidential Democracy in Thought and Practice, 1927–1952*, Ph.D. dissertation (Columbia: forthcoming).

[68] Schumpeter, *Capitalism, Socialism, and Democracy*, 274.

democratic government ... has worked itself out most completely in the English practice" that emerged in the eighteenth century with Walpole.[69] It was from parliamentarism – as depicted by Burke, Bagehot, and Weber – that Schumpeter derived his influential theory of competitive democracy.[70]

If the tradition of thought explored in this book has cast such a shadow over the emergence of twentieth-century democratic theory, this may be because its account of political life remains compelling. We still have no good substitute for representative assemblies when it comes to achieving the values of responsibility, representation, and deliberation. And our polities are still defined by how they place such assemblies within a larger constitutional fabric. Across the world, democratic regimes are facing a political crisis that is very much characterized by these old questions. On the one hand, the populist and authoritarian leaders who have recently risen to power are shockingly disdainful of normal political responsibility, making legislative opposition crucial to the survival of liberal values. On the other hand, scholars have traced the rise of populism to the way in which legislative assemblies have been increasingly displaced since the Second World War, their functions appropriated by constitutional courts, bureaucratic agencies, and independent administrative authorities.[71] Whereas the aim of liberal parliamentarism was to moderate political contestation, the liberal regimes of the postwar period sought instead to place individual rights and social goods beyond political contestation – but the result is a political system that feels increasingly opaque and unrepresentative to many citizens.[72]

By reconnecting with the tradition of thought explored in this book, we can begin to see our current situation in a larger historical perspective. We are not yet beyond the history and dilemmas of classical parliamentarism. Nor have we escaped the logic of its greatest theorists.

[69] Ibid.

[70] For a more extended argument to this effect, see William Selinger, "Schumpeter on Democratic Survival," *Tocqueville Review*, vol. 36, no. 2 (2015), 127–157.

[71] For this general history of the displacement of legislative assemblies, see Peter Lindseth, *Power and Legitimacy: Reconciling Europe and the Nation-State* (Oxford: 2010), 61–90; Jan-Werner Mueller, *Contesting Democracy: Political Ideas in Twentieth-Century Europe* (New Haven: 2011), 146–150; Gauchet, *L'avènement de la démocratie*, vol. 3, 555–657; as well as vol. 4: *Le nouveau monde* (Paris: 2017). For discussions of similar trends, specifically focused on the United States, see Theodore Lowi, *The End of Liberalism: The Second Republic of the United States* (New York: 1979); Theodore Lowi, "Two Roads to Serfdom: Liberalism, Conservatism, and Administrative Power," *American University Law Review*, vol. 36 (1987), 295–322; Orren and Skowronek, *The Policy State*.

[72] The connection between the rise of populism and the displacement of traditional parliamentary politics is a theme in Rosanvallon, *Counter-Democracy*; Pierre Rosanvallon, *Democratic Legitimacy: Impartiality, Reflexivity, Proximity* (Princeton: 2011); Nadia Urbinati, *Democracy Disfigured: Opinion, Truth and the People* (Cambridge, MA: 2014); Jan-Werner Müller, *What Is Populism?* (Philadelphia: 2016); Yascha Mounk, *The People vs. Democracy: Why Our Freedom Is in Danger and How to Save It* (Cambridge, MA: 2018).

Bibliography

PRIMARY SOURCES

Aiken, Peter. *A Comparative View of the Constitutions of Great Britain and the United States of America*. London, 1842.

Anon. *The Subjects Case: Or Advice to All Englishmen*. London, 1701.

Officers Good Members: Or the Late Act of Settlement Consider'd. London, 1701.

An Enquiry into the Danger of Multiplying Incapacities on the Gentlemen of England to Sit in Parliament. London, 1739.

A Letter to a Member of Parliament: Concerning the Present State of Affairs at Home and Abroad. London, 1740.

A Second Letter to a Member of Parliament Concerning the Present State of Affairs. London, 1741.

A Dialogue on the Actual State of Parliament. London, 1783.

The Liverpool Tractate: An Eighteenth-Century Manual on the Procedure of the House of Commons. Edited by Catherine Stratham. New York, 1937.

Archives Parlementaires: recueil complet des débats législatifs et politiques des chambres françaises, sér. 1. 82 volumes. Edited by E. Laurent and E. Clavel. Paris, 1879–1913.

Arendt, Hannah. *The Origins of Totalitarianism*. New York, 1973.

Bagehot, Walter. *The Collected Works of Walter Bagehot*. 15 volumes. Edited by Norman St. John-Stevas. Cambridge, MA, 1965–1986.

Barante, Prosper de. *Questions constitutionnelles*. Paris, 1849.

Barrot, Odilon. *Mémoires posthumes de Odilon Barrot*. 4 volumes. Paris, 1875.

Bastiat, Frédéric. *Collected Works of Frédéric Bastiat*. 3 volumes. Edited by Jacques Guenin. Indianapolis, 2011–2017.

Beaumont, Gustave de. *De l'Intervention du pouvoir dans les élections*. Paris, 1843.

Blackstone, William. *Commentaries on the Laws of England*. 4 volumes. Edited by George Sharswood. Philadelphia, 1893.

Bolingbroke, Henry. *Political Writings*. Edited by David Armitage. Cambridge, 1997.

Boyer, Abel. *An Essay towards the History of the Last Ministry and Parliament*. London, 1710.

Brougham, Henry. "The State of the Parties." *Edinburgh Review* 46, no. 92 (1827): 415–432.

Contributions to the Edinburgh Review by Henry Lord Brougham. 3 volumes. London, 1856.

The Works of Henry Lord Brougham. 11 volumes. Edinburgh, 1873.

Bryce, James. *The American Commonwealth.* 2 volumes. New York, 1908.

Modern Democracies. 2 volumes. New York, 1921.

Burgh, James. *Political Disquisitions.* 3 volumes. Philadelphia, 1774–1775.

Burke, Edmund. "Debate in the Commons on the Regency Bill." In *The Parliamentary History of England,* vol. 27, 1171–1177. London, 1816.

The Correspondence of Edmund Burke. 10 volumes. Edited by Thomas Copeland. Cambridge, 1959–1978.

Further Reflections on the Revolution in France. Edited by Daniel Ritchie. Indianapolis, 1992.

Writings and Speeches of Edmund Burke. 8 volumes. Edited by Paul Langford. Oxford, 1970–2015.

Chateaubriand, François-René, Vicomte de. *La monarchie selon la charte.* Paris, 1816.

Clermont-Tonnerre, Stanislas Marie Adélaïde, Comte de. "Rapport par M. le comte Stanislas de Clermont-Tonnerre contenant le résumé des cahiers au point de vue de la Constitution." *Archives parlementaires,* ser. 1, t. 8. Edited by E. Laurent and E. Clavel, 283–284. Paris, 1875.

Condorcet, Marie Jean Antoine Nicolas de Caritat, Marquis de. *Oeuvres de Condorcet.* 12 volumes. Edited by A. O'Connor and M. F. Arago. Paris, 1847–1849.

Constant, Benjamin. *De la liberté des brochures, des pamphlets et des journaux.* Paris, 1814.

Réflexions sur les constitutions, la distribution des pouvoirs, et les garanties, dans une monarchie constitutionnelle. Paris, 1814.

De la responsabilité des ministres. Paris, 1815.

Principes de politique applicables à tous les gouvernements représentatifs et particulièrement à la constitution actuelle de la France. Paris, 1815.

Political Writings. Edited by Biancamaria Fontana. Cambridge, 1988.

Recueil d'articles 1829–1830. Edited by Éphraïm Harpaz. Paris, 1992.

Oeuvres complètes. 18 volumes. Edited by Paul Delbouille et al. Berlin, 1993–2013.

Commentary on Filangieri. Edited by Alan Kahan. Indianapolis, 2015.

Croly, Herbert. *Progressive Democracy.* New York, 1914.

de Lolme, Jean Louis. *An Essay on Constitutional Liberty: Wherein the Necessity of Frequent Elections of Parliament Is Shewn to Be Superseded by the Unity of the Executive Power.* London, 1780.

The Constitution of England. Edited by David Lieberman. Indianapolis, 2007.

de Mably, Gabriel Bonnot. *Du gouvernement et des loix de la Pologne.* Paris, 1781.

de Staël, Auguste. *Lettres sur l'Angleterre.* Paris, 1825.

de Staël, Germaine. *Considérations sur les principaux événemens de la révolution Françoise.* Paris, 1818.

Considerations on the Principal Events of the French Revolution. Edited by Aurelian Craiutu. Indianapolis, 2008.

Oeuvres complètes. 7 volumes. Edited by Florence Lotterie. Paris, 2000–2017.

Dicey, A. V. "Democracy in Switzerland." *Edinburgh Review* 171, no. 349 (1890): 113–145.

"Ought the Referendum to Be Introduced into England." *Contemporary Review* 57 (1890): 489–511.

Introduction to the Study of the Law of the Constitution. Edited by E. C. S. Wade. London, 1961.

Duguit, Léon. *Manuel de droit constitutionnel: théorie génerale de l'état – organisation politique.* Paris, 1907.

Ellys, Anthony. *The Spiritual and Temporal Liberty of Subjects in England.* 2 volumes. London, 1765.

Ferguson, Adam. *Remarks on a Pamphlet Lately Published by Dr. Price.* London, 1776.

Greg, William Rathbone. "Historical Painting – Macaulay." *North British Review* 24, no. 49 (1856): 41–58.

"Cabinets and Statesmen" *North British Review* 24, no. 49 (1856): 183–196.

Grey, Henry George, Third Earl. *Parliamentary Government Considered with Reference to a Reform of Parliament.* London, 1858.

Guizot, François. *Du gouvernement représentatif et de l'état actuel de la France.* Paris, 1816.

Du gouvernement de la France depuis la restauration et du ministère actuel. Paris, 1820.

Sir Robert Peel: étude d'histoire contemporaine. Paris, 1858.

Mémoires pour servir à l'histoire de mon temps. 8 volumes. Paris, 1858–1867.

Histoire parlementaire de France, recueil complet des discours prononcés dans les Chambres de 1819 à 1848. 5 volumes. Paris, 1863–1864.

Des moyens de gouvernement et d'opposition dans l'état actuel de la France. Edited by Claude Lefort. Paris, 1987.

The History of the Origins of Representative Government in Europe. Translated by Andrew Scoble. Edited by Aurelian Craiutu. Indianapolis, 2002.

Guizot, François, and George Hamilton-Gordon, Lord Aberdeen. "Guizot et Lord Aberdeen en 1852. Échange de vues sur la réforme électorale et la corruption." Edited by Douglas Johnson. *Revue d'histoire moderne et contemporaine* 5, no. 1. 1958: 57–70.

Hare, Thomas. *The Election of Representatives Parliamentary and Municipal, a Treatise by Thomas Hare.* London, 1865.

Halifax, George Savile. *The Works of George Savile, Marquess of Halifax.* 3 volumes. Edited by Mark Brown. Oxford, 1989.

Hauranne, Duvergier de. *De la réforme parlementaire et de la réforme électorale.* Paris, 1847.

Hearn, William. *The Government of England: Its Structure and Its Development.* London, 1867.

Hegel, G. W. F. *Elements of the Philosophy of Right.* Translated by H. B. Nisbet. Edited by Allen Wood. Cambridge, 1991.

Herle, Charles. *A Fuller Answer to a Treatise Written by Doctor Ferne.* In *The Struggle for Sovereignty: Seventeenth-Century English Political Tracts,* vol. 2. Edited by Joyce Malcolm, 223–261. Indianapolis, 1999.

Hume, David. *Essays Moral and Political*. Edited by Eugene Miller. Indianapolis, 1985.
Jaucourt, Chevalier. "English Parliament." In *Encyclopedic Liberty: Political Articles in the Dictionary of Diderot and D'Alembert*, 451–462. Translated by Henry Clark and Christine Dunn Henderson. Indianapolis, 2016.
Jeffrey, Francis. "Cobbett's Political Register." *Edinburgh Review* 10, no. 20 (1807): 386–421.
"Parliamentary Reform." *Edinburgh Review* 14, no. 28 (1809): 277–306.
"Mad. de Staël sur la Revolution Françoise." *Edinburgh Review* 30, no. 60 (1818): 275–317.
"Madame de Staël." *Edinburgh Review* 36, no. 71 (1822): 54–82.
Jenyns, Soame. *Thoughts on a Parliamentary Reform*. London, 1784.
Journal of the House of Commons. 277 volumes. London, 1802–2015.
Kelsen, Hans. *The Essence and Value of Democracy*. Translated by Brian Graf. Edited by Nadia Urbinati and Carlo Invernizzi Accetti. Lanham, 2013.
Laboulaye, Edouard. *Considérations sur la Constitution*. Paris, 1848.
Questions constitutionnelles. paris, 1872.
"Rapport fait, au nom de la commission des lois constitutionnelles (a) chargée d'examiner le projet de loi organique sur les rapports des pouvoirs publics." *Journal officiel de la République française* 7, no. 157 (1875): 4160–4162.
L' état et ses limites suivi d'essais politiques. Paris, 1886.
Lanjuinais, Jean-Denis. *Oeuvres de J. D. Lanjuinais*. 4 volumes. Paris, 1832.
"Suite de la discussion de la motion de M. comte de Mirabeau relative à l'entrée des ministres dans l'Assemblée." In *Archives parlementaires*, ser. 1, t. 9. Edited by E. Laurent and E. Clavel, 716. Paris, 1877.
"Suite de la discussion du projet de Constitution—Discussion de l'article 10." In *Archives parlementaires*, ser. 1, t. 29. Edited by E. Laurent and E. Clavel, 446–447. Paris, 1888.
Laveleye, Émile. *Le gouvernement dans la démocratie*. 2 volumes. Paris, 1891.
Lecky, William Edward. *Democracy and Liberty*. 2 volumes. Edited by William Murchison. Indianapolis, 1981.
Lewis, George Cornewall. "Earl Grey on *Parliamentary Government*." *Edinburgh Review* 108, no. 219 (1858): 271–297.
Low, Sydney. "If the House of Commons Were to Be Abolished." *Littel's Living Age* 204, no. 2636 (1895): 88–100.
"The Decline of the House of Commons." *Littel's Living Age* 205, no. 2654 (1895): 411–420.
The Governance of England. London, 1914.
Lowell, Abbott Lawrence. *The Government of England*. 2 volumes. New York, 1908.
Macaulay, Catherine. *Observations on a Pamphlet Entitled Thoughts on the Cause of the Present Discontents*. London, 1770.
Macaulay, Thomas. *The Complete Writings of Thomas Babington Macaulay*. 10 volumes. Boston and New York, 1900.

The History of England from the Accession of James II to the Present. 4 volumes. Philadelphia, 1856.

Mackintosh, James. "France." *Edinburgh Review* 24, no. 48 (1815): 505–536.

"Universal Suffrage." *Edinburgh Review* 31, no. 61 (1818): 165–203.

"Parliamentary Reform," *Edinburgh Review* 34, no. 68 (1820): 461–501.

Vindiciae Gallicae. Edited by Donald Winch. Indianapolis, 2006.

Mackworth, Humphrey. *A Vindication of Rights of the Commons of England.* London, 1701.

Maine, Henry. *Popular Government.* Indianapolis, 1976.

Massey, William. "May's *Constitutional History of England:* 1760–1860." *Edinburgh Review* 115, no. 233 (1862): 211–242.

May, Thomas Erskine. *A Practical Treatise on the Laws, Proceedings, and Usages of Parliament.* London, 1851.

A Treatise on the Law, Privileges, Proceedings, and Usage of Parliament. London, 1868.

Mill, John Stuart. *The Collected Works of John Stuart Mill.* 33 volumes. Edited by J. M. Robinson. Toronto, 1963–1991.

Millar, John. *An Historical View of the English Government.* Edited by Mark Phillips and Dale Smith. Indianapolis, 2006.

Milton, John. *Political Writings.* Edited by Martin Dzelzainis and Claire Gruzelier. Cambridge, 1991.

Mirabeau, Honoré Gabriel Riqueti, Comte de. "Discussion de diverses motions relatives au renvoi des ministres et au rappel de M. Necker," In *Archives parlementaires*, ser. 1, t. 8, edited by E. Laurent and E. Clavel, 242–243. Paris, 1875.

"Motion concernant : 1* les subistances; 2* la création d'une banque nationale; 3* l'entrée des ministres dans l'Assemblée." In *Archives parlementaires*, ser. 1, t. 9, edited by E. Laurent and E. Clavel, 706–11. Paris, 1888.

Montesquieu, Charles-Louis de Secondat, Baron de. *The Spirit of the Laws.* Edited by Anne Cohler et al. Cambridge, 1989

Oeuvres complètes de Montesquieu. 21 volumes. Edited by Jean Ehrard et al. Paris and Oxford: 1998–2019.

My Thoughts (Mes Pensées). Translated by Henry Clark. Indianapolis, 2012.

Mounier, Jean Joseph. *Considérations sur les gouvernements et principalement sur celui qui convient à la France.* Paris, 1789.

Recherches sur les causes qui ont empêché les Français de devenir libres, et sur les moyens, qui leur restent pour acquérir la liberté. 2 volumes. Paris, 1792.

"Discussion de diverses motions relatives au renvoi des ministres et au rappel de M. Necker." In *Archives parlementaires*, ser. 1, t. 8. Edited by E. Laurent and E. Clavel, 242. Paris, 1875.

"Présentation par M. Mounier du projet contenant les premiers articles de la Constitution." In *Archives parlementaires*, ser. 1, t. 8. Edited by E. Laurent and E. Clavel, 285–287. Paris, 1875.

"Rapport fait par M. Mounier contenant les articles concernant l'organisation du pouvoir législatif." In *Archives parlementaires*, ser. 1, t. 8. Edited by E. Laurent and E. Clavel, 522–527. Paris, 1875.

"Suite de la discussion relative à la sanction royale. Rapport de M. Mounier sur la nécessité de cette sanction." In *Archives parlementaires*, ser. 1, t. 8. Edited by E. Laurent and E. Clavel, 554–564. Paris, 1875.

Necker, Jacques. *Oeuvres complètes de M. Necker*. 15 volumes. Edited by Auguste de Staël. Paris, 1821.

"Mémoire de M. Necker sur la sanction royale." In *Archives parlementaires*, ser. 1, t. 8. Edited by E. Laurent and E. Clavel, 612–615. Paris, 1875.

Ostrogorski, Mosei. *Democracy and the Organization of Political Parties*. 2 volumes. Translated by Frederick Clarke. New York, 1902.

Paine, Thomas. *Political Writings*. Edited by Bruce Kuklick. Cambridge, 2000.

Paley, William. *The Principles of Moral and Political Philosophy*. Indianapolis, 2002.

Park, J. J. *The Dogmas of the Constitution*. London, 1832.

Parker, Henry. "The Political Constitution of the Spanish Monarchy. Promulgated in Cadiz, the Nineteenth Day of March, 1812." In *Cobbett's Political Register* 26, (1814): 25–32.

The Case of Shipmony Briefly Discoursed. In *The Struggle for Sovereignty: Seventeenth-Century English Political Tracts*, vol. 1. Edited by Joyce Malcolm, 93–125. Indianapolis, 1999.

Observations upon Some of His Majesties Late Answers and Expresses. In *Tracts on Liberty in the Puritan Revolution, 1638–1647*, vol. 2. Edited by William Haller, 167–213. New York, 1979.

Prévost-Paradol, Lucien Anatole. *La France nouvelle*. Paris, 1868.

Price, Richard. *Political Writings*. Edited by D. O. Thomas. Cambridge, 1992.

Rémusat, Charles. "Députés fonctionnaires publics." In *Annales du Parlement français*, vol. 9. Edited by M. T. Fleury, 364–372. Paris, 1848.

Robespierre, Maximilien. "Suite de la discussion du projet de Constitution – Discussion de l'article 10." In *Archives parlementaires*, ser. 1, t. 29. Edited by E. Laurent and E. Clavel, 445. Paris, 1888.

Rousseau, Jean-Jacques. *The Social Contract and Other Later Political Writings*. Translated. by Victor Gourevitch. Cambridge, 1997.

Royer-Collard, Pierre-Paul. *La vie politique de M. Royer-Collard: ses discours et ses écrits*. 2 volumes. Edited by Prosper de Barante. Paris, 1861.

"Suite de la discussion du projet de loi relatif à l'organisation des colléges électoraux." In *Archives parlementaires*, ser. 2, t. 18. Edited by E. Laurent and E. Clavel, 293. Paris, 1870.

Russell, John. *An Essay on the History of the English Government and Constitution: From the Reign of Henry VII. to the Present Time*. London, 1823.

An Essay on the History of the English Government and Constitution: From the Reign of Henry VII. to the Present Time. London, 1865.

Schmitt, Carl. *The Crisis of Parliamentary Democracy*. Translated by Ellen Kennedy. Cambridge, MA, 1985.

Constitutional Theory. Translated by Jeffrey Seitzer. Durham, 2008.

The Guardian of the Constitution. In *The Guardian of the Constitution: Hans Kelsen and Carl Schmitt on the Limits of Constitutional Law.* Translated by Lars Vinx. Cambridge, 2015.

Schumpeter, Joseph. *Capitalism, Socialism, and Democracy.* New York, 1942.

Serre, Hercule de. "Discussion de project de loi sur les élections." In *Archives parlementaires*, ser. 2, t. 16. Edited by E. Laurent and E. Clavel, 238–242. Paris, 1869.

"Suite de la discussion du projet de loi relatif à l'organisation des colléges électoraux." In *Archives parlementaires*, ser. 2, t. 18. Edited by E. Laurent and E. Clavel, 90–91. Paris, 1870.

Sieyès, Emmanuel Joseph. "Reprise de la discussion sur l'organisation du pouvoir législatif et la sanction royale." In *Archives parlementaires*, ser. 1, t. 8. Edited by E. Laurent and E. Clavel, 592–597. Paris, 1875.

"Bases de l'ordre social." In *Sieyès et l'invention de la constitution en France* by Pasquale Pasquino, 181–191. Paris, 1995.

Political Writings. Edited by Michael Sonenscher. Indianapolis, 2003.

Emmanuel Sieyès: The Essential Political Writings. Edited by Oliver W. Lembcke and Florian Weber. Leiden and Boston, 2014.

Sismondi, Sismonde de. *Examen de la constitution Française.* Paris, 1815.

Études sur les constitutions des peuples libres. Paris, 1836.

Smith, Adam. *Lectures on Jurisprudence.* Edited by R. L. Meek et al. Indianapolis, 1982.

Spelman, Edward. *A Fragment out of the Sixth Book of Polybius.* London, 1743.

Spencer, Herbert. *The Man versus the State: With Six Essays on Government, Society, and Freedom.* Indianapolis, 1982.

Stewart, Dugald. *Collected Works.* 11 volumes. Edited by William Hamilton. London, 1854–1860.

Sydney, Algernon. *Discourses Concerning Government.* New York, 1999.

Thiers, Adolphe. *Études historiques sur la vie privée: politique et littéraire de M. A. Thiers.* 2 volumes. Edited by Alexandra Lava. Paris, 1846.

Discours parlementaires de M. Thiers. 16 volumes. Edited by M. Calmon. Paris, 1879–1889.

Tocqueville, Alexis de. *Memoirs, Letters, and Remains of Alexis de Tocqueville.* 2 volumes. London, 1861.

Oeuvres complètes. 20 volumes. Edited by J. P. Mayer. Paris, 1951–2003.

Recollections: The French Revolution of 1848. Edited by J. P. Mayer. New Brunswick, 1987.

Lettres choisies; Souvenirs: 1814–1859. Edited by Françoise Mélonio. Gallimard, 2003.

Democracy in America. 2 volumes. Edited by Eduardo Nolla. Translated by James Schleifer. Indianapolis, 2012.

Tocqueville, Alexis de, and Nassau William Senior. *Correspondence & Conversations of Alexis de Tocqueville with Nassau William Senior from 1834 to 1859.* 2 volumes. Edited by M. C. M. Simpson. London, 1872.

Todd, Alpheus. *On Parliamentary Government in England.* 2 volumes. London, 1867.

Parliamentary Government in the British Colonies. Boston, 1880.

Trenchard, John, and Thomas Gordon. *Cato's Letters, or Essays on Liberty, Civil and Religious, and Other Important Subjects.* 2 volumes. New York, 1971.

Vitrolles, Eugéne, François Auguste d'Arnaud, Baron, de. *Du ministère dans le gouvernement représentatif.* Paris, 1815.

Voltaire, François-Marie Arouet de. *Lettres Philosophiques.* Amsterdam, 1733.

Walpole, Robert. *The Celebrated Speech of Sir Robert Walpole, against Short Parliaments; to Shew That a Parliamentary Reform Is Both Unnecessary and Dangerous.* Edited by Henry Dundas. London, 1793.

"Debate in the Commons on the Place Bill." In *The Parliamentary History of England,* vol. 11, 362–369. London, 1812.

Weber, Max. *Political Writings.* Edited by Peter Lassman and Ronald Speirs. Cambridge, 1994.

Wilkins, John Williams. "Parliamentary Government and Representation." *North British Review* 28, no. 54 (1858): 437–464.

Wilson, Woodrow. *Congressional Government: A Study in American Politics.* Boston, 1885.

Cabinet Government in the United States. Stamford, 1947.

Wollstonecraft, Mary. *Vindication of the Rights of Men and a Vindication of the Rights of Women.* Edited by Sylvana Tomaselli. Cambridge, 1995.

SECONDARY MATERIAL

Alexander, Robert. *Re-writing the French Revolutionary Tradition.* Cambridge, 2003.

"Benjamin Constant as a Second Restoration Politician." In *The Cambridge Companion to Constant.* Edited by Helena Rosenblatt, 146–170. Cambridge, 2009.

Armitage, David. "A Patriot for Whom? The Afterlives of Bolingbroke's Patriot King." *Journal of British Studies* 36, no. 4 (1997): 397–418.

Foundations of Modern International Thought. Cambridge, 2013.

Austin, Granville. *The Indian Constitution: Cornerstone of a Nation.* Oxford, 1966.

Baehr, Peter, and Melvin Richter. "Introduction." In *Dictatorship in History and Theory: Bonapartism, Caesarism and Totalitarianism.* Edited by Peter Baehr and Melvin Richter, 1–26. Cambridge, 2004.

Baranger, Denis. *Parlementarisme des origines: Essai sur les conditions de formation d'un exécutif responsable en Angleterre (des années 1740 au début de l'âge victorien).* Paris, 1999.

Bastid, Paul. *Les institutions politiques de la monarchie parlementaire française (1814–1848).* Paris, 1954.

Bastid, Paul. *Benjamin Constant et sa doctrine.* Two volumes. Paris, 1966.

Biefang, Andreas, and Andreas Schulze. "From Monarchical Constitutionalism to a Parliamentary Republic: Concepts of Parliamentarism in Germany since

1818." In *Parliament and Parliamentarism*. Edited by Pasi Ihaleinen et al., 62–80. New York, 2016.

Blaas, P. B. M. *Continuity and Anachronism: Parliamentary and Constitutional Development in Whig Historiography and in the Anti-Whig Reaction between 1890 and 1930*. The Hague, 1978.

Blackburn, Robert. "Laying the Foundations of the Modern Voting System: The Representation of the People Act 1918." *Parliamentary History* 30, no. 1 (2011): 33–52.

Boesche, Roger. "Tocqueville and *Le Commerce*: A Newspaper Expressing His Unusual Liberalism." *Journal of the History of Ideas* 44, no. 2 (1983): 277–292.

Bouchet, Thomas. "French Parliamentary Discourse, 1789–1914." In *Parliament and Parliamentarism*. Edited by Pasi Ihaleinen et al., 162–175. New York, 2016.

Bourke, Richard. *Empire and Revolution: The Political Life of Edmund Burke*. Princeton, 2015.

Brewer, John. "The Misfortunes of Lord Bute: A Case-Study in Eighteenth-Century Political Argument and Public Opinion." *Historical Journal* 16, no. 1 (1973): 3–43.

Party, Ideology and Popular Politics in the Era of George III. Cambridge, 1976.

The Sinews of Power: War, Money and the English State. London, 1989.

Brogan, Hugh. "America and Walter Bagehot." *Journal of American Studies* 11, no. 3 (1977): 335–356.

Alexis de Tocqueville: A Life. New Haven, 2006.

Bromwich, David. *The Intellectual Life of Edmund Burke: From the Sublime and the Beautiful to American Independence*. Cambridge, MA, 2014.

Burdeau, François, and Marcel Morabito. "Les expériences étrangères et la première constitution française." *Pouvoirs* 50, (1989): 97–112.

Burdiel, Isabel. "Myths of Failure; Myths of Success: New Perspectives on Nineteenth-Century Spanish Liberalism." *Journal of Modern History* 70, no. 4 (1998): 892–912.

Burrow, John. *Whigs and Liberals: Continuity and Change in English Political Thought*. Oxford, 1988.

Cannon, John. *The Fox-North Coalition: Crisis of the Constitution, 1782–1784*. Cambridge, 1970.

Aristocratic Century: The Peerage of Eighteenth-Century England. Cambridge, 1984.

Chandaman, C. D. *The English Public Revenue, 1660–1688*. Oxford, 1975.

Cherniss, Josh. "An Ethos of Politics between Realism and Idealism: Max Weber's Enigmatic Political Ethics." *Journal of Politics* 78, no. 3 (2016): 705–718.

Chubb, Basil. *The Control of Public Expenditure: Financial Committees of the House of Commons*. Oxford, 1952.

Clark, J. C. D. *The Dynamics of Change: The Crisis of the 1750s and English Party Systems*. Cambridge, 1982.

English Society, 1688–1832: Ideology, Social Structure and Political Practice during the Ancien Regime. Cambridge, 1985.

Revolution and Rebellion: State and Society in England in the Seventeenth and Eighteenth Centuries. Cambridge, 1986.

English Society, 1660-1832: Religion, Ideology and Politics during the Ancien Regime. Cambridge, 2000.

Collingham, H. A. C. *The July Monarchy: A Political History of France, 1830–1848.* Edited by R. S. Alexander. New York, 1988.

Collini, Stefan, et al. *That Noble Science of Politics: A Study in Nineteenth-Century Intellectual History.* Cambridge, 1983.

Conniff, James. "Burke, Bristol, and the Concept of Representation." *Western Political Quarterly* 30, no. 3 (1977): 329–341.

Conti, Gregory. *Parliament the Mirror of the Nation: Deliberation, Representation, and Democracy in Victorian Britain.* Cambridge, 2019.

Conac, Gérard, and Jean-Pierre Machelon, eds. *La Constitution de l'an III: Boissy d'Anglas et la naissance du libéralisme constitutionnel.* Paris, 1999.

Courtney, Cecil Patrick. *A Bibliography of Editions of the Writings of Benjamin Constant to 1833.* Hudson, 1981.

Craiutu, Aurelian. "Tocqueville and the Political Thought of the Doctrinaires." *History of Political Thought* 20, no. 3 (1999): 456–493.

"Guizot's Elitist Theory of Representative Government." *Critical Review* 15, nos. 3–4 (2003): 261–284.

Liberalism under Siege: The Political Thought of the French Doctrinaires. Lanham, 2003.

A Virtue for Courageous Minds: Moderation in French Political Thought, 1748–1830. Princeton, 2012.

de Dijn, Anelien de. *French Political Thought from Montesquieu to Tocqueville: Liberty in a Levelled Society?* Cambridge, 2008.

de Ruggiero, Guido. *The History of European Liberalism.* Translated by R. G. Collingwood. London, 1927.

Dickinson, H. T. "George III and Parliament." *Parliamentary History* 30, no. 3 (2011): 395–413.

Dickinson, Reginald, ed. *Summary of the Constitutions and Procedures of Foreign Parliaments.* London, 1890.

Dickson, P. G. M. *The Financial Revolution in England: A Study in the Development of Public Credit, 1688–1756.* London, 1967.

Dragnich, Alex. *The Development of Parliamentary Government in Serbia.* New York, 1978.

Drolet, Michael. "Carrying the Banner of the Bourgeoisie." *History of Political Thought* 32, no. 4 (2011): 645–690.

Duguit, Léon, and Henry Monnier. *Les constitutions et les principales lois politiques de la France depuis 1789: collationnées sur les textes officiels, précédées des notices historiques et suivies d'une table analytique détaillée.* Paris, 1908.

Einzig, Paul. *The Control of the Purse: Progress and Decline of Parliament's Financial Control.* London, 1959.

Elofson, W. M. *The Rockingham Connection and the Second Founding of the Whig Party, 1768–1773.* Montreal, 1996.

Eulau, Heinz. "Early Theories of Parliamentarism." *Canadian Journal of Economics and Political Science* 8, no. 1 (1942): 33–55.

Fearon, James. "Deliberation as Discussion." In *Deliberative Democracy*. Edited by Jon Elster, 44–68. Cambridge, 1998.

Fletcher, F. T. H. *Montesquieu and English Politics: 1750–1800*. London, 1939.

Flynn, Phillip. *Francis Jeffrey*. Camden, 1978.

Fontana, Biancamaria. *Rethinking the Politics of Commercial Society. The Edinburgh Review, 1802–1832*. Cambridge, 1985.

Benjamin Constant and the Post-Revolutionary Mind. New Haven, 1991.

Germaine de Staël: A Political Portrait. Princeton, 2016.

Foord, Archibald. *His Majesty's Opposition: 1714–1830*. Oxford, 1964.

Fröhlich, Klaus. *The Emergence of Russian Constitutionalism, 1900–1904*. The Hague, 1981.

Furet, François. *Revolutionary France 1770–1880*. Translated by Antonia Nevill. Malden, 1995.

"The Intellectual Origins of Tocqueville's Thought." In *Tocqueville et l'espirit de la Démocratie*. Edited by Laurence Guellec, 121–140. Paris, 2005.

Gannett, Robert. "Tocqueville and the Politics of Suffrage." *Tocqueville Review* 27, no. 2 (2006): 209–226.

Garsten, Bryan. "Representative Government and Popular Sovereignty." In *Political Representation*. Edited by Ian Shapiro, 90–110. Cambridge, 2009.

"From Popular Sovereignty to Civil Society in Post-Revolutionary France." In *Popular Sovereignty in Historical Perspective*. Edited by Richard Bourke and Quentin Skinner, 236–269. Cambridge, 2016.

Gash, Norman. *Politics in the Age of Peel: A Study in the Technique of Parliamentary Representation, 1830–1850*. New York, 1971.

Gauchet, Marcel. *La Révolution des droits de l'homme*. Paris, 1989.

La Révolution des pouvoirs. La souveraineté, le peuple et la représentation (1789–1799). Paris, 1995.

La condition politique. Paris, 2005.

L'avènement de la démocratie. Four volumes. Paris, 2007–2017.

Gerard, Christine. *The Patriot Opposition to Walpole: Politics, Poetry, and National Myth, 1725–1742*. Oxford, 1994.

Gildea, Robert. *Children of the Revolution: The French, 1799–1914* (Cambridge, MA: 2010), 246–260.

Girard, Louis. "La réélection des députés promus à des fonctions publiques, 1828–1831." In *La France au XIX siècle: Mélanges offerts à Charles Hippolyte Pouthas*, 227–244. Paris, 1973.

Goldie, Mark. "Situating Swift's Politics in 1701." In *Politics and Literature in the Age of Swift*. Edited by Claudia Rawson, 31–51. Cambridge, 2015.

Goodwin, Craufurd D. *Walter Lippmann: Public Economist*. Cambridge, MA, 2014.

Grange, Henri. *Les idées de Necker*. Paris, 1974.

"Mme de Staël et la Constitution de l'an III: avant et après." In *La Constitution de l'an III: Boissy d'Anglas et la naissance du libéralisme constitutionnel*. Edited by Gérard Conac and Jean-Pierre Machelon, 183–199. Paris, 1999.

Gunn, J. A. W. "Influence, Parties and the Constitution: Changing Attitudes, 1783–1832." *Historical Journal* 17, no. 2 (1974): 301–328.

Beyond Liberty and Property: The Process of Self-Recognition in Eighteenth-Century Political Thought. Montreal, 1983.

When the French Tried to Be British: Party, Opposition, and the Quest for Civil Disagreement, 1814–1848. Montreal, 2009.

Habermas, Jürgen. *The Structural Transformation of the Public Sphere: An Inquiry into a Category of Bourgeois Society.* Translated by Thomas Burger. Cambridge, MA, 1989.

Harling, Phillip. "Rethinking 'Old Corruption.'" *Past and Present* 147, no. 1 (1995): 127–158.

Hawkins, Angus. *Parliament, Party and the Art of Politics in Britain, 1855–59.* London, 1987.

"Lord Derby and Victorian Conservatism: A Reappraisal." *Parliamentary History* 6, no. 2 (1987): 280–302.

"'Parliamentary Government' and Victorian Political Parties, c. 1830–c. 1880." *English Historical Review* 140, no. 412 (1989): 638–669.

British Party Politics: 1852–1886. London, 1998.

Victorian Political Culture: "Habits of Heart and Mind." Oxford, 2015.

Hayton, David. "The Reorientation of Place Legislation in England in the 1690s." *Parliaments, Estates and Representation* 5, no. 2 (1985): 103–108.

Heffernan, Richard, and Paul Webb. "The British Prime Minister: Much More than 'First among Equals.'" In *The Presidentialization of Politics: A Comparative Study of Modern Democracies.* Edited by Thomas Poguntke and Paul Webb, 26–52. Oxford, 2005.

Hewitson, Mark. "The *Kaiserreich* in Question: Constitutional Crisis in Germany before the First World War." *Journal of Modern History* 73, no. 4: 725–780.

Holmes, Geoffrey. *British Politics in the Age of Anne.* London, 1987.

Holmes, Stephen. *Benjamin Constant and the Making of Modern Liberalism.* New Haven, 1984.

Hont, Istvan. *Jealousy of Trade: International Competition and the Nation-State in Historical Perspective.* Cambridge, MA, 2005.

Politics in Commercial Society. Edited by Béla Kapossy and Michael Sonenscher. Cambridge, MA, 2015.

Hoppen, K. Theodore. *The Mid-Victorian Generation, 1846–1886.* Oxford, 1998.

Hoppit, Julian. "Patterns of Parliamentary Legislation." *Historical Journal* 39, no. 1 (1996): 109–131.

Hunt, Lynn. *Politics, Culture, and Class in the French Revolution.* Berkeley, 1986.

Ihaleinen, Pasi, et al. "Parliament as Conceptual Nexus." In *Parliament and Parliamentarism.* Edited by Pasi Ihaleinen et al., 1–16. New York, 2016.

Innes, Joanna. "Legislating for Three Kingdoms." In *Parliaments, Nations and Identities in Britain and Ireland: 1660–1860.* Edited by Julian Hoppit, 15–38. Manchester, 2003.

Jainchill, Andrew. *Reimagining Politics after the Terror: The Republican Origins of French Liberalism.* Ithaca, 2008.

Jardin, André. *Tocqueville: A Biography.* Translated by Lydia Davis and Robert Hemenway. Baltimore, 1988.

Jaume, Lucien. *L'Individu effacé ou le paradoxe du libéralisme français.* Paris, 1997.

"Le concept de 'responsabilité des ministres' chez Benjamin Constant." *Revue française de droit constitutionnel* 42, (2002): 227–243.

"La théorie de l'autorité chez Benjamin Constant." *Historical Reflections / Réflexions Historiques* 28, no. 3 (2002): 455–470.

"Tocqueville et le problème du pouvoir exécutif en 1848." *Revue française de science politique* 41, no. 6 (1991): 739–755.

"Necker: examen critique de la Constitution de l'an III." In *La Constitution de l'an III: Boissy d'Anglas et la naissance du libéralisme constitutionnel.* Edited by Gérard Conac and Jean-Pierre Machelon, 167–182. Paris, 1999.

Jenkins, T. A. *Parliament, Party, and Politics in Victorian Britain.* Manchester, 1996.

Jennings, Jeremy. "Conceptions of England and Its Constitution in Nineteenth-Century French Political Thought." *Historical Journal* 29, no. 1 (1986): 65–85.

"Constant's Idea of Modern Liberty." In *The Cambridge Companion to Benjamin Constant.* Edited by Helena Rosenblatt, 69–91. Cambridge, 2009.

"A Note on Freedom of the Press in Restoration France." *Journal of Modern Italian Studies* 17, no. 5 (2012): 568–573.

Jones, Emily. *Edmund Burke and the Invention of Modern Conservatism, 1830–1914: An Intellectual History.* Oxford, 2017.

Julien-Laferrière, Francois. *Députés fonctionnaires sous la monarchie de Juillet.* Paris, 1970.

Kahan, Alan. *Liberalism in Nineteenth-Century Europe: The Political Culture of Limited Suffrage.* New York, 2003.

Kalyvas, Andreas, and Ira Katznelson. *Liberal Beginnings: Making a Republic for the Moderns.* Cambridge, 2008.

Kelley, Robert. "Midlothian: A Study in Politics and Ideas." *Victorian Studies* 4, no. 2 (1960): 118–140.

Kelly, George Armstrong. *The Humane Comedy: Constant, Tocqueville, and French Liberalism.* Cambridge, 1992.

Kelly, Paul. "Constituents' Instructions to Members of Parliament in the Eighteenth Century." In *Party and Management in Parliament, 1660–1784.* Edited by Clyde Jones, 169–189. New York and Leicester, 1984.

Kim, Kyu Hyun. *The Age of Visions and Arguments: Parliamentarianism and the National Public Sphere in Early Meiji Japan.* Cambridge, MA, 2007.

Kishlansky, Mark. *Parliamentary Selection: Social and Political Choice in Early Modern England.* Cambridge, 1986.

A Monarchy Transformed: Britain, 1603–1714. London, 1996.

Kloppenberg, James. *Toward Democracy: The Struggle for Self-Rule in European and American Thought.* Oxford, 2016.

Koepke, Robert. "The Failure of Parliamentary Government in France, 1840–1848." *European Studies Review* 9, no. 4 (1979): 433–455.

Kramnick, Isaac. *Bolingbroke and His Circle: The Politics of Nostalgia in the Age of Walpole.* Cambridge, MA, 1968.

Kwan, Jonathan. *Liberalism and the Habsburg Monarchy, 1861–1895.* Basingstroke, 2013.

Landemore, Hélène. *Democratic Reason: Politics, Collective Intelligence, and the Rule of the Many.* Princeton, 2012.

Langford, Paul. *The First Rockingham Administration, 1765–1766.* Oxford, 1973.

A Polite and Commercial People: England, 1727–1783. Oxford, 1989.

"Swift and Walpole." In *Politics and Literature in the Age of Swift.* Edited by Claudia Rawson, 52–78. Cambridge, 2015.

Laquièze, Alain. "Adolphe Thiers, théoricien du régime parlementaire. Ses articles dans Le National en 1830." *Revue française d'histoire des idées politiques* 5 (1997): 59–88.

"Le modèle anglais et la responsabilité ministérielle selon le Groupe de Coppet." In *Coppet, creuset de l'esprit libéral: les idées politiques et constitutionnelles du Groupe de Madame de Staël.* Edited by Lucien Jaume, 157–174. Paris, 2000.

Les origines du régime parlementaire en France: 1814–1848. Paris, 2002.

"Benjamin Constant et l'Acte Additionnel aux Constitutions de l'Empire du 22 Avril 1815." *Historia Constitucional,* no. 4 (2003): 197–234.

"La Charte de 1814 et la question du gouvernement parlementaire." *Jus Politicum* 13 (2014): 1–13.

Larmore, Charles. "Liberal and Republican Conceptions of Freedom." *Critical Review of International Social and Political Philosophy* 6, no. 1 (2001): 96–119.

Laski, Harold. *The Rise of European Liberalism: An Essay in Interpretation.* London, 1936.

Parliamentary Government in England. New York, 1938.

Lebovitz, Adam. *The Colossus: Constitutional Theory in America and France, 1776–1799.* Ph.D. dissertation, Harvard University, 2018.

Lembcke, Oliver, and Floria Weber. "Introduction to Sieyès' Political Theory." In *Emmanuel Joseph Sieyès: The Essential Political Writings.* Edited by Oliver W. Lembcke and Florian Weber, 1–42. Leiden and Boston, 2014.

Levy, Jacob. *Rationalism, Pluralism, and Freedom.* Oxford, 2014.

Leydet, Dominique. "Pluralism and the Crisis of Parliamentary Democracy." In *Law as Politics: Carl Schmitt's Critique of Liberalism.* Edited by David Dyzenhaus, 109–130. Durham, 1998.

Lieberman, David. "Codification, Consolidation, and Statute." In *Rethinking Leviathan: The Eighteenth-Century State in Britain and Germany.* Edited by John Brewer and Eckhart Hellmuth, 359–390. Oxford, 1999.

Lindseth, Peter. *Power and Legitimacy: Reconciling Europe and the Nation-State.* Oxford, 2010.

Lock, F. P. *Edmund Burke. Two Volumes: 1784–1797,* vol. 2. Oxford, 1998–2006.

Loewenstein, Karl. "The Balance between Legislative and Executive Power: A Study in Comparative Constitutional Law." *University of Chicago Law Review* 5, no. 4 (1938): 566–608.

Lowi, Theodore. *The End of Liberalism: The Second Republic of the United States.* New York, 1979.

"Two Roads to Serfdom: Liberalism, Conservatism, and Administrative Power." *American University Law Review* 36 (1987): 295–322.

MacIntyre, Alasdair. *After Virtue: A Study in Moral Theory.* South Bend, 2007.

Magalhães, Pedro T. "A Contingent Affinity: Max Weber, Carl Schmitt, and the Challenge of Modern Politics." *Journal of the History of Ideas* 77, no. 2 (2016): 283–304.

Manin, Bernard. *Principles of Representative Government.* Cambridge, 1997.

Mansfield, Harvey. "Party Government and the Settlement of 1688." *American Political Science Review* 58, no. 4 (1964): 933–946.

Statesmanship and Party Government: A Study of Burke and Bolingbroke. Chicago, 1965.

Mazower, Mark. *Dark Continent: Europe's Twentieth Century.* New York, 1998.

McCormick, John. *Carl Schmitt's Critique of Liberalism: Against Politics as Technology.* Cambridge, 1999.

McDaniel, Iain. "Jean-Louis De Lolme and the Political Science of the English Empire." *Historical Journal* 55, no. 1 (2012): 21–44.

"Constantin Frantz and the Intellectual History of Bonapartism and Caesarism: A Reassessment," *Intellectual History Review*, vol. 28, no. 2 (2018): 317–338.

Meinecke, Friedrich. *Weltbürgertum und Nationalstaat.* Munich, 1908.

Cosmopolitanism and the National State. Translated by Robert Kimber. Princeton, 1970.

Milgate, Murray, and Shannon Stimson. "The Figure of Smith: Dugald Stewart and the Propagation of Smithian Economics." *European Journal of the History of Economic Thought* 3, no. 2 (1996): 225–253.

Mises, Ludwig von. *Liberalism.* Translated by Ralph Raico. San Francisco, 1985.

Mitchell, C. J. *The French Legislative Assembly of 1791.* Leiden, 1988.

Mommsen, Wolfgang. *Max Weber and German Politics 1890–1920.* Translated by Michael Steinberg. Chicago, 1990.

Mounk, Yascha. *The People vs. Democracy: Why Our Freedom Is in Danger and How to Save It.* Cambridge, MA, 2018.

Muel, Léon. *Gouvernements, ministères et constitutions de la France depuis cent ans: Précis historique des révolutions, des crises ministérielles et gouvernementales, et des changements de constitutions de la France depuis 1789 jusqu'en 1890.* Paris, 1891.

Mueller, Jan-Werner. *Contesting Democracy: Political Ideas in Twentieth-Century Europe.* New Haven, 2011.

What Is Populism? Philadelphia, 2016.

Namier, Lewis. *England in the Age of the American Revolution.* London, 1930.

The Structure of Politics at the Accession of George III. London, 1957.

Nelson, Eric. *The Greek Tradition in Republican Thought.* Cambridge, 2004.

The Royalist Revolution: Monarchy and the American Founding. Cambridge, MA, 2014.

"Are We on the Verge of the Death Spiral That Produced the English Revolution of 1642–1649?" *History News Network* December 12, 2014.

O'Gorman, Frank. *Edmund Burke: His Political Philosophy.* Bloomington, 1973.
Voters, Patrons, and Parties: The Unreformed Electoral System of Hanoverian England, 1734–1832. Oxford, 1989.
O'Neill, Daniel. *The Burke-Wollstonecraft Debate: Savagery, Civilization, and Democracy.* University Park, 2007.
Orren, Karen, and Stephen Skowronek. *The Policy State: An American Predicament.* Cambridge, MA, 2017.
Osterhammel, Jurgen. *The Transformation of the World: A Global History of the Nineteenth Century.* Translated by Patrick Camiller. Princeton, 2014.
Palonen, Kari. *The Politics of Parliamentary Procedure: The Formation of the Westminster Procedure as a Parliamentary Ideal Type.* Opladen: 2014.
"Parliamentarism as a European Type of Polity: Constructing the Parliamentarism versus Presidentialism Divide in Walter Bagehot's English Constitution." In *The Meanings of Europe: Changes and Exchanges of a Contested Concept.* Edited by Claudia Wiesner and Mieke Schmidt-Gleim, 74–90. New York, 2014.
From Oratory to Debate: Parliamentarisation of Deliberative Rhetoric in Westminster. Baden-Baden, 2016.
A Political Style of Thinking: Essays on Max Weber. Colchester, 2017.
Pares, Richard. *King George III and the Politicians.* Oxford, 1953.
Parsons, Floyd. *Thomas Hare and Political Representation in Victorian Britain.* Basingstoke, 2009.
Pasquino, Pasquale. "Sur la théorie constitutionelle de la monarchie de Juillet." In *François Guizot et la culture politique de son temps.* Edited by Marina Valensise, 110–128. Paris, 1991.
Sieyès et l'invention de la constitution en France. Paris: 1995.
Phillips, John. *Electoral Behavior in Unreformed England: Plumpers, Splitters, and Straights.* Princeton, 1982.
The Great Reform Bill in the Boroughs: English Electoral Behaviour, 1818–1841. Oxford, 1992.
Pincus, Steven. *1688: The First Modern Revolution.* New Haven, 2009.
Pitkin, Hannah. *The Concept of Representation.* Berkeley, 1967.
Pitts, Jennifer. *A Turn to Empire: The Rise of Imperial Liberalism in Britain and France.* Princeton, 2006.
Plumb, J. H. *Sir Robert Walpole: The King's Minister.* Boston, 1961.
The Growth of Political Stability in England. London, 1967.
Pocock, J. G. A. *The Machiavellian Moment.* Princeton, 2003.
Price, Don. "The Parliamentary and Presidential Systems." *Public Administration Review* 3, no. 4 (1943): 317–334.
Prutsch, Markus. *Making Sense of Constitutional Monarchism in Post-Napoleonic France and Germany.* New York, 2013.
Rabb, Theodore. "The Role of the Commons." *Past and Present* 92 (1981): 55–78.
Reid, Christopher. "Whose Parliament? Political Oratory and Print Culture in the Later 18th Century." *Language and Literature* 9, no. 2 (2000): 122–134.

Reitan, Earl A. "The Civil List in Eighteenth-Century British Politics: Parliamentary Supremacy versus the Independence of the Crown." *Historical Journal* 9, no. 3 (1966): 318–337.

Politics, Finance and the People: Economical Reform in England in the Age of the American Revolution, 1770–1792. Basingstroke, 2007.

Richards, P. G. *Patronage in British Government.* London, 1963.

Richter, Melvin. "Tocqueville and Guizot on Democracy: From a Type of Society to a Political Regime." *History of European Ideas* 30, no. 1 (2004): 61–82.

"A Family of Political Concepts: Tyranny, Despotism, Bonapartism, Caesarism, Dictatorship, 1750–1917." *European Journal of Political Theory* 4, no. 3 (2005): 221–248.

Robbins, Caroline. "'Discordant Parties': A Study of the Acceptance of Party by Englishmen." *Political Science Quarterly* 73, no. 4 (1958): 505–529.

The Eighteenth-Century Commonwealthman: Studies in the Transmission, Development and Circumstance of English Liberal Thought from the Restoration of Charles II until the War with the Thirteen Colonies. Cambridge, MA, 1959.

"Edmund Burke's Rationale of Cabinet Government." *Burke Newsletter* 7, vol. 1 (1965): 457–465.

Roberts, Clayton. "The Constitutional Significance of the Financial Settlement of 1690." *Historical Journal* 20, no. 1 (1977): 59–76.

Rosales, Jose Maria. "Parliamentarism in Spanish Politics in the Nineteenth and Twentieth Centuries: From Constitutional Liberalism to Democratic Parliamentarism." In *Parliament and Parliamentarism.* Edited by Pasi Ihaleinen et al., 277–291. New York, 2016.

Rosanvallon, Pierre. *Le moment Guizot.* Paris, 1986.

Le sacre du citoyen: Histoire du suffrage universel en France. Paris, 1992.

La monarchie impossible: Les Chartes de 1814 et de 1830. Paris, 1994.

Le peuple introuvable: Histoire de la representation démocratique en France. Paris, 1998.

La démocratie inachevée: Histoire de la souveraineté du peuple en France. Paris, 2000.

Counter-Democracy: Politics in an Age of Distrust. Cambridge, 2008.

Democratic Legitimacy: Impartiality, Reflexivity, Proximity. Princeton, 2011.

Le bon gouvernement. Paris, 2015.

Rosenblatt, Helena, ed. "Why Constant? A Critical Overview of the Constant Revival." *Modern Intellectual History* 1, no. 3 (2004): 439–453.

The Lost History of Liberalism: From Ancient Rome to the Twenty-First Century. Princeton, 2018.

Rosenblum, Nancy. *On the Side of the Angels: An Appreciation of Parties and Partisanship.* Princeton, 2008.

Rosenblum, Noah. *The Tribe of the Eagle: Presidential Democracy in Thought and Practice, 1927–1952.* Ph.D. dissertation, Columbia University, forthcoming.

Roseveare, Henry. *The Treasury: Evolution of a British Institution.* London, 1969.

Roussellier, Nicolas. *Le Parlement de l'éloquence: La souveraineté de la délibération au lendemain de la Grande Guerre*. Paris, 1997.

Rubini, Dennis. *Court and Country, 1688–1702*. London, 1968.

Saunders, Robert. *Democracy and the Vote in British Politics, 1848–1867: The Making of the Second Reform Act*. Burlington, 2011.

Sawyer, Stephen. *Demos Assembled: Democracy and the International Origins of the Modern States, 1840–1880*. Chicago, 2018.

Sedgwick, Romney. *The House of Commons, 1715–1754*. Oxford, 1970.

Seaward, Paul. "Parliament and the Idea of Political Accountability in Early Modern Britain." In *Realities of Representation: State Building in Early Modern Europe and European America*. Edited by Maija Jannson, 45–62. New York, 2007.

Selinger, William. "Schumpeter on Democratic Survival." *Tocqueville Review* 36, no. 2 (2015): 127–157.

"*Le grand mal de l'époque*: Tocqueville on French Political Corruption." *History of European Ideas* 42, no. 1 (2016): 73–94.

"The Politics of Arendtian Historiography: European Federation and *The Origins of Totalitarianism*." *Modern Intellectual History* 13, no. 2 (2016): 417–446.

"Fighting Electoral Corruption in the Victorian Era: An Overlooked Dimension of John Stuart Mill's Political Thought." *European Journal of Political Theory*, forthcoming.

Shackleton, Robert. *Montesquieu: A Critical Biography*. Oxford, 1961.

Silberman, Bernard. *Cages of Reason: The Rise of the Rational State in France, Japan, the United States and Great Britain*. Chicago, 1993.

Skinner, Quentin. *Liberty before Liberalism*. Cambridge, 1998.

"A Third Concept of Liberty." In *Proceedings of the British Academy* 115 (2002): 237–268.

"Hobbes on Representation." *European Journal of Philosophy* 13, no. 2 (2005): 155–184.

Smith, Paul. "Introduction." In *The English Constitution* by Walter Bagehot. Edited by Paul Smith, vii–xxvii. Cambridge, 2001.

Sonenscher, Michael. *Before the Deluge: Public Debt, Inequality, and the Intellectual Origins of the French Revolution*. Princeton, 2007.

Sans-Culottes: An Eighteenth-Century Emblem in the French Revolution. Princeton, 2008.

Spitzer, Alan. "Restoration Political Theory and the Debate over the Law of the Double Vote." *Journal of Modern History* 55, no. 1 (1983): 54–70.

Starobinski, Jean. "The Pulpit, The Rostrum, and the Bar." In *Realms of Memory: The Construction of the French Past*, vol. 2: *Traditions*. Translated by Arthur Goldhammer. Edited by Pierre Nora and Lawrence Kritzman, 418–440. New York, 1997.

Stedman-Jones, Gareth, and Gregory Claeys, eds. *The Cambridge History of Nineteenth-Century Political Thought*. Cambridge, 2013.

Stockdale, Melissa. *Paul Miliukov and the Quest for a Liberal Russia, 1880–1918*. Ithaca, 1996.

Stoetzer, O. Carlos. "Benjamin Constant and the Doctrinaire Influence in Hispanic America." *Law and Politics in Africa, Asia and Latin America* 11, no. 2 (1978): 145–165.

Swanson, Donald, and Andrew Trout. "Alexander Hamilton, 'The Celebrated Mr. Neckar,' and Public Credit." *William and Mary Quarterly* 47, no. 3 (1990): 422–430.

Thomas, P. D. G. "The Beginning of Parliamentary Reporting in Newspapers, 1768–1774." *English Historical Review* 74, no. 293 (1953): 623–636.

The House of Commons in the Eighteenth Century. Oxford, 1971.

Trevor-Roper, Hugh. "Lord Macaulay: The History of England." In *History and the Enlightenment.* Edited by John Robertson, 192–223. New Haven, 2010.

Troper, Michel. *Terminer la Révolution: la Constitution de 1795.* Paris, 2006.

Tuck, Richard. *The Sleeping Sovereign: The Invention of Modern Democracy.* Cambridge, 2015.

Turkka, Tapani. *The Origins of Parliamentarism: A Study of Sandys' Motion.* Baden-Baden, 2007.

Urbinati, Nadia. "Schmitt's Critique of Liberalism." *Cardozo Law Review* 21 (2000): 1645–1651.

Mill on Democracy: From the Athenian Polis to Representative Government. Chicago, 2002.

Representative Democracy: Principles and Genealogy. Chicago, 2006.

Democracy Disfigured: Opinion, Truth and the People. Cambridge, MA, 2014.

Urbinati, Nadia, and David Ragazzoni. "Theories of Representative Government and Parliamentarism in Italy from the 1840s to the 1920s." In *Parliament and Parliamentarism.* Edited by Pasi Ihaleinen et al., 243–261. New York, 2016.

Varouxakis, Georgios. "Guizot's Historical Works and J. S. Mill's Reception of Tocqueville." *History of Political Thought* 20, no. 2 (1999): 292–312.

Victorian Political Thought on France and the French. Basingstroke, 2002.

"'Negrophilist' Crusader: John Stuart Mill on the American Civil War and Reconstruction." *History of European Ideas* 39, no. 5 (2013): 729–754.

Vile, M. J. C. *Constitutionalism and the Separation of Powers.* Indianapolis, 1998.

Villa, Dana. "The Legacy of Max Weber in Weimar Political and Social Theory." In *Weimar Thought: A Contested Legacy.* Edited by Peter E. Gordon and John McCormick, 73–100. Princeton, 2013.

Vincent, K. Steven. *Benjamin Constant and the Birth of French Liberalism.* New York, 2011.

Vovelle, Michel. *The Fall of the French Monarchy: 1787–1792.* Translated by Susan Burke. Cambridge, 1984.

Waldron, Jeremy. "The Dignity of Legislation." *Maryland Law Review* 54, no. 2 (1995): 633–665.

The Dignity of Legislation. Cambridge, 1999.

Welch, Cheryl. *De Tocqueville.* Oxford, 2001.

Weston, Corrine. *English Constitutional Theory and the House of Lords, 1556–1832.* London, 2010.

Whatmore, Richard. *Against War and Empire: Geneva, Britain, and France in the Eighteenth Century.* New Haven, 2012.

Woodhouse, Diana. *Ministers in Parliament: Accountability in Theory and Practice.* Oxford, 1994.

Yack, Bernard. "The Rationality of Hegel's Concept of Monarchy." *American Political Science Review* 74, no. 3 (1980): 709–720.

Zeldin, Theodore. *The Political System of Napoleon III.* London, 1958.

"English Ideals in French Politics during the Nineteenth Century." *Historical Journal* 2, no. 1 (1959): 40–58.

Index

IDEAS IN CONTEXT

Edited by

David Armitage, Richard Bourke, Jennifer Pitts, and John Robertson

The Development of an Aristocratic Liberalism
HB 9780521473835
PB 9780521024761

38. NANCY CARTWRIGHT, JORDI CAT, LOLA FLECK AND THOMAS E. UEBEL
Otto Neurath: Philosophy between Science and Politics
HB 9780521451741

39. DONALD WINCH
Riches and Poverty
An Intellectual History of Political Economy in Britain, 1750–1834
PB 9780521559201

40. JENNIFER PLATT
A History of Sociological Research Methods in America
HB 9780521441735
PB 9780521646499

41. KNUD HAAKONSSEN (ed.)
Enlightenment and Religion
Rational Dissent in Eighteenth-Century Britain
HB 9780521560603
PB 9780521029872

42. G. E. R. LLOYD
Adversaries and Authorities
Investigations into Ancient Greek and Chinese Science
HB 9780521553315
PB 9780521556958

43. ROLF LINDNER
The Reportage of Urban Culture
Robert Park and the Chicago School
HB 9780521440523
PB 9780521026536

44. ANNABEL BRETT
Liberty, Right and Nature
Individual Rights in Later Scholastic Thought
HB 9780521562393
PB 9780521543408

45. STEWART J. BROWN (ed.)
William Robertson and the Expansion of Empire
HB 780521570831

46. HELENA ROSENBLATT
Rousseau and Geneva

HB 9780521652506
PB 9780521616218

CPSIA information can be obtained
at www.ICGtesting.com
Printed in the USA
LVHW011917101022
730376LV00002B/364